STEPHEN SPENDER

STEPHEN SPENDER

A Life in Modernism

DAVID LEEMING

Duckworth

First published in UK in 1999 by
Gerald Duckworth & Co. Ltd.
61 Frith Street, London W1V 5TA
Tel: 0171 434 4242
Fax: 0171 434 4420
Email: enquiries@duckworth-publishers.co.uk

First published in USA in 1999 by
Henry Holt and Company, New York

A catalogue record for this book is available
from the British Library

ISBN 0 7156 2948 4

Grateful acknowledgement is made for permission to reproduce the
photographs appearing in the plate section: plates 1-4, 6, 7, 8, 12, Princeton
University Library; 5, Weidenfeld Publishers Ltd.; 9, Hulton Getty/Liaison
Agency; 10, Rollie McKenna; 11, Carlos Freire.

Printed in Great Britain by
Redwood Books Ltd, Trowbridge

For Margaret, Juliet, and Paul

CONTENTS

Plates between pages 144 and 145

PREFACE

During my first semester as a faculty member at the University of Connecticut in Storrs, I was told by my graduate student friends that the next semester would be "better" because Stephen Spender was coming back. It was the fall of 1969 and Spender had been a writer in residence at Storrs during the previous semester. The students spoke of the poet's "cool" parties, his being an attentive and stimulating teacher and leader of poetry workshops.

At that time I knew little about Stephen Spender. I had met W. H. Auden during my college years and knew that Spender was associated with him, and I had read "I Think Continually of Those Who Were Truly Great." I had also read Spender on Henry James. But I had no conception of him as a personality until I met him at the beginning of the spring semester of 1970, when, for some reason, we were placed in the same office.

That Spender was given an office with a young and untried assistant professor was in keeping with the undervaluation that marked the attitude of some of the English department faculty toward him during this stay and several others during the seventies in Storrs. The author of

World Within World, the friend of Auden, Sartre, Virginia Woolf, and T. S. Eliot, the first non-American poetry consultant (poet laureate) at the Library of Congress, was not infrequently dismissed as an academic globe-trotter, interested only in money. In part this reaction was to be expected in the somewhat provincial atmosphere of a place such as Storrs, where the temporary presence of the famous can conflict with a general complacency. No such attitude attached itself to Spender's old Oxford friend Rex Warner, who was also well known but who was at the time happily settled in Storrs as a permanent writer in residence. It was partly Warner's popularity as a particularly friendly and outgoing presence on the campus that inevitably contributed to the undervaluing of the shier, more remote Spender, who by his many excursions to places like Boston and New York to meet with "Wystan" or "Christopher" or "Reynolds" seemed to imply that there was a more important life away from Storrs.

Spender did have faculty friends—including Warner—people who would invite him for meals and were more than willing to accept his invitations to dinner. In fact, he was to write in his journals "this was the most congenial English faculty I was to know in all my years of teaching in America."[1] But he was most comfortable with the students he met in classrooms and at the poetry workshops over which he presided and with friends in New York, Cambridge, and Washington.

Not all students loved Spender. A black graduate student considered him a racist because he was not talkative one evening when, at the request of others, he picked her up and drove her to a party. This incident gave rise to a terrible dinner-party argument between Spender's defenders and his detractors, led by the graduate student in question. The argument as to whether he was a racist, or just shy in front of women he did not know, came to an end only when the host literally stood on the dinner table and demanded silence.

Several characteristics stand out in my memories of Spender during the seventies and later. There was the innocence of his smile, the enjoyment of "pretty" youths and a tendency to create elaborate fantasies about their lives, an ever-present willingness to attend a party or go on an outing—unless he was engaged in writing, in which case he would go nowhere. There was also the genuine pleasure he took in discussing famous friends and important events. Underneath the characteristic nervous giggle and the childlike smile was a deep commitment to a better world and an unwillingness to compromise on serious priorities.

Spender's dinner parties became famous for loud arguments about the issues of the day between Storrs faculty members, graduate students, and younger, long-haired, pot-smoking, gothic-looking students of sometimes indeterminate gender, whom Spender imported from Trinity College in Hartford, where he also taught a class. These were the days of Vietnam protest and general rebellion, but there were few faculty living rooms in which such a mixture of people and ideas could be found. Spender, who took the role of moderator but usually came down on the more liberal side of arguments, provided a haven for revolutionary interchange and poetry supported by a good meal.

He also joined public events of protest. One afternoon, during one of many student strikes, we left our office and joined a march to the ROTC building to sign our names with many others on a petition of protest against that organization. A friend would later chide us for being so mild, for not burning the building down. Spender agreed that she had a point but added that he was glad we had not done that. Radical principles and good manners were always at war in him.

Spender had amazing energy and prided himself on that energy. Once on the way back from a long, alcohol-laced lunch with Rex Warner and another faculty member, I asked Stephen if he planned to take a nap when he got home. "I don't take naps," he snapped. This was the only time he would ever speak to me in an unfriendly way. It was only years later that I read in Spender's published journals the account of how "maddened" he would become when, very tired himself, someone in his company would yawn "unthinkingly, not accepting the necessity I saw of never revealing that one was tired."[2]

Legends developed around Spender's absentmindedness and his generally bumbling but endearing awkwardness. One day, on his way back from a visit to friends at Harvard, his long legs squeezed into his baby blue Volkswagen Beetle, he was busy composing a poem in his mind and "woke up" in Albany, well over one hundred miles past his exit. He

turned around and rushed back to Storrs to find a houseful of guests
waiting for the dinner party to which he had invited them. Was it that
night or another on which, as I was helping him to cook a roast beef, for
waiting guests, he telephoned his wife, Natasha, in London—the time
difference made the call especially awkward—to ask her how to do roast
potatoes? I had suggested that I knew how to prepare them, but he
insisted on calling Natasha. The point was, he was lonely for home and
for his wife, who was always, in spite of the ambivalence of his lifestyle,
quite evidently the centre of his emotional life.

Spender became a frequent guest at my home during his Storrs visits.
There he told spicy stories about the rich and famous, always with a tone
of naïveté, as if he did not quite understand the significance of the spice.
The young Hugh Walpole had told him about Henry James's affairs with
the royal horse guardsmen. In an interview with Virginia Woolf she had
answered Spender's naive question about the importance of sex in marriage by saying it was "as important as cocks and cunts." Although he
clearly enjoyed a particularly witty Oxonian form of gossip, with an emphasis on sex, he avoided giving the impression that he admired the great
any less for their foibles.

He enjoyed joking about his students, too, even though he liked them.
He had the Britisher's fascination with casual American student ways
and approaches to poetry. He told the story of the student who had raised
her hand and suggested that Prufrock's ragged claws "scuttling across the
floors of silent seas" had to do with a man who wished he could "grab" a
girl.

On a spring afternoon in the early seventies Spender suggested that
we take an outing to Stonington to visit "Jimmy" Merrill. My wife and I
and our two daughters, who were then aged about five and six, readily
agreed. Merrill was not there, but Spender decided to do some shopping
for casserole dishes so that he could try some casseroles at his dinner parties. The women of Storrs cooked casseroles, he said; he would cook
casseroles from now on instead of "joints." We were very poor at the time
and our children were used to our careful spending of money. They
watched in amazement as Spender paid with cash dredged out of various
pockets and bought casserole cookbooks at the Stonington bookstore,

expensive cheeses and other ingredients at the deli, and finally the dishes
at the hardware store. As we drove away from Stonington, one of them
whispered to their mother, "Is Mr. Spender called that because he spends
so much?" Later I told Spender about the question and he responded
with much laughter and reminded me that only days before an attendant
at the Museum of Modern Art in New York had written the name "Mr.
Spent" on a new membership card he had requested. During a much
later visit to Storrs, the poet was introduced by a student at a poetry reading as "Sir Spender"—sounding like *suspender*. Spender liked that, too.

In the 1980s I saw Spender more often in London and in France than
in Storrs. I was invited to several lunches at the Spender home in St.
John's Wood and at the old farm in Maussane, near Les Baux. On a few
occasions Stephen took me to the Savile Club. One such lunch was after
a long interview he gave me in preparation for my article on him in the
Scribner's British Writers Series. That day he also took me on a tour
of art galleries and to the Tate, where he commented with emotion
and great perception on modernism and on the paintings of his friends
Lucian Freud, Frank Auerbach, and Francis Bacon.

In London Spender seemed much more English than he had seemed
in the United States, where he had always tried to fall in with American
ways. It was clear that London was very much his city and that he loved it
in spite of political differences with the Conservative establishment.

Spender was always in the "in crowd" anywhere he was. During one
of my wife's and my stays in London, the Spenders invited us to dinner at
the Garrick Club. There would be other guests, Stephen nervously told
us in several phone calls the day before the dinner, and a dark suit and
somewhat formal dress would be required. Upon entering the club—the
Spenders had arrived earlier—Pam was ushered up the side set of stairs,
and I was directed up the main stairway apparently reserved for men.
In the women's cloakroom Pam met a middle-aged woman who held
the door for her into the upper hallway and chatted about the weather.
The woman, who, it turned out, was one of the other Spender guests,
was Mrs. T. S. Eliot. We were, of course, thrilled to hear stories during
dinner about "Tom" doing and saying this and that. We were told, for
example, that the ancient maître d' who seated us had told Valerie Eliot

that he had seen "Mr. Eliot" walk by the club and look up wistfully at the dining room windows the evening after his death.

Spender's final academic visit to the University of Connecticut was during the fall semester of 1987. By that time my wife and children and I had moved to Stonington, where he had first taken us. Residents of note were James Merrill, whom we had sought in vain on that visit of many years ago, photographer Rollie McKenna, and writer Eleanor Perenyi, all of whom were also friends of Spender. It seemed that it would make more sense for Stephen to live in Stonington, where Lady Spender would join him later in the semester, so that he would be spared the strain of life at the university itself. It fell to me to drive him to Storrs for classes and appointments. To pass the time on these trips we recorded stories of Spender's life and work, and his comments on music and art. We also did an interview on a mutual interest, Henry James, an interview that was published in the *Henry James Review*. And we taught a graduate seminar on James together.

In Storrs that last semester, graduate students and faculty members interviewed Spender on various aspects of his life and work. These interviews have been a valuable resource, as have notes on the poetry workshop he led in his Stonington house. When he left that house to return to London in November, he left some important photographs behind, and a sock and a yellow sweater were found under the sheets. I returned the sweater and the photographs when I saw him next in London.

In October of 1994 Spender did a poetry-reading tour in the New York–Boston area, had a fall, and became seriously ill. When I visited him several times at the hospital in New York, he was still cheerful and was determined to get home. A month earlier he had somewhat reluctantly given me written permission to write a "literary biography," although at first he had resisted the idea of a biography of any kind. We agreed that my book was not to be the official or authorized biography but that I might quote from published material. Spender felt that if there had to be an official biography, it had better be written by an Englishman. Although my father was English, I felt more comfortable with an unauthorized book in any case. My primary interest is in Spender not as an Englishman particularly but as a cosmopolitan man of letters and as a witness to the development of modernism, in its sociopolitical and aesthetic aspects.

My last meeting with my subject was at lunch at the Spenders' London home, a few months before he died. The conversation was, as always at the Spender table, lively and funny. Stephen laughed a great deal, but he did not talk as much as usual, and he left the table early, this time, I noted regretfully, to take a nap.

STEPHEN
SPENDER

INTRODUCTION

Stephen Spender was an enduring presence on the cultural landscape of the twentieth century. Like Virginia Woolf's long-lived hero(ine) Orlando, he was somehow always in place to document the significant sociopolitical and aesthetic events of his time. His long life spanned the immense space between W. B. Yeats and Joseph Brodsky, between Picasso and Frank Auerbach, between Lloyd George and Margaret Thatcher, between the war of the trenches and that of atomic bombs and guided missiles. A social historian of the twentieth century finds the nine-year-old Orlando-Spender in a taxi in front of 10 Downing Street waiting for his father and Lloyd George to emerge. A few years later he is printing the early poems of W. H. Auden; having tea with Ottoline Morrell, W. B. Yeats, and Virginia Woolf; revelling in the hedonism of the Weimar Republic; watching the rise of Fascism in Germany; living with a male lover in London; visiting a female one in Vienna; touring the front of the Spanish Civil War as a Communist, then serving in the National Fire Service during World War II; editing two important literary and political journals; and becoming a husband and father. In the 1950s and '60s the former Communist is found confronting the unwanted support of the CIA and the power of the anti-Communist right of the McCarthy era in America. He is also writing an autobiography, *World Within World,* a daring depiction of the struggle of a man to reconcile public events with the ambivalent development of his inner life and his sexuality. The sixties and seventies find him often in America— in New York, in Berkeley, in Washington as American poet laureate, and in many places as a teacher, often at the very centre of the student political and sexual revolution and Vietnam protest that would change American life. In his later years, now Sir Stephen, he is discovered working tirelessly against the repression of intellectuals in totalitarian—especially Communist—regimes. During many of those years, he continues to be a teacher—in both England and America. Spender was the professional witness par excellence of the phenomenon we call modernism in its overall historical and cultural context.

Two aspects in particular give a certain cohesiveness to this long and varied life. Spender was a collector of "the great." He made a practice of cultivating the socially powerful—the T. S. Eliots, the Henry Kissingers, the Baron de Rothschilds—not because he was a snob or a name-dropper, as some have suggested, but because he wished to be close to and to understand the significant currents of the cultural life of his time. But the most important of his activities was his writing. From childhood until the end of his life he thought of himself as primarily a writer. In introductory remarks to Spender's last New York poetry reading in October of 1994, Edward Mendelson rightly called Spender "perhaps the only complete man of letters in the English language in this century." He wrote verse plays, a formal autobiography, journals, novels, short stories, an opera libretto, translations, art and music criticism, books and articles of literary criticism and sociopolitical analysis, and above all he wrote verse, long poems and especially the lyric poems that are at the centre of his vocation. In fact, it must be said that the lyric poet's approach colours all of the other aspects of his composite life's work. When the rise of Hitler and events of the Spanish Civil War are described in *World Within World* or the "political-moral" context of Henry James's novels in *The Destructive Element*, the voice we hear is

that of the lyric poet straining for the right word to convey not only concrete reality but ambiguous essence.

"The poet is essentially sensitive to the life of his time," Spender once
wrote.[1] But what makes him different from other poets who record the
events of their day is that he was, above all, confessional, determined to
bring the events of his day into focus by way of his innermost life and personal development. To put it another way, as Spender does in *World
Within World*, he looked at the world around him—the homosexual culture at Oxford and in the Germany of the thirties, the Spanish Civil War,
the student revolution of the sixties and seventies—to find metaphors to
describe his inner self: he was an "autobiographer restlessly searching for
forms in which to express the stages of my development," and the various
elements of his literary and journalistic production were, finally, "fragments of autobiography."[2] Thus it is that any consideration of Stephen
Spender's work and his place in cultural history demands a biographical
approach.

Samuel Hynes suggests that Spender's approach to his art depends on
"a romantic notion of the artist, as a man with a superior morality and a
higher responsibility [to reveal] the truth about public issues."[3] It can also
be said that another romantic notion was his need to bare his personal
life in the service of that mission. In this aspect Spender was very different from his friend W. H. Auden, with whom he is commonly associated
by literary criticism. In his writing Spender was not given to Auden's
sharp wit, satire, or hard, self-contained images. In his verse, especially,
he analyses his world by way of the disarmingly honest and sometimes
seemingly naive attitude that marked his personality as much as wit and
satire marked Auden's. Spender's poetry, like Spender himself, is always
lyrical, sometimes awkward, always revealing of his ambivalence and the
scars of his upbringing and social class. His poetry expresses his essential
innocence and his extreme humility and self-deprecation, as well as a
delight in the life of the senses. The poet's personality itself provides him
with a rich basis for metaphor and for the kind of spiritual and moral
exploration that reminds us more of Wordsworth or Wilfred Owen, or
perhaps even T. S. Eliot, than it does of Auden.

It is these very characteristics of his personality combined with a freedom from dogma and a basic tolerance and curiosity about the world around him—a true cosmopolitanism—that make Spender so astute a witness to the development of Western culture from the 1920s to the 1990s. Spender absorbed with enthusiasm all that was around him, including the modernist lessons in verse-making he found in contemporaries like Auden, Robert Lowell, and even Allen Ginsberg. His life is a record of the movement from Edwardian liberalism to postmodernism. Again the ever-tolerant, ever-present Orlando comes to mind in the image of a small boy overhearing with deep pleasure his father's late-night recitation of a Wordsworth poem in the Lake District and the much later version of that boy as a bent old man, still a romantic of sorts, wrestling with a word processor in London to express his personal connection with the postmodernist world of computers, Gulf War syndrome, and the enduring but broken humanity whose experiences he so loved to share and observe.

1

CHILDHOOD AND HERITAGE

Stephen Harold Spender was born on February 28, 1909, at 47 Campden House Court in London. The Spenders were the epitome of the reasonably well-to-do, upper-middle-class late-Edwardian family with liberal-progressive views on politics and somewhat "low church" Victorian ones on morality and lifestyle. Stephen Spender would ultimately absorb the essence of the former and reject the latter.

Spender's liberal social and political attitudes and his role as a public man of letters and a consummate insider were inevitably influenced by the presence and priorities of his strong father. Harold Spender was a reformist journalist with the *London Daily News* and a sometimes Liberal politician. He was a man who "knew everybody" in the Liberal Party during its last years of power, including the prime minister, David Lloyd George, whose authorized biographer he was.

The outsider side of Stephen Spender's personality, the side characterized by shyness and awkwardness, can be attributed in part to his sense of being cornered by his father's Victorian values of duty, purity, and discipline in both the public and private spheres. From an early age Spender rejected and rebelled against his father's abstract principles and his tendency to be rhetorical rather than personal. He revelled instead in the concrete and the physical and in the exploration of his inner self and by adolescence had developed a desire to experiment in activities of which his parents would have disapproved. He sensed that his father's world was a dying one, that his father was essentially a "failure" in spite of his rhetoric and his dominance in the family. The Spender household was one of "Puritan decadence" that led Stephen to a retreat into himself.

If Spender's predilection for confessional poetry and self-searching autobiography was attributable in part to his rejection of his father, it was perhaps even more attributable to the personality of his mother, Violet Hilda Schuster, whom Harold had married in 1904. A poet and painter, and a chronic victim of heart problems and other ailments, Violet Spender was very much the sensitive, self-absorbed outsider. Spender always felt, too, that the sense of his Jewishness, inherited from his mother, contributed to his tendency toward self-deprecation—a "self-hatred and self-pity, an underlying perpetual mourning amounting at times to spiritual defeatism"—and, more positively, to a certain softness and inquisitiveness that contrasted with the "aloof, hard, external English" ways that he simultaneously envied, feared, and loved.[1] In later years Oxford friend and fellow poet Louis MacNeice would tell Spender that he had always thought of him—even at Oxford—as being Jewish "because under everything there is an underlying quality of melancholy or sadness about your character," a characteristic MacNeice associated with Jews.[2]

In his relationships with both of his parents, young Stephen felt dissatisfaction, then. Before his rebellion he longed especially for the approval of his exacting father, even deciding at a young age that he must strive to be prime minister one day in order to please him. Stephen always felt, however, that Harold much preferred his more athletic and academically successful older son, Michael, who had a great deal of that "aloof, hard, external English" aspect. Michael was able to tolerate Harold's impersonal and rhetorical approach to his children. Spender describes in *World Within World* how Harold Spender once visited Michael at school and was asked to read the lesson at the evening chapel service. The lesson was the parable of the Prodigal Son. Michael was the organist that day, seated, therefore, in the organ loft far away from where his father was standing. At a crucial point in the lesson, Harold Spender, "with a flourish," removed his glasses "and gazing up at my brother in the distance exclaimed in the voice of the father beholding his prodigal son: 'But when he was as yet a great way off, his father saw him. . . .' "[3]

Harold Spender was born to a family of successful and progressive physicians and writers. His maternal grandfather, Edward Headland, was known for his "modern" ideas about the education and the role of women in society. He married the daughter of a Spanish nobleman, who gave birth to Lily Headland in 1835. Lily would be educated far beyond the level of most women of her time. She became a linguist and a writer (under the name of Mrs. J. K. Spender). Her novel *Parted Lives* (1873) achieved some considerable success, as did several others after it. In 1858 she had married John Kent Spender, a prominent physician of progressive leanings, whose father was also a doctor who held similar views. The Bath Spenders were descended from an old Bradford-on-Avon family. John Kent Spender achieved fame for his medical writings, but it was Lily's publications that created the trust money that would provide their children and grandchildren with some financial security. Stephen Spender never knew his paternal grandparents, as they both died before he was born.

Harold was the second son of Lily and John Kent. There were eight children in all, one of whom, Hugh, followed in his mother's footsteps by becoming a popular novelist. Throughout his life Harold stood in the shadow of his older brother, Alfred, who later went by the name J. A. Spender when he was chairman of the Liberal Federation, influential editor of the *Westminster Gazette*, and authorized biographer of his friend the prime minister H. H. Asquith, archrival in the Liberal Party of Harold Spender's hero, David Lloyd George. The rivalry between Asquith and Lloyd George was reflected in a certain coldness between the two brothers.

All of the Spender children, male and female, were formally educated. Both Alfred and Harold excelled at the local Bath College—a progressive

school, developed as an alternative to the great public boarding schools, and committed to the highest academic standards. Harold
followed Alfred as head boy at the school before also following him
to Oxford, but to University College rather than to Alfred's much
more prestigious Balliol College. Both men did well at the university,
Harold a bit better than Alfred, but it was Alfred who, on their arrival in
London, quickly became the greater success in their chosen profession of
journalism.

Stephen's mother, Violet, was as difficult to please as her husband, but
for different reasons, and young Stephen felt that she kept him at a distinct distance. Perhaps because of her chronically "delicate" state, she was
self-absorbed and impatient with the noise of children. One of Spender's
early memories of her places her with "a plaid rug over her knees, . . . on
a chaise longue, perpetually grieving over I know not what."[4] Another
time, when he was a small child, she appeared at the door of the nursery,
"with a white face of Greek tragedy, and exclaimed like Medea: 'I now
know the sorrow of having borne children.' "[5] Although Stephen shared
her sensitivity and love of things artistic, he sensed his mother's impatience with him, and rather than consider her an ally, he associated her
with his father's Victorian emphasis on duty, purity, and discipline.

Violet came from a family as formidable in its way as the Headlands
and Spenders. Her grandfather Sir Herman Weber was a German Catholic
whose mother had been partly Italian. After his migration
from the Rhineland in Germany to England he became a prominent
physician, was close to the great Liberal prime minister William
Gladstone, and was knighted in 1899. He died on Armistice Day in 1918.
Sir Herman's wife was a Danish Lutheran whose family name was Grun-
ing. Among their children was Hilda Weber, who was artistic,
interested in modern art and literature, liberal in her views, and always
committed to "good causes." During the First World War, she would
become a Quaker. In 1876 Hilda married Ernest Joseph Schuster, the son
of a German Jewish banker-lawyer who had immigrated to England from
Frankfurt am Main in the 1840s. Ernest's mother was also a German Jew, a

strong woman who led her family in their conversion to a particularly devout Christianity. Ernest had been sent to Germany for his education as a lawyer, and there he obtained a doctor of law degree from the University of Munich. In 1869 he returned to England, became a British subject, and entered his father's firm, now Schuster, Son and Company.

Ernest and Hilda's marriage produced four children: Edgar, a scientist and inventor, George (later Sir George Schuster), Alfred, who was killed during World War I, and Violet, Stephen Spender's mother. The Schusters lived a comfortable life until Ernest died in 1924, three years after his daughter Violet's death. At that point Hilda moved, in effect, to one room of her apartment in London and lived according to a somewhat extreme and eccentric frugality. Young Stephen became particularly attached to his grandmother after his grandfather's death and even more so after his father's, when she became, with J. A. Spender, the de facto guardian of Harold and Violet's children.

It was the death of both his parents, Violet when Stephen was twelve, Harold when he was seventeen, that was, to the sensitive child, the ultimate act of desertion. "The death of both my parents, in the middle of their lives after operations," Spender would write, "gave me a sense of death as an almost voluntary act within a tragic family relationship."[6] The Spenders left four children, all born before the First World War: Michael in 1906, Christine in 1907, Stephen in 1909, and Humphrey in 1910.

Although somewhat ill at ease with his parents and constantly embarrassed by his awkwardness and his shyness, Stephen's was not an altogether unhappy childhood. Its positive aspects included a great deal of exposure to nature, to public events and people, and to poetry. If the Spenders were stiff and undemonstrative, they were at least intelligent and highly civilized.

When Stephen was four, his mother's health took a turn for the worse and doctors recommended time in the country. For this reason the family moved from London to Sheringham in Norfolk. The Sheringham house, called the Bluff, was on a cliff overlooking the sea. This would be the Spender home until 1919.

In *World Within World* Spender suggests, "My childhood was the nature I remember"—primarily the nature that surrounded him at Sheringham and that he encountered during stays in the Lake District.[7] He always felt that it was these natural surroundings that led more than anything else to his interest in the romantics and to the lyrical aspect that differentiated his poetry from that of his modernist friends and contemporaries, including especially W. H. Auden.

Spender, who always loved flowers, remembers a world in Sheringham of pansies, speedwells, scabious, hollyhocks, and cornflowers:

Sometimes, stuck as though glued to the stem of a flower, just below the cup of the petals, there was a chalk-blue butterfly— milky blue its widespread wings: and pale russet chalky colour the short under-wings, with small copper rings and spots as though stamped on to them by a minute hammer. . . .

The scent of a rose was a whole world, as though when I buried my nose in the petals the day was instantly canopied with a red sky.

And in the fall and winter there was the wind off the sea. The boy

started singing into the wind. Then I stopped singing, and I heard a very pure sound of choral voices answering me out of the blowing sky. It was the angels.[8]

In trying through his prose to re-create the sense of his childhood, Spender reveals himself to have had the temperament of a lyric poet with clear romantic tendencies and to have been in many ways happy. The child he describes even enjoyed his usually pompous father's company as Harold took his children on romps along the coastal paths and told them stories of his past. While in Miss Harcourt's kindergarten in nearby East Runton he would long to get back to the flowers and fields. His childhood ambition "was to be a naturalist, an old man with a long white beard, like a photograph I had seen of Charles Darwin."[9] Stephen's hobby was collecting furry caterpillars, a large number of which, at age seven, he "allowed to escape" in a Leeds hotel elevator, much to the consternation of fellow guests onto whose clothes the caterpillars attached themselves.

It was in Wordsworth's Lake District, however, that the young Spender associated his love of nature with the possibility of poetry. In the summer of 1916, during a German zeppelin bomb attack on England, an explosive fell near the Sheringham house and led to Harold Spender's decision that a vacation in the less vulnerable north country would be wise.

The Spenders rented Skelgill Farm, which still stands at the foot of Catbells Mountain near Derwent Water in the Lake District. Young Stephen loved the wildness of the lake scenery as much as he loved that of Sheringham. On rainy days his father would read Wordsworth aloud—the simple ballads, like "We are Seven" and "A Lesson to Fathers."

> The words of these poems dropped into my mind like cool pebbles, so shining and so pure, and they brought with them the atmosphere of rain and sunsets, and a sense of the sacred cloaked vocation of the poet.[10]

And in the evening Stephen would overhear his father reading aloud to his mother the longer, more complex Wordsworth poems, the words of which he did not understand but the sound of which thrilled him.

Many years later Spender would revisit Skelgill Farm and would remember the birth of his vocation in the last lines of a poem called "Worldsworth":

> *Rhythms I knew called Wordsworth*
> *Spreading through mountains, vales,*
> *To fill, I thought, the world.*
>
> *"Worldsworth," I thought, this peace*
> *Of voices intermingling—*
> *"Worldsworth," to me, a vow.*[11]

If nature was the first theme of Stephen's early life, the quest for friendship was the second. He observed that despite their liberal politics, both parents strove to keep their children away from the "lower elements" of the world around them.

> *My parents kept me from children who were rough*
> *And who threw words like stones and wore torn clothes. . . .*
>
> *I feared the salt coarse pointing of those boys*
> *Who copied my lisp behind me on the road.*
>
> *They were lithe they sprang out behind hedges*
> *Like dogs to bark at my world. They threw mud*
> *While I looked another way, pretending to smile.*
> *I longed to forgive them but they never smiled.*

The somewhat hypocritical attitude of Stephen's parents was typical of middle-class Liberal reformers of the day. The politics of Gladstone, Asquith, Lloyd George, and people like the Spenders envisioned a reformed and caring society, but they did not envision a breakdown of the class system. The family's attitude on class mixing contrasted with young Stephen's thirst for friendship with those whom the social system rendered unreachable. But Stephen also made friends among his "own kind." At Miss Harcourt's kindergarten there was Penelope "with whom at the age of seven I was in love," and there was also Forbes, a boy he liked with whom, however, he fought from time to time. Once, when Stephen happened to be on top of Forbes in one of their struggles, he experienced something of the thrill of physical love, "a sensation like the taste of a strong sweet honey . . . spreading wave upon wave, throughout my whole body."[12]

The First World War days were by no means all nature and friendship. An early memory was of the visit to Sheringham of Stephen's uncle Alfred Schuster and of the word that came soon afterward of his death on the front. Words that remained with him all of his life were those of his mother on the night before the news of her brother's death. She suddenly stopped painting that night, sighed, and muttered, "This terrible war."[13] The Spenders and Schusters were attacked in certain right-wing and anti-Semitic elements of the press for both their German and Jewish backgrounds. When a Christian zealot confronted Stephen's grandfather, Ernest Schuster, with the "impertinence" of allowing his son, a German Jew, to serve in the Christian British Army, Schuster handed the man a copy of the telegram announcing his son's death and asked him to leave.

At the age of nine Stephen entered a period of suffering that was brought on by his own request that he be allowed to join his older brother, Michael, as a boarder at Old School House Preparatory School, of Gresham's School, Holt. It is of interest to note that later, after Stephen had left the school, his future friend W. H. Auden would join Michael Spender in its upper forms.

It was a desire to take on something of his brother's grown-up English ways that motivated Stephen's decision to attend Old School House. As soon as he arrived there, however, it was made clear that he was not to associate with his brother, who was in a higher form. Once again he was faced with an impenetrable social system, and a period of painful homesickness began. Stephen's parents, in the interest of making their awkward son "a man," ignored his pleas to be taken back home. Spender would later capture the sense of his homesickness at Old School House and other schools in his novel *The Backward Son* (1940), in the memoir "Day Boy" (1934), and in his autobiography, *World Within World*. Bothered by unfair discipline administered by older boys and the headmaster, embarrassed by the public nakedness in cold showers, and intimidated by academic and social requirements, Spender withdrew into himself, finding support in the teaching of a Miss Bristowe about the romantic poets, who did not follow classical rules and who explored their inner beings. In the quiet of his dormitory bed at night he experienced the understanding that would one day lead to the title of his autobiography:

Within each there is a world of his own soul as immense as the external universe, and equally with that, dwarfing the little stretch of coherent waking which calls itself "I."[14]

Stephen and his younger brother, Humphrey, who joined his older brothers during Stephen's second year at Old School House, were particularly teased for their German ancestry. They were "Huns" among the English and sometimes "Jews."

After one particularly bad day of bullying, Stephen broke down at the home of his music teacher, Mr. Greatorex, who put his arm around the boy's shoulder, coaxed the agony from him, and comforted him with words his pupil would remember and remind the teacher of in later years: "I can assure you that a time will come, perhaps when you are about to go to University, when you will begin to be happy. You will be happier than most people."[15]

It was during a vacation from school, just after the war, that the nine-year-old Stephen accompanied his father to 10 Downing Street to see Lloyd George. This marked one of the few occasions in his life that Spender would miss an opportunity to make the most of a significant moment. Left in the taxi while his father went in to talk with the prime minister, the boy became overwhelmed by a desire to urinate, and after much inner debate relieved himself into the fog outside of the cab window. The taximan turned to the now humiliated Stephen and commented on the fact that the prime minister had just walked by. Stephen, huddled face down in the back seat, had missed him.

By the time of the Lloyd George experience the Spenders had moved back to London, this time to 10 Frognal in Hampstead. Here Violet's condition steadily worsened and, after an emergency operation, she died on December 4, 1921, at the age of forty-four. To the twelve-year-old Stephen his mother's death seemed the inevitable result of her constant and very visible suffering; it was, in fact, "the lightening of a burden." If he felt anything at the time, it was "a stimulating excitement." His father's reaction was predictable, too. It was dramatic and rhetorical and it somehow isolated the children from him:

> I remember entering a room and seeing my father seated on a chair with his head in his hands. When he saw us he raised his arms, embraced us and exclaimed: "My little ones. You are all your old father has left."[16]

The immediate effect of Harold Spender's grief was to attempt to keep all the children but Michael close to him at home. There was no question of any more emotional closeness than there had been before, however, so Stephen felt imprisoned but unfulfilled by his father's possessiveness.

Still, there was a distinct advantage in not being sent back to boarding school. Instead, Stephen was enrolled as a day student in the prestigious Hall School of Hampstead and after two very successful terms there—his first happy school experience—he went on to University College School just up the road, also a prestigious institution, which would lead, it was hoped, to a place at Oxford. University College School was considered liberal and relatively progressive, yet academically demanding. Bullying was rare, corporal punishment was forbidden, and a general atmosphere of caring prevailed there. It was not unlike the Bath school that had prepared Harold for Oxford in his youth. Now on the verge of adolescence the thirteen-year-old Spender entered the fourth form in the fall of 1922.

At University College School Spender flourished. He disliked sports because his father had instilled in him the idea that sports were character-building activities rather than entertainment. But in spite of chronic health problems, which he would outgrow, he succeeded academically because he found courses and instructors he liked enough to make it possible for him to separate learning from his father's dictums on duty and discipline. He also became interested in political issues and joined clubs such as the Debating Society and the League of Nations Union. At debates, especially, he established a reputation for originality, humour, and enthusiasm, even announcing midway through one that he had been converted by his opponent's argument.

Stephen read a great deal on his own, painted landscapes, took a special interest in the vegetable garden at 10 Frognal, wrote sonnets of the Miltonic sort for *The Gower*, the school publication, was elected to the student government, worked through the ranks of the Officer Training Corps, and grew into a tall young man who was considered to be exceptionally handsome, if still a bit awkward. In a 1925 journal he reveals something of his poetic, intellectual, and philosophical interests. He is reading Shaw's *Back to Methuselah* and enjoys the portraits of Asquith and Lloyd George he finds there. He notes with appreciation the dynamics between his uncle Hugh and aunt Edith when they come for dinner. He especially appreciates Aunt Edith's famous elaborate headdress. He goes to church with his father and meditates on the nature of prayer and its "power." But organized religion is not something that particularly appeals to him. Yet he finds Christ's use of what he considers to be symbolic language of great interest: "This is my body" expresses an abstract idea concretely with great power. Actually eating Christ's body and blood would amount to something grotesque, but the symbolic idea behind the image contains great power. Young Spender feels closest to God when he is involved in the creation of poetry; his creation helps him to understand God's. When he is sent off to Officer Training Corps camp on Salisbury Plain in July, he is bored by the conversations of the other boys; they seem primarily interested in prurient matters. But a visit to Stonehenge is something else. The monument as a whole disappoints the young poet. But when he comes upon a particular set of three stones, he is reminded of the work of Epstein and of Greek art. What he sees before him is a suggestion of the meaning of the Trinity, and he remembers the visit of Tess to Stonehenge in Hardy's *Tess of the D'Urbervilles*.[17]

Harold Spender continued to be overly possessive during Stephen's secondary school years, and increasingly the boy rebelled against his father's Victorian values, particularly those related to work, morality, and discipline: "Secretly I was fascinated by the worthless outcasts, the depraved, the lazy, the lost, and wanted to give them that love which they were denied by respectable people."[18]

If Harold Spender was the epitome of respectability, he was excruciatingly embarrassing to his teenage son. His rhetorical pronouncements became increasingly absurd, and Stephen felt mortified when at the age of fourteen he was forced to participate in his father's unsuccessful run for the Bath seat in Parliament. He and Humphrey were made to ride around Bath in a donkey cart bearing the words "Vote for Daddy."[19]

Stephen was encouraged in his rebellion and provided with some ideological ammunition for it by a history teacher who came to University
College School during Stephen's sixth form year. Late in his life Spender
would write in his journals about this teacher, whom he called Mr.
Bunch and then Mr. Branch. Mr. Branch was, in fact, Geoffrey Thorp, a
socialist who believed in revolution, in free love, and in "freedom for the
masses."[20] He encouraged Spender and several other sixth-formers to
form a literary club in which radical politics and alternative values were
discussed. Through Thorp, Ramsay MacDonald, the first Labour Party
prime minister, began to replace Lloyd George as the model for
admirable political ideology. By 1926 the young Spender considered his
political and social views to be "modern," as opposed to his father's old-
fashioned ones.

It was in April of 1926 when, while Stephen was on a walking tour in
Dartmoor (walking tours had been a part of the Spender lifestyle since the
childhood of Harold and Alfred), Harold Spender died after a failed operation on his spleen. Spender was surprised by his lack of emotional
response at first to his father's death. In fact, he felt a certain release, a
sense of relief even. Harold Spender and everything he stood for—his
middle-of-the-road politics, his belief in discipline and good form, his
emotional blandness and upper-middle-class respectability—stood in the
way of everything young Stephen now had become. In fact, for some time
he had felt isolated from his parents, who, he felt, had always wanted him
to be something he was not. Later Spender would describe his feelings on
his loss in a poem called "The Public Son of a Public Man." In that poem
Spender remembers how he had been hurt by his father:

> My mind a top whipped by the lashes
> Of your rhetoric, windy of course.

On his way back from the funeral Stephen's resentment and "contempt
for your failure" gave way briefly to tears, but somewhat resentful tears,
as he recognized the public man in himself:

> *It was then I made my appointment*
> *With fame, beyond the gates of Death.*

The later Spender, recognizing his father's influence on his own quest for fame and "the Bitch Goddess called success," regrets a quieter life of inner reflection and anonymity:

> *O father, to a grave of fame I faithfully follow*
> *Yet I love the glance of failure, tilted up,*
> *Like a gypsy's amber eyes that seem to swallow*
> *Sunset from the evening like a cup.*

At age seventeen, then, Stephen Spender was left an orphan. Michael remained away, now at Oxford; Humphrey was sent off to boarding school. Stephen, who was nearly finished at University College School, and Christine, who came home from her domestic science college, remained at 10 Frognal under the care of longtime servants Bertha and Ella, sisters always collectively called "Berthella" by the family. Orders to Berthella were given by the children's grandmother, Hilda Schuster, now their legal guardian, and sometimes by their formidable uncle J. A. Spender. A young woman, Caroline Alington, a niece of a close friend of Mrs. Schuster's, was hired to serve primarily as a companion for eighteen-year-old Christine.

Both Stephen and Christine very quickly came "to like Caroline with an intensity which was perhaps rather dangerous." Caroline was independent and had an "amoral attitude on sexual subjects" and a distinctly un-Victorian modern approach to morality. She was the first woman with whom Spender was able to speak freely about love and sex and relationships and he "simply fell in love with her."[21] It seems, too, that Caroline genuinely loved Stephen but in a more sisterly or even maternal way. Inevitably the relationship remained platonic. But near the end of his life Spender began outlining a novel based in part on fantasies he had had of its being otherwise.

The other great female influence of Stephen's middle and late teens was his grandmother, Hilda Schuster. Perhaps surprisingly, Mrs. Schuster was not unsupportive of the "modern" morality espoused by Caroline and now her grandson. "Dear Stephen, say something quickly to shock me," she would sometimes say, and they discussed "everything, including art, religion and sex."[22] And although she would often have doubts about the propriety of such talk and even apologize for it to Stephen's stern uncle, she genuinely encouraged Stephen in his interest in things "modern." They went to galleries and the theatre together and shared books. Perhaps more than anyone, Mrs. Schuster's open-mindedness and love helped Stephen to overcome whatever sense he might have been expected to feel over the loss of his parents. Her defence of modernism and of Stephen's interest in writing poetry was particularly surprising and even rebellious in light of the well-known disapproval of both Harold and J. A. Spender of "modern art" of any kind, and their belief in the frivolity of any ambition that included writing poetry.

But the situation for the now seventeen-year-old Spender after his father's death was finally difficult. As much as he loved Caroline, she was unattainable, and to live in a household directed by two female servants and a woman in her late twenties was not easy for an adolescent anxious to experience "life." Furthermore, Mrs. Schuster became understandably more possessive and watchful and less "modern" upon becoming Stephen's guardian after Harold's death. To do them credit, Berthella, Caroline, and Mrs. Schuster realized that something needed to be done about Stephen's restlessness and it was decided that he should take a trip abroad before going up to Oxford.

The question of the trip brought up a France-versus-Germany argument that would remain a part of Spender's cultural makeup for many years to come. The Schusters were German and Mrs. Schuster, who considered the French to be immoral, wanted Stephen to discover his roots in Germany. Caroline, however, was part French and strongly encouraged Stephen in his need for experience that had nothing to do with his roots. Stephen found Caroline's advice more appealing and begged to be sent to France. Mrs. Schuster relented and arranged through some French Quaker connections for her grandson to stay with a Protestant clergyman in Nantes—sufficiently far away from corrupt Paris. Stephen had a miserably lonely and uneventful time in Nantes and missed Caroline. He asked to be sent elsewhere and, following Caroline's recommendation, his grandmother approved of a move to Lausanne. There he fell in love with an English boy of great "beauty" with whom he had an intense but unfulfilled relationship—it "remained at a stage of mutual frustration and irritation because we were both afraid"—which was a mixture of "attraction and repulsion."[23] Stephen was sufficiently infatuated, however, to postpone his trip back to England in spite of Caroline's sudden illness (from which she recovered).

It was in the midst of the Lausanne infatuation that Stephen wrote in pencil in a small notebook an autobiographical novella he called "Torso," which describes the "affair" in some detail. What the writer concentrates on is the psychological effect of the situation on Charles Baldock, the Spender figure, and the strangely erotic innocence of the boy, Donald. In a dramatic scene Charles describes sexual experimentation with a rough boy in his boarding school and eventually he reveals that he feels able to love Donald in the way others love women. "Torso" became "By the Lake" in a later collection called *The Burning Cactus* (1936).

When Spender finally did leave Lausanne to make his way to London and then to a new life at Oxford, he did so in what had been, and would be for some time, a characteristic state of mind. It was one in which mingled self-consciousness, guilt, political and aesthetic idealism, a desire for something forbidden, and an almost overwhelming desire for deep friendship.

2

OXFORD

The tall, blond eighteen-year-old Stephen Spender who entered University College, Oxford, in October of 1927 was by all reports awkward but handsome. Poet Louis MacNeice describes him as a "towering angel not quite sure if he was fallen."[1] Seemingly naive and shy, he was nevertheless determined to make a personal mark. At first he assumed a role: he hung modern paintings by Klee, Gauguin, van Gogh, and others in his rooms, "wore a red tie, cultivated friends outside the college, was unpatriotic, declared myself a pacifist and a Socialist, a genius."[2] When the weather was right, he sat on a cushion in the main university quadrangle and read poetry.

Part of the reason for Spender's apparent self-consciousness was his college. University College—his father's alma mater—although respectable, was not one of the most prestigious Oxford colleges. Inevitably Stephen was made to feel a certain inferiority in relation to his brother Michael, who was at the highly regarded Balliol College, and an Etonian cousin, who was at the equally distinguished New College. "Univ," as it was called, was at the lower end of the High Street and was known for its preponderance of "hearties"—athletes and men who were not particularly intellectually inclined and whose interests were "games, drinking, and girls."[3] Although the hearties were ex-public school and generally of the middle and upper classes, their reaction to what they saw as the eccentric in their midst was in a sense a late-adolescent version of the treatment Spender describes in his "My parents kept me from children who were rough." In *World Within World* he tells how the hearties at first treated him as an object of ridicule and played pranks on him, trying to "break up" his rooms, cutting his red tie into bits, and draping the pieces over his much-mocked modern paintings.[4]

But the disappointment Spender felt at Oxford was not centred on the hearties, who soon learned to tolerate and even like him well enough, but on the public school–dominated hierarchical system he found there. Having been happily exposed to the essentially classless system of University College School in Hampstead, Spender was distressed by the social and intellectual ranking of the various colleges; by the apparent expectation that one was to be either a hearty or an aesthete of the sort associated with such former Oxonians as Evelyn Waugh, Anthony Powell, and Harold Acton; and by the poor treatment of scholarship students by their public school colleagues. Instead of the modern Oxford he had envisioned of young men "caring for beautiful things, and caring also for social justice," he found an old-fashioned class snobbery that made it possible for the university "to ignore the proletarianization of European life which was going on everywhere outside it."[5]

In reaction against the prevailing attitudes and expectations, Spender took several actions in addition to the affectations that initially so outraged the hearties. Rather than confine himself to readings assigned by his tutor, the philosophy don Edgar Frederick Carritt (Spender's official academic field was politics, philosophy, and economics), he spent a great deal of time pursuing the literary interests that came more naturally to him. He attended and eventually became secretary of the Oxford University English Club, where he came to know such visiting notables as Walter de la Mare, Wyndham Lewis, Edmund Blunden, J. B. Priestley, Humbert Wolfe, J. C. Squire, and a man who would become one of his closest friends, William Plomer. On his own he read Shakespeare and Blake and his old favourite, Wordsworth, but he turned especially to the modernists and premodernists—to Henry James, W. B. Yeats, Edith Sitwell, Robert Graves, Laura Riding, Ezra Pound, Herbert Read, Virginia Woolf, James Joyce, D. H. Lawrence, Ernest Hemingway, T. S. Eliot, and various poets suggested by a new friend, W. H. Auden.

He was attracted by the connection made by these writers between external and internal experience. There was real excitement generated by the modernist use of ordinary, traditionally unpoetic material—especially in Eliot and Joyce. The writers Spender admired were those marked by their "boldness of experimentation."[6] In James, as in Proust, he discovered a writer who had pushed the novel beyond the Victorian borders of the form, treating the processes of consciousness as a subject. He found a further development of the Jamesian approach in both Woolf and Joyce, who, like Picasso and other modernist painters he admired, made the process of artistic creation itself the subject of their works. In Lawrence he was attracted by the serious aesthetic use of modern psychological theory and by a sexual frankness that reminded him of his own need for experience in that area. As for Eliot, he was in some ways the most interesting of all, using the modern fragmented idiom to speak in poems like *The Waste Land* and "Preludes" to the divide between the rising proletariat world and the blind class snobbery Spender was experiencing at Oxford.

This is not to say, however, that the work he did in connection with his tutorials was meaningless or uninteresting to Spender. On the contrary, the path from the liberal politics and philosophy he learned in his father's and uncle's houses to reading politics, philosophy, and economics at Oxford was a clear and natural progression. His official studies provided him, in fact, with a firm basis for discussions of cultural and sociopolitical issues that would dominate much of his later journalistic work. But it was the self-directed modernist reading that would affect his life most profoundly. By the summer of 1930, in fact, Spender would come to the conclusion that what he really wanted to follow was a career in literature, and he would give up working for his degree.

For friendship at Oxford the young poet turned to other "strange fauna who had wandered out of unpublic-school zoos."[7] These included two noblemen—Prince Radziwill from Poland and Count Czernin from Austria—and an American Rhodes scholar. He also took up with fellow Englishmen who, whether they had attended public school or not, shared something of his interest in modernism and often his sense of Oxford's shortcomings. Included among this group were his tutor's son, Gabriel Carritt, who in *World Within World* is called Tristan; Alec Grant, a half Russian who admired D. H. Lawrence; Archie Campbell, like Spender, a lifelong collector of interesting people; Sidney Thorpe, a visionary philosopher; Richard Crossman, a fellow and later a don, who would become an editor at the liberal *New Statesman and Nation* and still later a Labour politician; Rex Warner, the classicist and future novelist; and two poets whose names would be associated with his and Auden's, Louis MacNeice and C. Day-Lewis (Day-Lewis had left the university just before Spender got there but lived nearby). With MacNeice, whom Spender would later describe as in those days an aesthete who sported an ash-plant stick in the manner of Stephen Dedalus, he coedited *Oxford Poetry, 1929*, which contained four poems by Spender and four by MacNeice. He became particularly close to future writers Bernard Spencer, with whom he coedited *Oxford Poetry, 1930*, Humphrey House, and Arthur Calder Marshall, and to the philosopher Isaiah Berlin, with whom he shared a lifelong friendship marked by a special passion for music, particularly Beethoven.

Spender also developed romantic if unfulfilled relationships with a young woman called Polly and with a fellow undergraduate at University College whom he calls "Marston" in *World Within World*.[8] The "Marston" question is one that would remain with Spender throughout his life. In his autobiography he makes no secret of his bisexuality. He reports with candour his feelings for the English boy he had met in Lausanne in 1927 and spends several pages describing his feelings for Marston. Homosexuality among Oxford undergraduates of Spender's day was not particularly unusual, and if frowned upon by the hearties, it was at least tolerated by heterosexuals of the more aesthetic and intellectual sort. Like so many of his contemporaries, Spender had been raised somewhat strictly as far as sexuality was concerned, according to essentially Victorian principles. And from preadolescence he had attended all-male schools. His experience of women and heterosexuality by the time he reached Oxford had been limited to reasonably frank conversations with his sister's governess, Caroline. It is safe to say that he was a virgin when he arrived at the university and found himself, given his discomfort with the hearties, associated with a group of young men for many of whom homosexuality was an almost fashionable phase, if not a matter of sexual identity. In connection with his Marston friendship, Spender points out that whereas nowadays people seem to feel the need "to give themselves labels . . . to make a choice"—such as heterosexual or homosexual—this was not the case in the Oxford of the late 1920s.[9]

Spender admits that from the beginning Marston and he had little in common. Marston was, in fact, a hearty—one of the "rough," as it were; his interests were athletics and flying. In love and frustrated by his failure to establish a more-than-casual relationship with Marston on a walking tour in the area of Wordsworth's Tintern Abbey, Spender finally wrote a letter making his nonplatonic feelings clear. The result of the letter was a meeting during which Spender, at Marston's suggestion, explained his feelings in detail. Marston reacted kindly but explained that "he in no way responded to my emotion." In the months that followed, the two men continued to meet and to talk frankly, and in the spring holiday of 1930 Marston even invited Spender to his home. But Spender was at that time still in love and could not continue seeing Marston in a platonic manner.[10] He decided that, given his frustration and his friend's feeling "uncomfortable" with him, it would be better if they did not see each other at all, at least for a while. For weeks Spender avoided eating in the University College dining hall in order not to meet Marston there. By the fall of 1930 he could write to a friend that he was no longer in love with Marston (although the two men remained friends for many years) and that he was in search of a woman.[11] And, in fact, he soon began a brief love affair with a young Oxford woman named Doris. The relationship, apparently his first sexual one with a woman, was not successful. He wrote to his friend William Plomer (his letters to

Plomer, who made a point of masking his own feelings so as to be open to the troubles of his acquaintances, were always among his most intimate) that he agreed with Plomer's dislike of Doris: in fact, he thought of her with extreme distaste.[12]

On the other hand, although the interest in Marston was clearly in part sexual, what Spender most admired in his friend was "the purity of his ordinariness." In a sense he represented a kind of relief from the torments of the other hearties and from the high-toned wit and intellectual standards of most of his other associates. Spender later described the friendship with Marston as "one phase of a search for identification of my own aims with those of another man." The point of identification was "a kind of innocence and integrity in him which was also present in my poetry."[13] And the most lasting effect of the Marston relationship was, in fact, the stimulation it provided for Spender's poetry. For once he had a real situation that "crystallized feelings which until then had been diffused and found no object."[14]

W. H. Auden suggested that Spender loved Marston precisely because of the latter's indifference. Indifference, said Wilmot, the Auden figure in Spender's autobiographical novel, *The Temple,* was "irresistible." Spender loved Marston because "you are afraid of physical contact so you fall in love with people with whom you feel safe."[15]

Four of what can now be called the "Marston poems" were Spender's contribution to *Oxford Poetry, 1929.* Several others would be added in a later collection called *Twenty Poems* (1930). One feels in these poems that although they are based on a real "Marston," Spender is using his friend in an idealized way as a model for his art—much in the way Petrarch used his Laura, Shakespeare his "Dark Lady," or Dante his Beatrice. That is, by the time the poem is composed it is the poem rather than the lover who inspired it that is of primary importance. Even in a love poem, such as the Marston poem "Acts passed beyond," Spender is the studied modernist, making use of traditionally nonpoetic objects—factories, power plants, trains—for his imagery. Yet there is passion in the Marston poems, as in "Acts" when the persona realizes the power of his necessarily suppressed emotions. The realization is stimulated when his friend thanks him for waiting with him for a tram and shakes his hand. "Waiting was very kind" was all he said, yet the poet was deeply moved. He left his friend

> *Thinking, if these were tricklings through a dam,*
> *I must have love enough to run a factory on,*
> *Or give a city power, or drive a train.*[16]

A major influence on Spender's choice of industrial age imagery was W. H. Auden, who, during Spender's first year at Oxford, was in his final year there. Of all the friends and acquaintances Spender made at Oxford, Auden was without a doubt the most important and the most influential. Almost from the day they met, their lives were intertwined. Auden and Spender—contrary to the assumptions of several biographers—were never lovers, but at Oxford and after Oxford each was always aware of the other's whereabouts and projects, and they corresponded and saw each other at regular intervals. Forty-six years after their first meeting, Spender would stand by his friend's coffin at his funeral in Austria, and he would deliver a eulogy for him at Christ Church Cathedral, which also serves as the chapel for Auden's old Oxford college.

During his first months at Oxford, Spender was aware of Auden's presence almost as a myth and was anxious to meet him. Yet no one seemed willing to make the necessary introductions. Gabriel Carritt, who knew him well, "feared that the desire to meet famous people was a great weakness of mine."[17] Spender's brother Michael and their mutual friend Christopher Bailey also knew Auden; Michael, Bailey, and Auden had all been schoolmates before coming to Oxford. But neither Michael nor Bailey seemed anxious to bring the young poets together.

Everyone who mentioned Auden spoke of him with awe—he was a "creative genius," he was eccentric and difficult. He drank endless cups of tea, sat in a constantly darkened room amid scattered books and papers and ashes from his cigarettes. He disliked bathing and dressed carelessly. He used an inordinate number of blankets on his bed, and had once complained to Mrs. Carritt, the wife of Spender's tutor, that the tea she had brewed tasted "like tepid piss."[18]

Finally, a meeting was arranged by Spender's University College friend Archie Campbell, who hosted a luncheon party in his rooms. The occasion was, from Spender's point of view, a terrible failure. The flabby, pale young man with nicotine-stained bitten fingernails, "almost albino hair and weakly pigmented eyes set closely together, so that they gave the impression of watchfully squinting . . . cast a myopic, clinically apprais-ing glance" in Spender's direction and then proceeded to ignore him until the end of the meal.[19] Then suddenly he turned to him and asked what contemporary poets he liked. Embarrassed, Spender mentioned someone of whom Auden was disdainful. Thinking he had failed the poet's intelligence-and-taste test, Spender was surprised when Auden, who had already become a superior being in his eyes, suggested that they might meet soon at his rooms at Christ Church.

The Spender-Auden relationship was always based on the essential differences in their personalities. It was a genuinely deep friendship, but from the beginning it was a mentor-pupil arrangement. Spender was shy and retiring, often self-denigrating, always seemingly anxious for constructive criticism. Auden gave the impression of supreme con-fidence and was more than willing to criticize. He was a born teacher and Spender was a born pupil. And Auden seems from the first to have liked Spender for being different. He liked his openness, his almost disarming honesty about himself, and his willingness to stand up to the hearties who tormented him. And he saw potential in Spender's writing.

The first private meeting several days after the luncheon party was in Auden's darkened rooms at Christ Church, and immediately the tone was set for the forty-six years of friendship that would follow. After asking his guest to sit down, Auden began "a rather terse cross-examination" about Spender's views on life and poetry.[20] Intimidated, Spender characteristically "tried to please, gave away too much, was not altogether sincere." There was an "element of self-betrayal" in his answers. His choice of contemporary poets was usually wrong. One, according to Auden, had "written ravishing lines, but has the mind of a ninny." The real poets were Wilfred Owen, Gerard Manley Hopkins, Edward Thomas, A. E. Housman, and Eliot. Auden's lesson was that of the orthodox modernist: "The subject of a poem was only the peg on which to hang the poetry." Feelings and emotions might be useful only to bring to his mind "the idea of a poem."[21]

Inevitably, Spender was influenced by Auden in the weeks and months that followed. Auden at twenty-one already knew what he thought and could back up his arguments with theory. The nineteen-year-old Spender was anything but a theorist. He had a "reluctance to follow philosophical arguments" and "lacked the vocabulary" to understand everything Auden said about poetry, philosophy, and psychology.[22] As Spender himself described it, "Auden's life was devoted to an intellectual effort to analyse, explain and dominate his circumstances. Mine was one of complete submission to experience, which I approached with no preconceived theoretic attitudes."[23] Even as he experienced modernism and theories of detachment developed by Auden and backed up by T. S. Eliot's essay "Tradition and the Individual Talent," Spender remained in some ways a romantic at heart, for whom emotion was the essence of poetry. When Auden's opinions changed in later life, he remained an intellectual poet, whereas Spender remained an emotional one. Auden looked at the form of a poem, Spender at the "feeling" in it.[24]

And on the personality level Spender saw much that was "ludicrous" in his friend. When he was attacked in a university magazine, Auden said this was a clear indication that the writer was in love with him. Whereas on one day he would praise a writer as one of the best of the era, the next day he might declare the same writer to be a fool. When Spender invited him to Hampstead for dinner during the holidays, Auden horrified Berthella by lifting the top off the serving dish, making a face, and disdainfully hissing, "Boiled ham."[25]

Still, in Auden's presence in 1927, Spender was awed by "the altogether superior brilliance of his gifts over mine."[26] For a time Auden succeeded in curbing much of Spender's natural romanticism. He encouraged him to write less and to write more carefully, which was a good thing. He also urged his pupil to be more modern in his imagery. In conversations and later letters over the years Auden criticized Spender's work in detail. He might praise one or two lines of a poem and then dis-approve of a metaphor, such as one that compared machines twisting to necessity and humanity. Sometimes he sounds like a schoolteacher scold-ing a lazy pupil: "Stephen, you are just not trying."[27]

Auden's favourite walk in Oxford, one on which Spender sometimes accompanied him, took him not into the idyllic meadows behind Christ Church but past the gasworks. Poets, he told Spender, must make use of modern landscape and modern objects—trains, gasworks, electric wires. Before long Spender was writing "industrial" poetry. One poem began, "Come, let us praise the gas works." As late as 1938 Louis MacNeice would write that Spender, Auden, and Day-Lewis—also deeply influ-enced in the late twenties by Auden—"draw many images from the modern industrial world, its trappings and machinery."[28]

An indication of Auden's importance to Spender was the latter's delight when he heard that Auden considered him one of the "gang," a member of his hypothetical cultural cabinet of "colleagues and dis-ciples." He was to be "the Poet" (though later for a while Auden decided that Spender should write only autobiographical narrative); Auden's friend—soon to be Spender's—Christopher Isherwood would be "the Novelist"; Robert Medley would be "the Painter." Isherwood's friend Edward Upward (Allen Chalmers in Isherwood's autobiographical novel *Lions and Shadows*)—a Marxist—and Cecil Day-Lewis were also in the cabinet, of which Auden saw himself as clearly the prime minister.

Auden finished his studies at Oxford at the beginning of the summer of 1928 and paid a visit to Spender in Hampstead soon afterward. Spender had bought a hand printing press that had been used by a chemist to print prescriptions. When Auden arrived, he was busily printing up his first book of poems, a collection he later described as "quite awful poems" called *Nine Experiments: Being Poems Written at the Age of Eighteen*. Auden suggested that Spender might print some of his poems and Spender agreed. But there were problems: he used ordinary typing paper, which he did not dampen, he was not an accurate proofreader or typesetter, and the press did not work well in any case. In the fall, back at Oxford, he took the Auden poems to Holywell Press to have the work completed by them. The result was thirty copies of *Poems* by W. H. Auden with Spender's initials as the publisher and the year 1928 on the cover page. This was Auden's first book of poetry. In 1983 a signed copy of it sold at Christie's for £6,696.

An amusing anecdote in connection with the Auden volume involves Auden, Spender, and Isherwood. In 1940 Spender was short of money, and he sold to a London dealer a page of typescript for *Poems* with hand-written corrections by Auden. But he failed to notice that on the back side of the page was a letter to him from Auden in the minuscule handwriting he favoured. The letter—about the size of a postage stamp — contained an "indiscretion," which was discovered by an American who had bought the page and who wrote to Auden about the miniature letter. Auden was irritated at Spender and sufficiently embarrassed to ask Christopher Isherwood to meet the collector and to buy the material in question.

Early in 1928 the American Louis Untermeyer, the editor of *Modern British Poetry* (1920), had written to Spender asking to see some of his poetry for a possible later edition of his book. It may be that he had heard of Spender through T.S. Eliot. Spender sent a few poems and then wrote to Untermeyer saying that what he had sent were "wild oats," written at a time when he had not been concerned with "technique."[29] Later he sent some poems, including a copy of *Nine Experiments*, complete with a bio-graphical sketch, which Untermeyer had requested. The sketch is very much the work of a brash undergraduate. After describing himself as one-third Jewish, one-sixth German, and one-half English, he notes that he has always impressed his school examiners with his knowledge of modern French painting rather than of the subjects he has studied for-mally. He says he has written poems since the age of nine, that he read Samuel Butler and Bernard Shaw when he was a child, and that he had been confirmed and blessed by the bishop of London with no belief in his heart.

Untermeyer chose to publish the "wild oats" poems in his "third revised edition" of *Modern British Poetry* in 1930. The seven poems are uniformly romantic in tone, written in the style that Auden so wanted Spender to give up for something more modern. "Farewell in a Dream" ends:

> *I hailed your earth. Salute my Hades too.*
> *Since we must part, let's part as heroes do.*

"Winter Landscape" begins:

> *Come home with white gulls waving across grey*
> *Fields. Evening. A daffodil West.*

In his introduction to the poems Untermeyer, who sees some influence of Gerard Manley Hopkins, says Spender's poems are "propelled by something deeper than energetic youth; he is fecund, not merely facile."[30] In his collection Untermeyer also included some early poems of Louis MacNeice, whom he mistakenly referred to as Louise MacNeice, noting that "she" was coeditor of *Oxford Poetry* with Spender.

Spender's *Nine Experiments*, of which eighteen numbered copies were printed, was republished in a facsimile edition by the Elliston Poetry Foundation at the University of Cincinnati in 1964. One of the original copies sold at Sotheby's in 1990 for £38,000. The nine poems contained in the book are an attempt to reconcile Spender's emotions and penchant for romanticism with the social and cultural deterioration of the age and the frustrations of his personal life. The most famous of the poems is the "Come, let us praise the gas works" piece, which Spender would come to particularly despise—so much so that he attempted (with only partial success) to retrieve and destroy the copies of *Nine Experiments*. "Come, let us praise" is the fourth and last part of a longer poem called "Epistle (Near the Canal)" dedicated to "G.C." (Gabriel Carritt/Tristan). It is an ironical reaction to the more romantic first three sections. The first of these begins "Let us take beauty frankly" and contains lines that express extreme frustration—"I am sick of rhyming, Gabriel, life goes too madly/For this pleasant tinkling. . . ." Sections two and three are concerned with the repression of love, and the gasworks section seems to say, in effect, if I can't have romantic love—if we can't "take beauty frankly"—then "come, let us praise the gas works." The specific experiential source for the poem was Spender's sharing of Auden's favourite Oxford walk, as described in the lines

> *Walking beside a stenchy black canal,*
> *Regarding skies obtusely animal,*
> *Contemplating rubbish heaps, and smoke,*
> *And tumid furnaces, obediently at work.*

There is an echo of T. S. Eliot's "Preludes" and "The Love Song of J. Alfred Prufrock" in the poem, as well. Eliot, like Spender, was attempting to find a reconciliation between a complex inner life and the imagery of the modern environment. In an essay entitled "Poetry of Power," Louis Untermeyer made note of Spender's advanced modernism: "While the belated Georgians were still invoking literary laverocks, lonely lambs, and traditionally deathless nightingales, Spender was hailing the advent of another order. . . ."[31]

After Auden left Oxford, Spender's primary mentor, whom he visited in London as often as possible, became Christopher Isherwood. Isherwood, four years older than Spender, had left Cambridge in disgust over what he saw as its class snobbishness and its irrelevance to conditions in the world. He encouraged Spender not only in his writing but in his already developing desire to leave Oxford. A militant homosexual, Isherwood traced the inadequacy of Oxford and Cambridge and of England itself to repression—to "denied affection" and "fear of sex."[32] Spender and Isherwood were not lovers, but, in spite of difficult moments—some arising out of Spender's interest in women, of which Isherwood generally disapproved—their friendship lasted for the rest of Isherwood's life. Like Auden, Isherwood admired Spender's honesty and his openness to ideas.

Spender had met Isherwood in Auden's Oxford rooms in the spring of 1928. He was struck by Christopher's boyish face marked by worry wrinkles, his characteristic "giggle," and the formal manner in which he praised Spender's piece, shown to him by Auden, about his friendship with the English boy in Lausanne. As Auden had told him how much he valued Isherwood as a literary critic, Spender was very much encouraged by this praise. Isherwood's memory of the first meeting is contained in *Lions and Shadows*, where Spender becomes Stephen Savage to Auden's Hugh Weston. Stephen was irritating: one wanted to "kick . . . protect and shake him" all at once. He "burst in upon us, blushing, sniggering loudly, contriving to trip over the edge of the carpet— an immensely tall, shambling boy of nineteen, with a great scarlet poppy-face, wild frizzy hair, and eyes the violent colour of bluebells."[33] Another friend, William Plomer, describes Stephen the undergraduate in his home in Hampstead:

> The quiet Humphrey and the sister, Christine, with her enigmatic smile, listened in fascinated and affectionate silence to the gay and spontaneous talk of their brother Stephen, in which acuteness mingled with a certain naivety, innocence with sophistication, unworldliness with ambition, benevolence with a strain of satire. No wonder their attention was held: Here was a young poet "bursting . . . with vitality" and aimed at the future like a rocket.[34]

By all accounts these portraits are accurate and were applicable with slight alterations to Spender throughout his life.

It was Isherwood who urged his young friend to vacation in the new sexually liberated Weimar Germany during the summer of 1929 and to write prose as well as poetry. At Isherwood's suggestion he had submitted his essay "Problems of the Poet and the Public" to the *Spectator*, where it was published in August 1929.[35] The article called for a new tolerance for modernism in poetry on the part of the public and the critics. The modern poet's problem was twofold. The public expected traditionally "poetic" language and imagery, but the modern poet was unable to express the realities of the contemporary world in traditional forms. Robert Graves and Laura Riding had defined poets as "the psychologists of each generation." Spender agreed with that definition and suggested that it justified the modern poet's search for new language and new imagery. The honest poet had no choice but to move from the traditional forms, of which he should have knowledge in order to maintain a connection with the genre itself, to new forms to express a new age. The influences of Auden and of T. S. Eliot are evident in Spender's article.

Isherwood, a prose writer himself, also encouraged Spender to write his first novel, *Instead of Death,* a thinly disguised and lifeless autobiographical treatment of his Oxford days. When Spender gave the work to Virginia Woolf to read for possible publication by the Hogarth Press, she advised him to destroy it (he did not do so, but he refrained from publishing it and it can be found in the Spender papers at the University of Texas). Isherwood also encouraged his friend in the writing of the early version of *The Temple*, another autobiographical work—a fictional record of the 1929 and 1930 summers in Germany. In a letter to Edward Garnett, with whom he corresponded for the Oxford University English Club, Spender reveals that the title of his novel comes from Christ's having spoken of "the temple of his body."[36]

It was during that first German summer that Spender decided definitively to commit his life to his writing rather than to a career based on his official studies. In his journal he wrote of this and of his need to achieve independence even from mentors like Auden and Isherwood:

My own work is to write poetry and novels. I have no character or will power outside my work. In the life of action, I do everything that my friends tell me to do, and have no opinions of my own. This is shameful, I know, but it is so. Therefore, I must develop that side of me which is independent of other people. I must live and mature in my writing.[37]

As always, Spender had a clear view of his commitment and of his inadequacies. And in spite of the latter he managed at the age of twenty-one, on his return to Oxford from the vacation in Germany, to arrange to have a limited edition of poems accepted by Basil Blackwell. *Twenty Poems* (1930) demonstrates just how far the young poet had matured in his writing. The poems were noticed by literary figures of importance, including Harold Nicolson, G. S. Fraser, and T. S. Eliot.

One of the more influential of the older writers to take an interest in

Twenty Poems was Wyndham Lewis, with whom Spender would maintain cordial relations well into the 1950s in spite of strong political differences, mutual irritation over reviews written by each about the other, and Lewis's apparent satire of Spender and other young writers in his 1931 novel, *Apes of God*. In a *Spectator* review of Lewis's collection of poetry called *One Way Song*, Spender criticized Lewis for being Fascist and undemocratic in his tendencies, but praised his poetry.[38] Lewis remained "the Enemy," but an enemy whom one could "respect," whose passionate egotism provided a kind of honesty lacking in what the young Spender saw as the "disguised Fascism" of Bernard Shaw and H. G. Wells. A particularly low point of the relationship was reached in 1934 when Spender reviewed Lewis's *Men Without Art* in the *Spectator*, praising his treatment of Faulkner and Hemingway in the first part of the book but vehemently taking the older writer to task for "malice and ill temper" in his discussion of Virginia Woolf.[39] Lewis answered in his characteristically vituperative style a month later.[40] Spender took this public response, like the satire in *Apes of God*, in good humour and went out of his way to be helpful when in later years Lewis lost his sight. And in his 1978 *The Thirties and After*, he even somewhat excuses Lewis for his early admiration of Hitler.[41] In 1938 Lewis had been forgiving enough of Spender to paint his portrait.

Spender had met Lewis in Oxford in 1928, having invited him to speak at the English Club. At their first meeting Spender had one of the extreme nosebleeds to which he was prone, and Lewis in later letters teased him about this, including it in his *Apes of God* satire of Spender as Dan Boylen, "a latter-day metropolitan shepherd, fashioned in quick-silver, who melts into shining tears [and nosebleeds] at a touch." The Spender-Lewis relationship was at first a formal connection between a young writer and an older one to whom the younger looked for advice, guidance, and help in getting published. Lewis had suggested that Spender send him some samples of his poetry and the manuscript of the novel about Oxford. He accepted several of the poems—ones that would be published in *Twenty Poems*—for the fourth volume of his magazine called *Enemy*, a volume that never appeared. The two men met several times in London, and Spender introduced Auden and Isherwood to Lewis.

From Germany in the summer of 1929 and later in the early 1930s
Spender wrote several times to Lewis, who was still addressed formally as
"Mr. Lewis" (later he would simply become "Lewis"). In these letters
matters in connection with the publication of the poems in *Enemy* are
discussed, but at times Spender seems to look to Lewis as a father figure,
revealing his confused feelings and seeming to ask for personal advice.
For instance, when in August of 1929 Spender's grandmother paid him
an extended visit in Hamburg, Spender wrote to his mentor complaining
of feeling "lonely" in his grandmother's presence even though he loved
her and could talk freely with her. He needed to be around his contemporaries. He often felt insane, he said, and longed to be like everybody else.
Yet the dull respectability of most people made him appreciate his own
madness.[42] In this and other letters the younger man clearly lets down his
formal guard at least momentarily. Lewis does not appear to have
responded in kind or to have answered the younger man's concerns. In
fact, he told others that he did not like Spender, whom he considered to
be too soft and effeminate and too experimental in his politics and sex
life—Lewis had no tolerance for homosexuality or left-wing politics—
and he used the Spender letters as ammunition in the *Apes of God* satire.
But he did suggest changes to *Twenty Poems*, and he did encourage
Spender in spite of his own "old guard" prejudices against the younger
"bright lights," whom he considered sophomoric at best and arrogant
and even destructive at worst.

The central theme of *Twenty Poems* was still the conflict between
inner feelings and a crumbling society and world, and the attempt to reconcile one with the other. And there continued to be some Audenesque
industrial imagery. But in *Twenty Poems* the poet has clearly achieved a
voice of his own, which brings together his natural romanticism and his
concern for public affairs. Fourteen of the twenty poems met the higher
standards of Spender when he collected his poems in 1933 and again in
1955. There were Marston poems and several of his finest works, such as
"Written whilst walking down the Rhine," which—slightly revised—
would become "In 1929" in later collections. In this poem Spender with
great delicacy of emotion uses the temporary community of nakedness,
sun, and the love of three youths (one of whom is himself) to consider

the World War I past, the hedonistic Weimar present, and a possible Communist future.

The poem begins with the lines "A whim of Time, the general arbiter,/Proclaims the love, instead of death, of friends." The friends are a volatile combination unaware of their volatility—the Englishman, the bronzed godlike German, the Communist clerk who "Builds with red hands his heaven . . ." The last stanzas provide an emotional prophecy:

> *That the history of man, traced purely from dust,*
> *Is lipping skulls on the revolving rim*
> *Of war, us three each other's murderers—*

After taking his Oxford examinations in a state of extreme unpreparedness, Spender failed to receive a degree. He expressed his lack of enthusiasm for academics most fully in a letter to William Plomer, suggesting that Oxford had delayed his intellectual development because of its essential snobbism and the fact that intelligence at the university tended to be used for purposes of personal advancement rather than for honest moral development.[43] When it became clear that his Oxford career was over, he invited all of his friends to his rooms on St. John's Street, announcing that they should take anything they wanted, as he wished to make a fresh beginning. Richard Crossman took a bundle of manuscripts of Spender's poetry. Isaiah Berlin took a copy of *Twenty Poems*, which the author signed for him. Others took chairs, tables, even clothes.[44]

Spender left again for Germany in February, this time with the intention of remaining there indefinitely. What he longed for more than anything else was freedom from the restrictions embodied in his upbringing and his formal education. The angel who was not sure whether he was fallen needed to find out what he could make of this new paradise of sun and freedom.

3

GERMANY

There were several sources for Stephen Spender's fascination with Germany. From his childhood his German origins had been impressed upon him by Hilda Schuster. He heard stories from his grandmother of the sufferings of the German people during the First World War and their unfair treatment by the Allies after the war. Germany was held up as a place of high culture and beauty to which young Stephen was encouraged to travel one day. While he was at Oxford it was Auden and then Isherwood who idolized Germany and who eventually urged Spender to follow them there. For them the new Germany of the Weimar Republic—until the definitive rise of Hitlerism—represented enlightenment. There was the modernism of the Bauhaus and that of the expressionist painters, of course, but what attracted them especially was a social modernism—the apparent rejection by the young in Germany of what they saw as the archaic and repressive bourgeois values and mores of England. Germany was a place where homosexuality, for instance, like all sexuality, was accepted and even celebrated. In the bars and on the beaches there was a 1930s version of the flower children–hippie movement of the 1960s and '70s. Because of the influence of Auden and

Isherwood, Germany in Spender's mind, as he suffered through his last two years at Oxford, meant sun, friendship, freedom, and a chance to observe and perhaps participate in a new order of civilization.

As Spender would write in his 1987 preface to *The Temple*, the young Englishmen who went to Weimar went for reasons similar to those of American expatriates who went to France in the twenties. The Americans went to avoid the absurdity of Prohibition; the Englishmen went to avoid the sexual repression reflected in such actions as the banning of Joyce's *Ulysses* and the censorship of D. H. Lawrence's paintings in their own country. The denial of sexuality in British culture led to the new radical English writers' desire to experience moral freedom and to write about forbidden matters.

To some extent, the first visit to Germany was a convenient antidote to the frustrating failure of the relationship with Marston. When Spender received an invitation from a young German Jewish Oxford acquaintance, Eric Alport, to visit Hamburg during the summer of 1929, he accepted immediately. Ironically, it was Marston who indirectly brought about the invitation. Spender had shown a Marston poem to a young dean at University College, who in turn showed it to his friend Alport. Alport was sufficiently moved by it, and by Spender himself, to fall in love. Spender did not become aware of his host's motives until he was actually in Germany, and by then he was firm in his indifference to Alport. It was an indifference, as Spender noted, that precisely matched Marston's lack of sexual feelings for him.

The nature of the Alport-Spender relationship is described in *World Within World* (Alport is called Dr. Jessel there) and is reflected in the relationship between Dr. Ernst Stockmann and Paul Schoner—the Alport-Spender characters—in *The Temple*. It quickly became apparent to Spender that in spite of the scattering of modern paintings in the Alport family home, the house, with its heavy, dark, formal furniture and its stuffy, fastidious inhabitants, represented the very bourgeois values he had hoped to escape by coming to Germany. To make matters worse, Alport appeared to be even more repressed than Spender himself, hardly the guide he needed in Germany. If they did eventually sleep together, as Ernst and Paul do in *The Temple*, the experience was unsatisfying and guilt-ridden. In *The Temple* Spender has his hero, Paul, go out to the beach the morning after the experience with Ernst and have cleansing "normal" sex there with a young woman named Irmi, a character based on an Irmi whom Spender had, in fact, met and danced with "in a trance of sensuous freedom" at a party in Hamburg.[1]

As unsuccessful as the Alport-Spender relationship was, it was through Alport and his more adventuresome friends that Spender first met young Germans at swimming pools, beaches, and parties, and in the gay bars of the Sankt Pauli district of Hamburg.

In all of these places the young poet was astounded by the uninhibited sexuality of an apparently bisexual sort. The "naked liberation" was also expressed in the "modernist" art and architecture he saw everywhere. It was in the skylights of boxlike houses, the atonal music, the expressionist painting, the bright colours that prevailed, the "bare . . . tables and chairs made of tubes of steel and bent plywood."[2]

Spender was attracted to this modernism, but he sensed something disturbing about it, as well. The life he observed around him was "being led by people who seemed naked in body and soul. . . . It was easy to be advanced. You had only to take off your clothes."[3] There was "a certain heartlessness at the centre of it all."[4]

> *Here the pale lily boys flaunt their bright lips,*
> *Such guilty cups for money, and older whores*
> *Scuttle rat-toothed into the night outdoors.*[5]

At one party Spender struck up friendships with his host, Herbert List (Joachim in *World Within World* and *The Temple*), and List's friend Willi (Willy in *The Temple*). Herbert was a man for whom life was "bathing, friendship, travelling, lying in the sun." His photographs were "an enormous efflorescence of [his] taste for living." They were of youths depicted "as though leaning against the sun, rising from bulrushes and grasses." They had about them "the same glaze and gleam of the 'modern'" as Herbert's apartment "and the people in it." Spender was attracted to Herbert and also to Herbert's friend Willi, whose blond hair and blue eyes were in contrast to List's almost black eyes and dark hair.

Willi laughed when Spender sought him out to say good night at the party where they first met. "How very funny!" Willi said of such old-fashioned formality. "Good night!"[6]

In August Herbert invited his English friend to accompany him on a walking tour along the Rhine, and Spender accepted with pleasure. In haste he cancelled a planned meeting with Auden in Hamburg. Auden wrote back calling his friend a "damned nuisance" but admitting that "slate black eyes" were a real attraction.[7] The tour was a success until Herbert met and befriended one of the tribe of young unemployed wanderers "which had been born into war, starved in the blockade, stripped in the inflation—and which now, with no money and no beliefs and an extraordinary anonymous beauty, sprang like a breed of dragon's teeth waiting for its leader, into the centre of Europe."[8] Heinrich took Stephen's place as Herbert's roommate at night and the two Germans sang German songs and chattered in their own language as the trio walked during the days. Fascinated as he was by this new class of youths, Stephen felt distinctly like a third party and left the others at Cologne.

He also began to suspect that although the simple freedom of the German youths was admirable, there was an aspect of it that was little more than pornography. In part he was led to this suspicion by Ernst Robert Curtius, a professor at Bonn University who befriended Spender, introduced him to German poetry, and took him on several driving tours around northern Germany. Curtius was older than Spender and treated his fascination with the new Germany with gentle scepticism, encouraging him to get on with his poetry, which Curtius admired.[9]

Spender returned to Oxford early in September somewhat discouraged but by no means cured of his fascination with Germany. At the end of November he was again in Germany, where he finished the first draft of *The Temple*. He wrote to William Plomer that as soon as he arrived, he had found a boy outside the railway station in Cologne, had been robbed and threatened by the boy after sex in a seedy hotel, and had managed to contract crabs.[10] He went back to Oxford after Christmas in Hamburg.

In Oxford he seemed to revel in his newfound sexual freedom, deciding that, following the heroes of the past, he must be a risk taker.[11] Perhaps in this remark he indicates thoughts that would result eventually in his poem "The Truly Great." In any case, he was more sexually adventuresome in early 1930 than he had been in his first years at Oxford. There was not only the affair with Doris but one with a young man, with whom he enjoyed having "risky" sex; once the landlady caught them in a room Spender had rented in Oxford, and once they did what they could while brother Michael played short Bach pieces in the next room at 10 Frognal.[12] He was learning much of the "world of the body" from his reading of D. H. Lawrence, about whom he argued constantly with his tutor, who, like everyone else at Oxford, it seemed, laughed at his "craze" for Lawrence.[13] He loved going to bed with people because there he could "touch reality."[14]

The sexual liberation was reflected in moments of high self-esteem. In March he would tell Plomer that he felt "like a voice singing," that he was rewriting *The Temple*, now called *Escaped*, that he felt there could be "no rules" for artists, and that with his novel he was sure to succeed. In spite of this confidence and a claim that he no longer cared about the opinion of friends, however, he immediately agreed with Christopher Isherwood's opinion that the novel was not yet ready for publication.[15]

In June Auden and Isherwood were both in Germany, and Spender, in good spirits, in spite of his Oxford degree problems, was anxious to follow them. Auden had just had his first full volume of poetry accepted for publication, and Isherwood had lent a proof copy to Spender. Spender had managed to crumple the manuscript's jacket and he returned it to his friend with a note: "Written by Wystan, dedicated to Christopher, damaged by Stephen."[16] He left for Hamburg on July 22. Before leaving, he wrote to Plomer, sending endearments to him and his lover, Tony Butts (the brother of eccentric bohemian novelist Mary Butts), and expressing ecstatic pleasure at exchanging Oxford for Germany.

Back in Hamburg, Spender found rooms in a small hotel on Innocentiastrasse. The irony of the street name was not lost on him.[17] Hamburg had become Stephen's city, as Berlin was Wystan's and Christopher's. Spender understood that Berlin was Isherwood's territory for fiction and that his friend would not welcome competition on that score.

A few days after his arrival he met up again with Herbert List, who came to a cocktail party given by Spender's friend René Janin, son of a French general and friend also of Laurens van der Post, who had introduced Spender to William Plomer in 1929, and who, with Isaiah Berlin, was also on vacation in Germany. The party was in honour of Spender and Berlin, who shared a passion for music and would later spend some time at the music festival in Salzburg. Spender maintained a close life-long friendship with Berlin, who, unlike Auden and even Isherwood, did not attempt to overpower him intellectually.

It was through Herbert List that Spender met a boy named Walter (Lothar in *The Temple*) in a Sankt Pauli bar. From the beginning it was clear that Walter was a thief and a liar and that he was taking full advantage of Spender's modest pocketbook. Yet Spender saw himself as "a member of a class whose money enabled me to benefit automatically from its institutions of robbery, to assume automatically its disguises of respectability." If Walter was an "anti-social" robber, he was a "social" one, and given his "sense of social guilt" he was in no position to be critical. So he found himself supporting Walter in his semicriminal escapades by constantly giving him money until Herbert List helped to extricate him from the relationship.[18] The Walter affair was the first in a series of connections based as much on socioeconomic and even political concerns and interests as on physical ones.

In fact, by the late summer of 1930, Spender's interest in Germany was at least as political as it was sexual. Having experienced some of the "new freedom," he increasingly turned his attention to what he saw as the struggle of the working classes (as represented, for instance, by boys like Walter and List's friend Heinrich) and to the ominous rise of Fascism, a cloud that had already darkened the Weimar world of sun and freedom that Spender had experienced the year before.

The political interest developed quickly when Spender left Hamburg and went to Berlin at the invitation of Christopher Isherwood, who, with a new friend named Otto, had first visited Spender in Hamburg in August. Then a struggling young author, Isherwood was working on a novel, *The Memorial*, which would be published by Hogarth Press after Spender recommended it to John Lehmann, the Hogarth editor and a close acquaintance. Isherwood lived in a slum tenement and was joined there by Spender in September.

During Spender's first visit to Berlin and regular stays in the next few years, it was impossible to avoid the growing conflict between the rich and the poor, the Fascists and the Communists, the proliferation of elegant modernist buildings and unspeakable slums. Christopher was adamant in his championing of the poor, in part because he, himself, was poor. When the composer Roger Sessions, whom Spender had met in London, and Michael Spender visited Berlin, Spender felt he had "betrayed" Christopher when he ate with them in a posh Russian restaurant.[19]

In the midst of the turmoil of his Hamburg social life, the affair with Walter, and his travels, Spender managed to write what he would later call some of his best early poetry, which, characteristically, he nevertheless compared unfavourably to the release of Auden's first professionally published book of poems.[20] Spender's poems included a particularly fine one, "My Parents Quarrel," which contains the mixture of sentiment and modernist imagery that increasingly marked his poetry:

> How can they sleep, who eat upon their fear
> And watch their dreadful love fade as it grows?
> Their life flowers, like an antique lover's rose
> Set puff'd and spreading in the chemist's jar.[21]

And he worked on *The Temple*, changing the main character from a woman to a more autobiographical male. Having done that, he nevertheless informed his friends of his growing attraction to women, informing William Plomer that he had had a heterosexual dream.[22] In fact, by the fall of 1930 he had begun to fantasize about a seventeen-year-old girl he had met the winter before on a skiing vacation in Switzerland. Gisa Soloweitschik was a wealthy German Jew whose family lived in Berlin. In November of 1930 Spender, back in Oxford, had confided in Isherwood that he intended to marry her. Only a month earlier, however, from a hotel in Vienna he had written to Plomer bemoaning his lack of a male lover and describing overwhelming nocturnal erotic longings.[23] And later, after it was evident that the relationship with Gisa, who several years later would marry a nephew of André Gide, would go nowhere, he would write to Plomer from a pension in Berlin that there was a woman there who sang horribly and that he thought he disliked the female gender.[24]

In January of 1931 Stephen, now definitively finished with Oxford and in Germany for what he hoped would be a long stay, paid his second visit to Berlin. By then Christopher had moved to a tenement presided over by a Fraulein Thurau and populated by people who would become characters in his novels—people such as eccentric Bobbi the gay bartender and the wildly dressed nightclub singer Jean Ross (the fictional Sally Bowles). Spender lived not far away in slightly better quarters but took his meals with Christopher—watery tripe or lung soup, horse meat and other unappetizing foods that Spender always said "for some years ruined my digestion, and for all time my teeth."[25] As for the teeth, they were more likely ruined by an addiction to the sweets the two Englishmen found in the ubiquitous Berlin coffeehouses.

Christopher argued for the political necessity of poverty and saw corruption in bourgeois "self-conscious aesthetic and intellectual pretensions." Concerts and intellectual conversations were a waste of time. He stood for honest self-realization and encouraged his younger friend in his work as they observed "the uniformed armies [Communist and Fascist] of youths" practising "their violence against the Republic and against one another."[26]

By early 1931 "the feeling of unrest in Berlin" was permanent. The paradise of the summer of 1929 was giving way to nationalistic and ideological songs and uniforms. When in the summer of 1931 Christopher, his friend Otto, and Stephen, joined by Auden, took a summer vacation at Insel Ruegen, "where the naked bathers in their hundreds lay stretched on the beach under the drugging sun, sometimes we heard orders rapped out, and even shots, from the forest . . . where the Storm Troopers were training like executioners waiting to martyr the naked and self-disarmed."[27] A new leader, Hitler, was constantly in the news. When members of the new Hitler Youth movement sunbathed in Ruegen, they would raise little Nazi flags on the beach. In his 1939 journal Spender tells how one day when he was with two of these youths, he lost his temper and told them he was a Jew.[28] The youths laughed at him, pointing out that with such Nordic features he could not be a Jew. After further argument Spender rushed off in a rage.

The 1931 summer trip was in many ways disappointing. Otto spent the evenings dancing with girls; Christopher cut his foot; Auden, unlike the others, avoided the sun; and there were the storm troopers in the woods. Stephen, who had taken up photography under the influence of his photographer brother Humphrey, took several Herbert List–like pictures of Otto in his scant bathing suit. Using an automatic shutter, he also took the now famous one of himself (see plate 3) standing with his arms around Auden and Isherwood with an expression on his face that to Isherwood "suggests an off-duty Jesus relaxing with 'these little ones.' "[29] Feeling restless, Spender went off to Salzburg and then to Berlin, where he stayed in Christopher's apartment until he returned.

On October 6, 1931, Spender wrote to William Plomer about a poem on which he was working. The poem, "The Truly Great," was to become perhaps his most famous work. It reflected what was becoming his approach to modernism, one that not only was clearly influenced by Auden and more particularly by T. S. Eliot, but was, nevertheless, his own:

> *I think continually of those who were truly great.*
> *Who, from the womb, remembered the soul's history*
> *Through corridors of light, where the hours are suns,*
> *Endless and singing. Whose lovely ambition*
> *Was that their lips, still touched with fire,*
> *Should tell of the Spirit, clothed from head to foot in song.*
> *And who hoarded from the Spring branches*
> *The desires falling across their bodies like blossoms.*

Spender told Plomer that the stimulus for this poem was phrases of music by the great classical composers. When he heard the music of Mozart or Beethoven, he understood that the truly great were those creative artists who "hoarded the best of every stage of their development." In writing the poem, he thought disparagingly of those who simply

reject the past in their use of the present. Echoing Eliot's "Tradition and
the Individual Talent," which he had read at Oxford, he announced that
the great are those who bring their knowledge of the past into their experience of the present. And once again Spender combines in his poetry the
sentiment and the lyricism of his knowledge and appreciation of romanticism with his images of the modern—in this case the noise and "fog" of
traffic: the poem's second stanza, which reminds us of Wordsworth's
image of the memory as a "dwelling place/For all sweet sounds and har-
monies" at the end of "Tintern Abbey," reads:

> What is precious, is never to forget
> The essential delight of the blood drawn from ageless springs
> Breaking through rocks in worlds before our earth.
> Never to deny its pleasure in the morning simple light
> Nor its grave evening demand for love.
> Never to allow gradually the traffic to smother
> With noise and fog, the flowering of the spirit.

Those who preserve the "flowering of the spirit," who do not cringe
before the necessity of risk-taking and full experience, are the saviours of
humanity:

> Near the snow, near the sun, in the highest fields,
> See how these names are feted by the waving grass
> And by the streamers of white cloud
> And whispers of wind in the listening sky.
> The names of those who in their lives fought for life,
> Who wore at their hearts the fire's centre.
> Born of the sun, they travelled a short while toward the sun
> And left the vivid air signed with their honour.

Meanwhile Spender continued his quest for a satisfying personal
life. He told Plomer that he felt at home in Germany, but that he still
lacked a viable relationship. He spent time, he said, in the baths, in the
indoor swimming pools, and at bicycle races, where boys could be

found.[30] In January 1932 he met a seventeen-year-old Russian boy named Staatlos, whom he called "Georg 101" in letters to Plomer. Once again the relationship was based as much on a fascination with the downtrodden as on physical desire. He told Plomer he felt as if he were more like a protector than a lover. When Harold Nicolson and a friend visited him in Berlin, they criticized the "young boy cult" of Isherwood and Spender, suggesting that there was nothing beyond the physical that they could "share" with these boys. Spender somewhat sheepishly agreed.[31] The relationship with Georg became strained and lasted only a short time.

In Berlin in 1931 and 1932 Spender came to know intellectual Germans of the Left, who struggled against the rise of National Socialism. There were Jews, like Wilfred Israel, who argued for peaceful protest that would "arouse the conscience of the world," and others who turned to Communism as the only hope.[32] Spender was an avid follower of the radical cinema, especially of the great Soviet films by Eisenstein— films like *Potemkin* and *Mother*, which were political in content and modernist in style and form, attacking their subjects, as Eisenstein said, "from within," using a new methodology of "purely cinematographic expressiveness."[33] These films became models to emulate as Spender, Isherwood, Auden, and others wrestled with the necessity of moving from poetry that was isolated from political and historical events to a new modernist poetry that expressed experience "from within" but served the common good.

Isherwood introduced Spender to Gerald Hamilton, an elderly Communist whose ideas interested him. Hamilton had been friendly with Oscar Wilde's Lord Alfred Douglas and with the spiritualist Aleister Crowley. Spender visited Crowley one afternoon in Berlin with Hamilton. Crowley's mistress changed her costume several times during the afternoon in an attempt to attract Crowley's attention. When she appeared wearing a turban announcing that she was "a Turk," Crowley scowled and said, "Well, then, if you're a Turk, make us some coffee."[34]

A more important political influence on Isherwood, Spender, and Auden was Edward Upward (Chalmers in Isherwood's books and in

World Within World). Upward had been Isherwood's close friend at Cambridge, and he was about to join the Communist Party. In 1932 Spender met him when he came to Berlin to visit Christopher, and they spent some time together. On long walks in Berlin they discussed the political situation and an appropriate response to it. Upward was full of enthusiasm for the Communist cause, having just returned from a visit to the Soviet Union. On one walk Spender told Upward that as much as he deplored Fascism, he could not condone the use of violence and the sacrifice of freedom that Communism demanded to oppose it. Upward smiled and called him "Gandhi."[35] But if Upward could not convince his new pupil of the validity of Communism, he succeeded in bringing him to a position from which he could view the politics of the early thirties in a more disciplined way. The old tolerant Liberalism of the Lloyd George era learned in the cradle, as it were, was giving ground to the view that something radical and highly organized would be necessary to confront the brutality that was Nazism. Perhaps this new force would be Communism, for all its own shortcomings. The alternative was an acceptance of the world depicted by Eliot in *The Waste Land*, of the "passive suffering" described by Yeats in poems like "The Second Coming." Spender recognized the "passive suffering" tendency in himself and was determined to find another way. With Upward's help Communism was now firmly planted in the back of his mind as a potential path to something better.

In November 1931 he finished the first of his better political poems, reflecting his new way of thinking combined with the sexual liberation achieved during the German years. "Oh Young Men" begins with a call to radical change in which the word *comrades* suggests the influence of Upward:

> *Oh young men oh young comrades*
> *it is too late now to stay in those houses*
> *your fathers built where they built you to breed*
> *money on money it is too late*
> *to make or even to count what has been made*

The poem includes a "Truly Great"–like call to value the body and the
soul as opposed to outworn social values:

> *Count rather those fabulous possessions*
> *which begin with your body and your fiery soul:—*
> *the hairs on your head the muscles extending*
> *in ranges with their lakes across your limbs*
> *Count your eyes as jewels and your valued sex*
> *then count the sun and the innumerable coined light*
> *sparkling on waves and spangled under trees*
> *It is too late now to stay in great houses where the ghosts are prisoned*
> *—those ladies like flies perfect in amber*
> *those financiers like fossils of bones in coal.*

The final stanza is both romantic in its idealization of manly love and
modern in its dramatic call to the comrades to rebel:

> *Oh comrades, step beautifully from the solid wall*
> *advance to rebuild and sleep with friend on hill*
> *advance to rebel and remember what you have*
> *no ghost ever had, immured in his hall.*

Still, in spite of the enthusiasm contained in "Oh Young Men,"
Spender was becoming disgusted with the real-life Communists in
Berlin. The ones he knew were for the most part foolishly intent on
spying on each other and gossiping about whether their comrades were
real Marxists. Although he disagreed with Middleton Murry on most
things, he agreed with his January 1932 essay in the *Adelphi* magazine claiming that the Communist movement had been "distorted" by
Russia.[36]

After a longish stay in London beginning in February 1932 Spender
returned to Berlin in May and paid a visit to Christopher Isherwood,
who was living with a new boy, a seventeen-year-old named Heinz, in
the village of Mohrin, north of the city. Isherwood resented the visit; he
"hated having Stephen and Stephen's camera invade the scene of his love

affair with Heinz."[37] Yet when Stephen left in a few days, Christopher missed his adult company and friendship.

In Berlin Spender worked still again on *The Temple*, the title of which he had changed for a while to *The Soldier's Disease*. He felt it ought to be published because it was honest about homoeroticism.[38] Rosamond Lehmann, the sister of John Lehmann, a woman Spender had met while he was at Oxford and much admired thereafter, had read it and suggested changes.

In June Spender once again settled for the summer in Sellin am Ruegen, this time alone in the village of Idyll. While there he read a great deal: Henry James's *The Ambassadors*—"the supreme example of the poetic novel"—Joyce's *Ulysses* for the second time, poetry by Pound, and Auden's *Orators*, which had just come out. He also read Goethe, whose *Faust* he greatly admired. An "invasion of schoolboys" marred the quiet of Idyll, however, so Spender joined Isherwood and Heinz in a nearby village. Humphrey Spender soon arrived, and the four invented a game called "Shelley" in which the winner was the one first washed up on the shore by waves.[39]

Late in August Spender travelled to Hamburg, where he met a boy named Arnold and fell in love. Arnold went with him to Berlin in September but soon returned to Hamburg, leaving Spender with a case of blood poisoning brought about by nicking himself with a rusty razor.[40] During his illness, Spender stayed with Gisa Soloweitschik, the woman he had once planned to marry.

In October Spender left Berlin. Although he would visit Germany often in the years to come, the German experiment effectively ended at this point. Back in London, still torn between the warring sides of his sexuality and between the political liberalism that came naturally to him and the Communism that was becoming more politically correct, he would take up the life of the man of letters.

4

THE MAN OF LETTERS

On September 8, 1930, Virginia Woolf received a letter with several poems from "a Mr Spender, saying he cares for my praise more than for that of any critic."[1] Stephen Spender was then twenty-one and still an undergraduate at Oxford. In April of that year he had written to Harold Nicolson and his wife, Vita Sackville-West, requesting a meeting, and in a diary entry of June 22 Nicolson notes that Spender had visited them at Long Barn in Kent—that he was "intelligent," that he had "wild blue eyes and a bad complexion," that he talked endlessly about whether he should be a poet or a novelist.[2] Spender would pay many subsequent visits to the Nicolsons at Long Barn and Sissinghurst Castle. He admired them for their advanced views on sexuality—especially bisexuality—and marriage, and in later years he and his wife would be guests of the younger Nicolsons at Sissinghurst.

From his position as a member of an Oxford club called the Martlets and as a member and later secretary of the Oxford University English Club, Spender had already by 1930 established contact with other literary notables, as well. These included Aldous Huxley, H. G. Wells, Julian

Huxley, Walter de la Mare, Wyndham Lewis, T. S. Eliot, and E. M. Forster. With many of these men Spender maintained friendships or professional associations. As has been noted, the Lewis-Spender relationship was marked by a combination of respect and conflicts. But even radical disagreements over an issue as serious as Lewis's defence of Hitler were not sufficient to alienate the younger writer completely. Spender and de la Mare would correspond several times, discussing literary matters and the need for sexual tolerance. The initial contact with Forster in 1929 would develop into a long, if sometimes fragile, friendship.

A meeting with Eliot at the Martlets in 1928 and a subsequent one in July of 1930 after a mutual friend had sent the older poet some poems by Spender would mark the beginning of a thirty-seven-year relationship in which Eliot served both as a publisher and encouraging father figure. In *World Within World* Spender describes a "grave, slightly bowed, aquiline, ceremonious" man with "something withdrawn and yet benevolent about his glance." At one lunch meeting Spender shocked Eliot by ordering smoked eel. "I don't think I dare eat smoked eel," said Eliot, putting his young guest in mind of Prufrock asking himself, "Do I dare to eat a peach?" Eliot often sounded like his poems.[3] In a letter to Spender he remembers the flies and heat and the oppressiveness of the mountains during a summer visit to the Salzkammergut. Mountains were only possible if there was water nearby to overcome the boredom and the sense of being in prison, wrote the author of *The Waste Land*.[4]

Once, when Spender asked him what he thought was the future of Western civilization, Eliot answered "internecine conflict ... people killing one another in the streets."[5] Like many a son, Spender, as much as he respected and admired him, was not able to accept his literary "father's" view of the world and its possibilities. And he was also not above criticizing his poetry or acting in a manner that would have displeased Eliot. In a letter to William Plomer from Vienna he calls one of Eliot's lines "unoriginal and silly" in practically the same breath as he jokes about the relationship between nose and penis sizes and bemoans the lack of a boy.[6]

Eliot, in fact, knew of Spender's escapades in Berlin from the reports of various mutual friends, particularly Auden.[7] But he always maintained the most discreet silence about such matters, merely suggesting in his early letters to Spender that it would be best if he were to return to London. In most of his letters Eliot concentrated on questions having to do with publications, both with Faber and Faber, where Eliot was Spender's editor for many years, and with *The Criterion*, the literary review Eliot edited and to which he encouraged Spender to contribute reviews and poetry.

When he was not discussing business, Eliot approached his younger colleague in a kindly if somewhat patronizing manner, only occasionally exchanging formal distance for somewhat revealing personal remarks. At first Eliot began his letters "Dear Spender" or "My Dear Spender" and signed them "Yours very truly, T. S. Eliot." It was not until 1935 that Spender became "Dear Stephen" or "My Dear Stephen" and the letters were signed "Affectionately, Tom."

Two early letters in particular suggest the intellectual intimacy and warmth that would gradually develop between the two men, however. In March 1931, after suggesting that Spender might look up Martin Heidegger, with whom Eliot had been struggling and whom he considered important, he expresses his delight that his new friend has attended a performance of the late Beethoven quartets. At the moment of writing, he notes, he is listening to the A minor quartet. He speaks of the divine joy of the piece, a joy that he supposes might result from release following terrible pain. Eliot then expresses a hope that he might be able to capture something of that feeling in verse of his own one day. As these words were written sometime before the publication of the first of the *Four Quartets*, which were inspired by the late Beethoven quartets, they mark what for Spender in hindsight was a significant moment in literary history. In the same letter Eliot compliments Spender on the poems he has just received from him, encourages him to write something with more scope, and suggests that although there is no hurry as far as a volume of poetry is concerned, it would be helpful in terms of self-esteem to see individual poems published— preferably in *The Criterion*.

The most revealing of the early letters is one of June 9, 1932, in which Eliot answers one of Spender's on March 13 in which the younger poet had somewhat brashly criticized the Church of England and suggested that people tend to use religion as an escape. In his letter Spender had somewhat obliquely defended his own "experimental" behaviour in Germany and suggested the need for a new morality. Eliot apologizes for quoting parts of Spender's letter without permission (he had not, in any case, named Spender as the writer of the letter) in a radio broadcast. He then argues that the problem as he sees it is not with the Church of England but with the English people, that the English wish above all to be gentlemen, but that gentlemanliness does not mix with real religious convictions. Real religion, he suggests, demands awkward, unstylish adjustments. Such religion is not an escape; for him it involves not only a realization that there are injustices that need to be attacked but an understanding that the world is doomed to be a place for individual testing. In these words one hears echoes of Eliot's "Journey of the Magi." As for morality, he adamantly proclaims that for him it has nothing to do with Puritanism, either the new kind contained in Spender's new morality or the kind taught to children in school chapels. Above all, Eliot avoids criticizing the younger man on any moral grounds. As far as he is concerned, how people behave is not nearly as important as the way their actions reveal self-image.

If Eliot was a literary father, Virginia Woolf often played the role of sympathetic, if sometimes irritated, mother. The 1930 letter to Mrs. Woolf mentioned above led to a genuine friendship based on Spender's need for approval and advice on both personal and literary matters. It led also to entry to the world of Bloomsbury. By late 1931, not only because of his original letter to Woolf, but through the Nicolsons and his friendship with Rosamond Lehmann Philipps, whose brother John was the editor at the Woolfs' Hogarth Press, he had begun to be a relatively frequent visitor at "Leonard and Virginia" 's for tea, dinner, after-dinner drinks, or even the occasional weekend. At first he was usually invited with William Plomer. Other guests might be E. M. Forster, Vanessa Bell, other members of "Bloomsbury," or Hugh Walpole, who loved telling outrageous stories, such as one about Henry James's supposed affairs with members of the King's Horse Guards. More often than not, however, the Woolfs preferred to have the young poet alone, usually instructing him not to dress formally.

The decorations at the Woolf house in Tavistock Square—especially the furniture and panels painted by Duncan Grant and Vanessa Bell— "represented a fusion of Mediterranean release with a certain restraint and austerity," which seemed to Spender to symbolize the odd mixture of freedom and form that was Bloomsbury.[8]

There was always some tension in Virginia's face as she fussed over her guests, encouraged them to gossip, and spoke archly of even some of her closest friends. In various diary entries and in letters to her sister Vanessa and her nephew Julian she was often snide in her comments on the young Spender, as well. Soon after one dinner party Virginia writes in her diary that Spender was "rattle-headed," and that he had an exaggerated sense of his talents.[9] After another dinner party, at which Spender had held forth on various personal and literary questions, she pronounced in her diary that he had the "makings of a long-winded bore."[10] In a letter to Quentin Bell written on the same day, she compared him to a "great thrush" and made remarks about his being "married to a Sergeant of the Guards."

But Woolf made equally devastating remarks about even friends as close as Vita Sackville-West and Hugh Walpole. Such remarks were the style of her circle and usually involved little or no malice. As much as anything they also reflected momentary irritation over literary and political disagreements, or simply a generation gap. Besides, in other remarks it is clear that Mrs. Woolf liked and felt protective of the young poet. She called him "handsome" and "poetic" and "ardent" in the same diary entry in which she called him "rattle-headed."[11] And she appreciated his defence of her against Wyndham Lewis's attack in *Men Without Art*.[12] She sent him books, and when he had personal problems, she gave him advice and comfort. She also discussed modern ways of approaching the art of novel writing. Whereas Eliot had little interest in a form that he felt had reached its peak in Henry James, Woolf encouraged Spender in his prose efforts. Although she urged him to scrap one early attempt, she encouraged him to try again, suggesting that the modern novel could be a mixture of verse, prose, and dramatic dialogue. Above all, the modern writer must experiment, she said.[13]

By the end of 1933 Spender had been "adopted" by Lady Ottoline Morrell, friend of Graham Greene, Aldous Huxley, Bertrand Russell, Augustus John, and D. H. Lawrence, and of Bloomsbury. It was William Plomer who introduced Spender to her. Lady Ottoline was the source for Hermione Roddice in Lawrence's *Women in Love*. Spender was invited often for tea as well as for Lady Ottoline's famous "Thursdays." At her home on Gower Street he met the likes of Russell, Huxley, and W. B. Yeats. The first meeting with Yeats was a near disaster, as the two men had difficulty hearing each other through the chatter around them, and an awkward silence resulted. Seeing the difficulty, Lady Ottoline called Virginia Woolf, who—much amused—soon arrived to "save the day." Spender happily listened as she and Yeats discussed her novel *The Waves*, which Yeats placed in the context of recent developments in physics having to do with "pulsations of energy throughout the universe." In later meetings Spender and Yeats would discuss the latter's late poetry. Yeats talked about the importance of maintaining a "Byronic lilt" even as he strove for ever more "starkness" and concreteness.[14]

Spender adored Lady Ottoline and continued to correspond with her until her death. He loved watching her eccentric aristocratic behaviour—the "air of falling apart" combined with the "grand manner." He was amused at this elderly woman with red (sometimes purple) hair and "rheumy" eyes who could walk the London streets and ride the buses with several Pekinese dogs attached by ribbons to a shepherdess's crook.[15]

"There was a sense of fulfilment" in meeting the people he met at the homes of Lady Ottoline and Virginia and Leonard Woolf. Spender always loved being among the talented. He was awkward and often shy around such people, but he needed the energy he found in them: "I did not actually enjoy social life, but I felt a strong compulsion towards it," he wrote.[16]

In addition to maintaining carefully his contacts with older writers, Spender, as early as the end of 1930, had made a minor reputation as a poet and was a leading figure in a group of younger modernists including

Rex Warner, John Lehmann, William Plomer, and Rosamond Lehmann, a particularly close friend who, with her husband Wogan Philipps, introduced him to Lytton Strachey. And, in the eyes of the literary world, he was a member of the group that consisted of Louis MacNeice, C. Day-Lewis, Christopher Isherwood, and W. H. Auden. With Auden and Isherwood and Plomer and to a lesser extent with the others, Spender would participate over many years in a process of constructive mutual criticism, which did not result in a "school" of poetry so much as in a commitment to standards that we now associate with the better works of the second generation of English modernists.

From the beginning of his literary career, then, Spender knew that if he was to be a poet and a novelist, he was also to be a personal and sometimes intimate witness to the modernist movement as it would develop through his lifetime in the careers of those he considered, with characteristic humility, to be more important than himself. "During this early period of my meetings with the great," he wrote in *World Within World*,

> I experienced those agonies of longing for their friendship which can hardly be explained to those who do not understand what it is for a young man to start trembling when he recognizes in a crowd the face of someone who means to him, Poet.[17]

The people who most meant "Poet" to him were the great modernists of the generation before him. Spender, Auden, and their friends had since their first Oxford days been excited by the "inclusion within new forms, of material which seemed ugly, anti-poetic, and inhuman." Eliot in *The Waste Land* and Joyce in *Ulysses* revealed that "modern life could be material for art." Spender particularly admired the "hard clear imagery," the "boldness of experimentation," and the "search for means of expressing complicated states of consciousness and acute sensibility" that he found in James, Joyce, Eliot, Woolf, Hemingway, the Sitwells, Pound, and his friend Herbert Read.[18]

Spender and his avant-garde contemporaries were greatly influenced by the works of these writers and of Lawrence, and the late Yeats. The politics of their role models, or the lack thereof, at first did not concern the younger generation. If Eliot and Lawrence and Yeats were reactionary, they were at least not members of the establishment or the Conservative Party. Their reactionary aspect was based on a belief in the importance of tradition in art and society, and they were not actively political. In fact, it seemed distinctly unmodernist to be political: politics were "alien to literature." Like their predecessor Henry James, writers such as Proust, Eliot, Woolf, Joyce, and even Hemingway and Faulkner, all of whom Spender read in the late twenties and early thirties, seemed to have decided that the purpose of art was not to change the world but to celebrate sensibility, the process of literary creation, and consciousness itself. Whether through Prufrock, Stephen Dedalus, or Mrs. Ramsay, they were political only insofar as they "had turned a hero or heroine into a passive spectator of a civilization falling into ruins." Only Lawrence "turned outwards from himself," but not toward politics but toward the relation between men and women and "towards nature."[19]

With the rise of Fascism, however, the so-called "Auden generation" turned with some reluctance, and in most cases only temporarily, to the idea that poetry and art in general must be used as a weapon against the enemy. Fascism was a frontal attack on what they saw as the very values of freedom of expression and experimentation—literary, social, sexual— that they associated with their apolitical and in some cases reactionary older modernist contemporaries.

If Spender most disagreed with his literary "father" on the subject of religion, it was the high modernist assumption that literature should not be tainted by politics, that literature should not in any way become pro-pagandistic, that came to some extent between Spender and his literary "mother." The disagreement was friendly and open, however. As part of a Hogarth Press letters series edited by John Lehmann, Virginia Woolf expressed her views on the subject in a mild attack on Auden, Spender, Day-Lewis, and Lehmann in the July 1932 *Letter to a Young Poet*, which the younger writers took in good spirits and to which Woolf hoped and expected they would respond.

If Yeats, Pound, and Wyndham Lewis were flirting with Fascism as a means of rediscovering order in society—recovering old values in a modern context—and if Woolf and Eliot were saying, in effect, "I told you the world was falling apart," Auden, Spender, Warner, Plomer, Day-Lewis, and others of their generation felt they had no choice but to become actively political. As they looked around at the writers they had most admired, they saw that, as Yeats had said in "The Second Coming," the "best" indeed lacked "all conviction." It was necessary therefore to attach oneself to a political movement that did have convictions and that concerned itself with the welfare of the downtrodden and, they hoped, with the aspirations of those who struggled to break through the barriers of Victorian English morality and classism.

Thus, in the face of what they saw as the failure of the old Liberalism, they all looked to Communism. And they wrote poetry "influenced by the diction and attitudes of Wilfred Owen—a kind of anti-Fascist paci-fist poetry" such as Spender's "Ultima Ratio Regnum," written during the Spanish Civil War, a poem that in the Marxist overtones of the first line and the sexual ones of the sixth is peculiarly Spenderesque, even as it reminds us of Owen's war poetry.[20] The poem begins:

> The guns spell money's ultimate reason
> In letters of lead on the Spring hillside.
> But the boy lying dead under the olive trees
> Was too young and too silly
> To have been notable to their important eye.
> He was a better target for a kiss.

For Spender, the political agenda inevitably merged with his pursuit of the "modern" in his poetry and in his sexual experimentation in Germany. Lehmann, Plomer, Auden, and Isherwood were all confirmed homosexuals and doubtless influenced Spender in his participation in the boy cult that was so much a part of life in a Weimar Germany overrun with unemployed and often desperate youths. Not surprisingly, when Spender sent Vita Sackville-West a copy of his "Oh young men oh young comrades" poem, she was "horrified" by the politics it suggested and probably worried about its sexual implications, even as she was "dazzled" by the poetry itself.[21]

In their appreciation of the young, somewhat blundering, Spender's sensitivity and honesty and his talents as a writer, his older modernist friends and sponsors stood by like good parents and aunts and uncles, recommending or publishing his work, nervously waiting for him to "come to his senses." They waited as patiently as possible, only occasionally offering advice and warnings, while he flirted with Communism, attempted to live a homosexual life, wrote confessional novels and essays and poetry about revolution, and made imagery of such objects as pylons and express trains.

Spender's contemporaries were for the most part supportive of what the older friends thought of as his extremism. In the autumn of 1931, for instance, Isherwood wrote to his friend, praising especially his poetry: "You are absolutely modern in feeling," he wrote.

At the end of 1931 the old house on Frognal in Hampstead was finally sold, and Michael and Stephen, accompanied by Bertha, moved to a large flat at 43 Boundary Road in South Hampstead. Because the flat was crowded and he needed a place to work, Spender rented a small study apartment nearby. Almost immediately, however, he left for Germany. From there he corresponded regularly with Eliot about a collection of poems contracted to be published in 1933 by Fabers. In the meantime he wished to participate in a project through John Lehmann at Hogarth Press and was able to obtain from Eliot a release of several poems to be included in that project, a volume published in February called *New Signatures*, edited by a Woolf protégé at Hogarth, Michael Roberts.

The idea of the anthology was to present to the public in one volume the best of the new second generation of modernist poetry, a poetry that would provide a positive alternative to the earlier twenties poetry of despair. The "stars" of the book were Auden, Day-Lewis, Lehmann, William Empson, and Spender, who immediately became known as the "New Signature poets" and later, after the Spender poem "The Pylons," as the "pylon poets." Spender's contribution dominated the book. It included several of the best poems he ever wrote, including "The Funeral," "The Express," "Oh Young Men," "My Parents," "The Prisoners," and "The Truly Great," all of which also appeared in the Fabers collection.

"The Express" is an example of the attempt of the new poets to assimilate apparently nonpoetic objects into poetry. Here, after "the first powerful plain manifesto/The black statement of pistons," the express train is personified as a woman: "Steaming through metal landscape on her lines/She plunges new eras of wild happiness." In these eras significance lies in the material inventions of the modern age rather than in the fields through which the train and her tracks go. "The Funeral" celebrates a dead worker who "excelled all others in making driving belts." It is an attempt at a poetry that gives value to the men in shirtsleeves who marked Prufrock's passage to his tea party: "This is festivity, it is the time of statistics/When they record what one unit contributed." This festivity of the new world order is compared at the end of the poem to "the decline of a culture"—the Eliot culture—"mourned by scholars who dream of the ghosts of Greek boys." In "My Parents" Spender blames his culture for the separation of the classes—"My parents kept me from children who were rough." "Oh Young Men" is a manifesto, the poet's call to revolution. He and the committed young men of his age are now, whatever their class, "comrades" who, in Spender's somewhat romantic revolution, will "sleep with friend on hill" even as they "advance to rebel."

New Signatures was so successful that Spender became almost overnight a literary lion. He was suddenly the most talked-about poet in London. The Nicolsons so admired his poetry that Harold requested and received a handwritten and signed copy of "The Truly Great" for Vita's birthday in 1932.[22] Virginia Woolf admired Spender's poems less; it was the "New Signature poets" she chided in her *Letter to a Young Poet*. In spite of her opinions, however, she welcomed lively controversy and encouraged Michael Roberts immediately to set to work preparing a second Hogarth anthology, this one with prose and poetry. *New Country,* which contained several Spender poems, all of them more personal than the *New Signatures* poems, would appear early in 1933. In "After Success," for example, Spender treats the subject of jealousy expressionistically in a domestic scene marked by pain and tension:

> *After success, your little afternoon success,*
> *You watch jealous perplexity mould my head*

To the shape of a dark and taloned bird
And fix claws in my lungs, and then you pass
Your silk soothing hand across my arm
And smile . . .

There was also an essay by Spender in *New Country*. It was entitled "Poetry and Revolution" and called on artists to allow their work to reflect social consciousness but not to sacrifice truth to propaganda.

In August 1932 Spender returned briefly to London, where he met for lunch with T. S. Eliot for the purpose of discussing the projected book of poems and the novel *The Temple*. Eliot was not enthusiastic about the latter but continued to be encouraging about the poetry. He had already written Spender suggesting that he should concentrate on poetry rather than wasting his talent on an old fashioned form of writing.[23]

Back in Berlin, Spender spent time with Edward Upward and continued to agonize over the struggle within himself between a traditional liberal's love of "freedom and truth" and the sacrificing of individualism for the common good in Communism. Under Auden's influence—Auden having adopted the views of the American psychologist Homer Lane on the importance of turning guilt feelings into positive energy and equating sin and neurosis—he feared that his worrying about his place in a bourgeois society was only the result of a sense of guilt. One way Spender dealt with these problems was to attempt to develop "guiltless" relationships with working-class youths. In January he had formed another liaison with a seventeen-year-old boy. Even Auden thought his fascination with "buggery" and "boys" was leading him nowhere. Eliot wrote to Spender in Berlin that both he and Auden felt he should come home.[24] By October, after breaking with his boy and being scolded by the Nicolsons about his obsession, he returned to London.

Christopher Isherwood was in London, too. Isherwood was uncomfortable in the literary society of which Spender had become so much a part and was angry at Spender for having somewhat indiscreetly told his best Berlin stories in that society. In reaction, he determined to "get him out of Berlin," which he "regarded as his territory." Isherwood demonstrated his anger by coldness and irritation toward his friend at a house party given by William Plomer and Tony Butts.[25] When Spender confronted him the next day, Isherwood was evasive, which led Spender to suggest that they at least "part like men." Isherwood "replied with a bitchy smile, 'But Stephen, we *aren't* men.'" Isherwood wrote Spender that day saying he would not return to Berlin if Spender did. Spender agreed to the "separation," and the two made up their quarrel. Isherwood realized that they "needed" each other, and for Spender the argument led to a healthy end to the kind of mentor-pupil dependence that had characterized the friendship.[26] One immediate result of the conflict was Spender's revoking of his announced decision to dedicate his 1933 *Poems* to Isherwood. Isherwood responded that he understood perfectly.[27] Nevertheless, when the undedicated *Poems* appeared, Spender sent Isherwood a copy inscribed "For Christopher in admiration and with love from the writer, Jan 10, 1933," and when the second edition was published in 1934, the planned dedication was restored.

For some time Spender had been concerned with what he saw as the essential loneliness of his life. Now twenty-three, never having felt at ease with the sexual "cruising" that was appealing to so many of his homosexual friends, and sensing the rightness of Harold Nicolson's disapproval of his wasting time with German street boys with whom he could have nothing in common, Spender looked about for some sort of permanent relationship. The Nicolsons knew a German of Spender's own age who worked as a cook/butler for a man in Barcelona. Something of Hellmut's character and his relationship with both the Nicolsons and his employer is captured in the Spender short story "The Burning Cactus," which he would begin writing in January of 1933 primarily as a vehicle to describe Hellmut's neurosis. The Nicolsons apparently enjoyed Hellmut's company well enough to suggest to Spender that he might be the perfect companion for him.

It is testimony to Spender's naïveté—and perhaps that of the Nicolsons—that he should have thought that by travelling to Barcelona to "rescue" from service a young man unknown to him, he could successfully fulfil a deep need for permanent companionship. Clearly Spender hoped the relationship could be sexual, and it seems likely that the Nicolsons thought it could be. The idea was that Hellmut would do

the domestic things that Spender knew so little about—shopping, cooking, cleaning. Spender would write. If things went as planned, Hellmut,
who was admittedly depressed and addicted to alcohol, would be "cured,"
and then Spender hoped they would become lovers. It seems, however,
that Spender cared less about the sexual aspect of the relationship, which,
as it turned out, amounted to little or nothing, than he did about nurturing Hellmut emotionally and making him happy. Not surprisingly, the
whole experiment was a disaster.

In an unpublished "Spanish Journal" Spender kept a daily record of
the couple's trek through Spain. From Barcelona they took a ship to
Valencia and then to Alicante. There they discussed sex for the first time.
After a terrible storm at sea they arrived at Málaga, where they stayed a
few days, Hellmut having difficulty tolerating the food. On the twenty-
third of November they began a planned walk, which took them as far as
Algeciras, where they were stoned by a group of children during a fruit-
less search for a decent hotel. Meanwhile, Hellmut suffered badly from
blisters. On the twenty-ninth they took a ship back to Málaga, where
Stephen received a letter saying Isaiah Berlin was ill, an old family friend
dead, and "Granny worried." When they failed to find decent housing,
Hellmut and Stephen gave up and returned to Barcelona. There, after
a few days of happiness, Hellmut became increasingly unbalanced
and things were made worse by the arrival of Spender's brother
Humphrey, who was being pursued by a lovesick alcoholic American
named Kirk, who remained behind after Humphrey left. After much
bitterness and the depletion of their limited financial resources, Hellmut
and Stephen ended their relationship. A letter from Vita Sackville-West
had greeted them on their arrival in Barcelona on December 6. Spender
must have felt the irony of her Orlando-like wish that she were
an "adventurous young man" in her twenties rather than a "middle-
aged woman about to tour the U.S." On January 5 Spender wrote to
Isherwood describing the great experiment as a "failure" and was made
miserable by news that Hellmut had gone to Berlin and attempted to
revive the Spender-Isherwood quarrel. Spender spent a few days in Paris
on his way back to London where he obtained treatment for the tape-
worm he had picked up in Spain.

In London he received the early copies of his *Poems*, the collection, as augmented in the second Faber edition (1934) and the first American edition (Random House, 1934) on which his reputation as a poet has primarily stood. As Spender notes in *World Within World*, this collection followed Auden's *Poems* and Day-Lewis's *Transitional Poem* and caused the linking of their names together as a "school" of poetry emerging from the "New Signature poets." Spender argues that the three poets were, in fact, very different. Auden was an "intellectual poet" who translated the "unconscious mind which had been made bare by psychoanalysts, and transformed it into a powerful poetic imagery." Day-Lewis's talent was "more traditional," one deeply influenced by the Georgian poets, whose "blurred quality" he had "corrected" by at first "introducing images drawn from factories and slums and machinery. . . ." As for Spender himself (who had also introduced this kind of "modernism" into his poetry), he was an "autobiographer restlessly searching for forms in which to express the stages of my development." Spender does admit to being influenced by Auden "in certain imagery, the tone of certain lines." And he points out that the three poets had in common the necessary effect on their work of "unemployment, economic crisis, nascent Fascism, approaching war." They were the "new generation," the new modernists as distinct from the older modernists who came into their own in the twenties.[28]

Poems was a critical success. Because of it, Spender's reputation was solidified. Gerald Bullet's review in *Weekend Review* was typical, calling Spender possibly "one of the most significant voices of the new age." In his jacket comment T. S. Eliot announced that "if Auden is the satirist of this poetical renaissance, Spender is its lyric poet." *Poems* contained thirty-three works, of which sixteen had already begun to establish Spender's reputation in *New Signatures* and *New Country*. There are forty poems in the second edition and forty-two in the definitive American edition. *Poems* provides the kind of objectification of Spender's overall poetic work that Eliot had wanted. In the forty-two poems of the definitive edition we find all of the approaches that we associate with the early Spender. In his sketchbooks of the 1931–33 period, he outlines the book according to the stages of his development. He begins with

"Marston poems" such as "Acts passed" or "Not to you, I sighed" in which we find the romantic and confessional element so favoured by Spender, but now tempered by the modern concreteness of Eliot and Auden:

> Not to you, I sighed. No, not a word.
> We climbed together. Any feeling was
> Formed with the hills. It was like trees unheard
> And monumental sign of country peace.

> But next day stumbling, panting up dark stairs,
> Rushing in room and door flung wide, I knew.
> Oh empty walls, book carcases, blank chairs
> All splintered in my head and cried for you.

The Marston poems are followed by "undergraduate introspective poems," most notably "My parents quarrel," "My parents kept me from children who were rough," "Beethoven's Death Mask," and "An 'I' can never be a great man," containing the lines of a young man who wishes he could be greater than he is:

> The 'great I' is an unfortunate intruder
> Quarrelling with 'I tiring' and 'I sleeping'

We move then to several poems reflecting the 1929 and 1930 experiences in Germany, pieces like "In 1929" and "The Port" hinting at the political turmoil to come.

Central to the collection are the "new generation" "pylon poems" such as "The Express" and "The Pylons" and especially "The Landscape Near an Aerodrome," which makes full use of the new generation's sense of beauty in things mechanical and modern. The airliner approaching the runway is "more beautiful and soft than any moth/With burring furred antennae feeling its huge path/Through dusk. . . ." And there are the socially conscious poems such as "In Railway Halls," in which the plight of the poor takes on an ominous air,

their eyes made big by empty staring
And only measuring Time, like the blank clock.

Openly political poems such as "Oh Young Men" and "Not Palaces" are included as well, with the fervent lines of a young poet moved by the possibility of a revolutionary new order—lines such as "Flag of our purpose which the wind engraves" and ". . . No man/Shall hunger: Man shall spend equally./Our goal which we compel: Man shall be man."

And, of course, there are the great signature poems for which the poet is best remembered—"The Truly Great" and "What I expected," a poem that perhaps more than any other captures Spender's mood at this stage of his life. It is a poem by a man who has longed to achieve the heroism of the "truly great" but who through experience has learned something of his own limitations and the world's.

What I expected was
Thunder, fighting,
Long struggles with men
And climbing. . . .

What I had not foreseen
Was the gradual day
Weakening the will
Leaking the brightness away, . . .

For I had expected always
Some brightness to hold in trust,
Some final innocence
To save from dust;
That, hanging solid,
Would dangle through all
Like the created poem
Or the dazzling crystal.

5

LOVE AND IDEOLOGY

With the publication of *Poems* in 1933, Stephen Spender realized an ambition that had coloured his life since those early childhood nights in the Lake District when he had overheard his father reading Wordsworth. "I will be a poet," he had thought then, and now all of literary London recognized him as such. Yet pure happiness did not come with fame. For one thing, Spender's political and personal hopes had to a great extent been dashed by circumstances. The idyllic and sexually exciting world of Weimar Germany, which he had discovered in the summer of 1929, had turned into a nightmare under the rise of Hitler. On February 27, the day before his twenty-fourth birthday, the Nazis had the Reichstag (Parliament) building set on fire, accused the Communists of the crime, and then, under a state of emergency, began arresting their enemies. On the twenty-first of March Spender's essay "Poetry and Revolution" appeared in Michael Roberts's *New Country*. The poet who felt most comfortable in a modernistic but confessional mode was now placing his talents in the service of political action. On March 23 Hitler obtained dictatorial powers. Clearly Germany had not and would not fulfil its promise as a positive moral alternative to the Victorian values of British society.

Even the release from sexual repression that Spender had at first found in his relations with German youths had led to nothing positive in his life. At twenty-four he remained alone and, less able than his circle of homosexual friends to find satisfaction in short-term relationships, he harboured an intense desire for domestic intimacy. He did not contemplate marriage, but he was "in the mood when people advertise for a companion in the newspaper."[1] It was in the context of this mood, which he had communicated to his London friends, that he was introduced to Tony Hyndman (Jimmy Younger in *World Within World*) late in March. Tony, a Welshman whose father ran a hotel near Cardiff, had left home as a teenager and eventually joined the army. Christopher Isherwood would describe him later:

> His appearance was attractive: curly red-brown hair, sparkling yellow-brown eyes, big smiling teeth. He would call Stephen "yer silly thing!" and tell him, "Don't be so daft!" with a Welsh accent. He was full of fun and the love of argument.[2]

The two men liked each other immediately. Tony told Isherwood that when he met Stephen, "that was when the curtain went up, for me."[3] And Spender, with the same impulsiveness that had led him to ask Hellmut to be his companion, asked Tony to live with him as his secretary. But as Spender had no flat of his own at this point, he and Tony, who had very quickly become lovers, decided to travel to Italy.

After a few days in Venice and Florence they settled in the Hotel Stella d'Italia in Levanto. Spender wrote to William Plomer that he and Tony were in love and happy. He also noted with interest that the *Daily Worker* had called him "a young poet turned revolutionary" and that a reader had responded to the effect that he was only a bourgeois intellectualizing leftist ideals.[4] Spender was not put out by this criticism, perhaps because he knew it was at least partly accurate. In any case, his literary life was, for the moment, keeping pace with his revolutionary one. He was happily reading T. E. Lawrence's (Lawrence of Arabia's) translation of the *Odyssey*, thinking about translating Rilke, and once again reworking *The Temple*, with some encouragement from T. S. Eliot. He had reviewed Eliot's recent American lectures, "The Uses of Poetry and the Uses of Criticism," and had been confident enough of his own judgment to criticize the master for some of his views and, characteristically, had then written to him to apologize for having done so. Eliot answered that the criticism was justified and that Spender's only shortcoming was in failing to see the irony in his work.[5]

Meanwhile, W. H. Auden wrote from his position as a schoolmaster from Downs School, Colwell, complaining of having to teach for money while Stephen and Tony and Christopher and his friend were free to live abroad and write.[6]

In spite of the apparent success of the Levanto stay, there were difficulties between Spender and Hyndman almost from the beginning. Spender discusses the relationship at some length in *World Within World*.[7] The problems were essentially class generated. Once again, as in the case of Hellmut, Spender was attempting to build a relationship based on his lover's working for him—in this case as a secretary. Although Tony was naturally intelligent, appreciative of his employer's work (he memorized several Spender poems), and more than willing to learn, it was apparent from the beginning that Spender did not really need a secretary. What he wanted was someone he could nurture in the same way he had tried to "cure" Hellmut. And he needed someone he could take to the homes of his friends as his steady companion. Once in Levanto, Tony said that as "nicely" as Spender treated him, he wanted to leave: "I feel that I am becoming completely your property." Yet when Spender said that of course he could leave whenever he wished to, Hyndman was placed in the position of being at once not needed and unable to leave without seeming ungrateful or unreasonable. At the same time, Spender would become irritated at his friend because he found it "difficult to force someone who is living on equal terms with me to work" and because, in fact, Tony had "so little to do" other than cook and clean up their living quarters. Life with Tony throughout the relationship was a "strain" that resulted from "the impression of being with someone whose life was empty." Spender was worried about being what today would be called an "enabler" and he sometimes thought it would be best for Tony if he simply broke off the relationship.[8]

Once again, as with Hellmut, Spender seems to have entered into a homosexual relationship somewhat arbitrarily because he wanted a "boy," particularly one who represented the lower orders he wanted so much to help. Still, the two men would come to love and respect each other and by the time they broke away, it would be with a great deal of pain on both sides.

By July, Spender and Hyndman were back in London staying in Humphrey Spender's flat on Upper Montague Street, and as a couple they became particularly friendly with E. M. Forster and his ex-policeman friend, Bob Buckingham. Although Forster and Buckingham did not live together and were not public about their relationship, the nature of their friendship was well known within the set that included William Plomer, John Lehmann, Bloomsbury, and Spender. Forster and Spender talked a great deal about the significance of their "marriages" to men of the blue-collar class. Forster advised his younger friend on the revision of *The Temple* and shared with him his own unpublished homosexual novel, *Maurice,* which he revealed was "wish fulfilment" rather than "autobiography."[9] In spite of his keeping his private life "closeted," Forster was a better role model and adviser in connection with sexual matters than Spender's other older-generation author confidants, Virginia Woolf and T. S. Eliot, who were both somewhat embarrassed by the open Hyndman relationship. During the troubles that would face Spender and especially Hyndman in the years to follow, Forster remained a faithful and supportive friend to both men.

Throughout the last months of 1933 and the early months of 1934, Spender continued in his role—now augmented by the publication of his *Poems*—as an active man of letters. There were numerous lunches with T. S. Eliot, dinners at the Woolfs', and tea at Lady Ottoline's with such notables as Woolf, Aldous Huxley, Bertrand Russell, T. S. Eliot, and W. B. Yeats, all of whom listened to young Spender's radical, if somewhat untidy, opinions on revolution, love, and poetry and doubtless marvelled at Tony Hyndman—"Stephen's Sergeant of the Guards"—whom he sometimes brought with him. Although Mrs. Woolf wrote to Lady

Ottoline calling Spender one of the current crop of egotistical "niminy piminies" with "refrigerators" for minds and "blank paper" for souls, she and Leonard and especially the Nicolsons continued to like him and to invite their "modern day Shelley" to their homes.[10] T. S. Eliot remained loyal, too, though according to Virginia Woolf, he felt there was "some melody some rhythm some emotion lacking in the Audens and Spenders."[11]

Spender was much in demand. Mrs. Munro at the Poetry Bookshop, encouraged by Eliot, requested permission to publish several of Spender's poems in an anthology. And there were constant requests by journals for reviews, poems, and short stories. On September 3, for example, Spender reviewed "That Sanity Be Kept," a poem by the then little-known Welsh poet Dylan Thomas, in the *Sunday Referee*. He and William Plomer took Thomas to lunch at the Cafe Royal and were so amused and impressed that Spender recommended Thomas's work enthusiastically to his some-times friend Geoffrey Grigson. Grigson published it in *New Verse*. Several years later Spender would lead a successful attempt to raise money for the then destitute Thomas and his wife. In his more-than-energetic work to get Isherwood's *The Memorial* published and in his assistance and encouragement of Thomas and later of many other writers, including William Goyen, George Barker, and Reynolds Price, to mention only a few, Spender always displayed a great deal of generosity of spirit.

In October Spender and Tony took a flat at 25 Randolph Crescent in Maida Vale, the Little Venice district of London, an area that, while shabby, reminded Spender of Berlin and had the advantage of a beauti-ful park accessible only to the houses on the crescent. William Plomer lived nearby with a policeman lover. Auden stayed there when he was on holiday from his school, and Joe Ackerley, author of *Hindu Holiday* and soon to become literary editor of the *Listener*, had a flat there. Always somewhat resentful of being lumped together with her friends as "Bloomsbury," Virginia Woolf now referred to this group as "Maida Vale" or, when she chose to be more arch, as the "Lilies of the Valley."[12]

For a while Stephen and Tony were happy at Randolph Crescent. They painted the flat together and instead of one working for the other they shared the cooking, and for a while Tony tried his hand at writing.

Spender did his best—but without success—to interest Eliot and Faber and Faber in a Hyndman novel, of which Tony finished several chapters.[13] The couple's primary social life was with an artistic set that included close gay friends such as Plomer, Forster, Buckingham, and Joe Ackerley, other friends and associates such as Geoffrey Grigson, Isaiah Berlin, Bernard Spencer, writers Cuthbert Worsley, Julian Huxley, and Gerald Heard, artists John Piper, Henry Moore, and William Coldstream, and, of course, Auden, Isherwood, MacNeice, and Day-Lewis when they were in town. John Lehmann was a part of the gay literary aspect of the set, but was not close to Spender. There were dinner parties at each other's flats and various outings to museums, plays, musical events, and restaurants. And there were occasional visits to Downs School, including particularly memorable ones during the early Christmas seasons to attend Wystan Auden's risqué school musicals full of innuendos created in part for the amusement of "Maida Vale."

During the mid- and late thirties, in spite of Eliot's disapproval, expressed on several occasions—Eliot still wanted his protégé to write poems only—Spender turned increasingly to literary criticism and the novel as modes of expression. In the fall of 1933 he began work on what he called his Henry James book. Spender had long admired James as one of the great premodernists, the ancestor of Joyce and Woolf and Eliot. Now he was anxious that James, the quintessential nonpolitical writer, be reread in the context of the crumbling of European values that marked the thirties. "The School of Experience in the Early Novels," an offshoot of the James work, would appear in a James issue of *Hound and Horn* edited by Lincoln Kirstein and would contribute to the mid-thirties revival of interest in the American novelist.[14]

In April Spender and Hyndman once again took up their travels. This time they settled in Mlini, a village near Dubrovnik in Yugoslavia. Spender worked on James, as well as on essays about Eliot, Lawrence, and Auden, which would, with the James piece, become *The Destructive Element*. He also agreed to Eliot's request that he do a second and enlarged edition of *Poems*.[15] And he began work on a play, which would emerge as *The Trial of a Judge*.

At the Pension Mlini Spender found an appropriate setting for another short story inspired in part by the Hellmut experience. "The Dead Island" was about the relationship between a character with Hellmut's and Kirk's alcohol and self-esteem problems and an unusual woman staying in a pension in a village near Dubrovnik.

Spender, in fact, met the partial source for the heroine of "The Dead Island" at the Pension Mlini. Muriel Gardiner ("Elizabeth" in *World Within World*) was, like the character in the story, twice divorced, independent, nurturing, and in possession of an air of having suffered.[16] She was an American, some eight years older than Spender. Unlike the fictional character, she was in Mlini with a little daughter and her nurse. Mrs. Gardiner was a student of psychology and medicine in Vienna. To the English writer working, among other things, on a book about Henry James, she was a real-life Jamesian heroine. Like Isabel Archer and Maggie Verver, she had "the freshness and newness of some dusty portrait from which the varnish had been removed, revealing the colours of the glowing flesh in their most shocking brilliance." With her "dark eyes, oval face . . . [and black] hair," which "if it had been plaited and braided into tresses would have had a snake-like sinuous quality," Muriel reminded Spender of Leonardo's *Leda*. She and Spender had in common a love of the English romantics, which Muriel had once studied at Oxford, and they had similar tastes in music and art. And, most important to Mrs. Gardiner, Spender was as "passionately concerned" with German-Austrian politics as she was.[17] She was in Mlini for only a few days, but when she learned that Tony's appendix needed medical attention, she suggested that she make hospital arrangements in Vienna and that the two men come to stay with her there.

At the end of May, Hyndman and Spender moved to Vienna. Although Tony's appendicitis would have justified a return to London, where there would have been familiar surroundings and English spoken in the hospital, Spender decided that Vienna would be more suitable. The couple had been fighting a great deal over minor issues, and Spender felt this was in part because of his growing fascination with Muriel Gardiner, whose invitation he was determined to accept. In Vienna Tony was immediately put into the hospital for his operation. Spender visited him regularly, finding a setting for much of still

another short story, "Two Deaths," in which, as in actual fact, the narrator's friend Tony has been operated on for appendicitis and is in a
bed next to that of an Englishman and across the room from a dying
Viennese man.

While Tony was in the hospital, Spender and Muriel had long
evening talks, and in his customary impulsive way, Spender announced
to Muriel that he was "attracted" to her. As the feelings were mutual, the
two became lovers.[18] In her memoir, *Code Name Mary,* Gardiner remembers that before the first time they made love, Spender spoke of his
embarrassment, as he "had never been in love with a woman before,
never even been attracted to a woman."[19]

So began what was until that time the most important of Spender's
relationships with women. Mrs. Gardiner was everything he could have
dreamed of in a woman. She was beautiful, a patient mother, an excellent cook and housekeeper, a dedicated student, and an exciting and
romantic lover, and, above all, she was understanding of his "ambivalence." In fact, "she understood, more than anyone has ever done, the
nature of the difficulty."[20] As far as the immediate situation was concerned, even as she and Stephen experienced their love affair—in
Vienna, in Muriel's small wooden house, the "Blockhaus," in Sulz, in the
Vienna woods, and in the flower-filled fields in front of the Blockhaus—
she understood his continuing sense of responsibility for and affection
for Tony. But although there was understanding, there was also "outraged frustration," as Muriel wanted Stephen only if he was capable of
deciding on his own what he must do about his "situation."[21]

When Tony was released from the hospital, Spender took him to the
village of Mariazell to convalesce. The village had a baroque church that
would serve later as a setting for an attempted assassination in "Two
Deaths." Spender disliked the village and wrote to William Plomer that
he was holed up in his room reading Eliot's "The Rock" with ambiguous
feelings about it and Eliot. And he spoke about Muriel—a figure out of
James whom he found attractive. He also expressed a sense of guilt;
his character was lacking. Here he was sleeping with Muriel even as he
lived with Tony and occasionally made love with others as well. But

Tony seemed to him to be most important, so he would proceed with things as they were.[22]

One way he would deal with the Muriel situation was somehow to idealize her. He would see her in the light of women he admired but not necessarily as lovers. At the beginning of his relationship with her he had told her she reminded him of his mother when she was young. Muriel had responded that this was not "a bad reason for falling in love."[23] Now he was rereading *To the Lighthouse*, paying particular attention to the character of Mrs. Ramsay, whom he much admired. He wrote to Virginia Woolf praising her novel, saying it was the only novel besides *War and Peace* that he had read several times. He did not mention Muriel, but she seems to have been on his mind as he described Winifred Carritt, the wife of his Oxford tutor, as his earliest experience of the "Mrs. Ramsay type."[24] Woolf asked about Mrs. Carritt, commenting that she wished there were a way of "circulating people ... as beautiful and charming as that."[25]

Meanwhile, Germany and Austria were on the point of explosion. On July 25 the autocratic Austrian chancellor Dollfuss, who was much hated by liberals and leftists for his brutal suppression of the Socialists, was assassinated in an attempted Fascist coup, an event Spender would incorporate into his "Two Deaths," in which the dying Viennese man in the hospital becomes the representative of the oppression of the Socialists. On June 30 Hitler had rival leaders murdered and turned to a more open policy of persecuting Jews and burning books. On August 2 he would be proclaimed führer.

During all of these events, Spender was in Germany and Austria— for a few days back at Sellin, then with Muriel and Tony in Vienna and Sulz. There was also a brief trip to the Tyrol to "get away" with Tony. The combination of political and personal confusion was overwhelming. Germany and Austria, in spite of past pleasures and present romances, were depressing, and he confided to Plomer that he wished he could "disentangle" himself from Tony.[26] He asked that Plomer and Winifred Paine, whom Spender often referred to as his "stepmother" because she had helped to care for him after his mother's death, serve as trustees of his estate. He wanted to be sure that in his will Tony was "looked after." In fact, Spender had drawn up an actual will stating that Tony should inherit £300 from the Ernest Joseph Schuster bequest fund and that the estate's trustees were to find work for him. The will was witnessed by Muriel.[27]

Earlier Spender had written to Geoffrey Grigson a particularly revealing letter in which he expressed a determination to avoid the kind of literary social life that had marked his recent life in London, to get on with his work—abroad if possible—to face his ambivalence once and for all, and, preferably, to settle into marriage—presumably with Muriel.[28]

In the summer Spender was working hard on a long poem called *Vienna*, which would attempt to make sense of the mixed emotions and political and personal confusion in his life: "I tried to relate the public passion to my public life."[29] The poem expressed Spender's sense that the individual must remain free—free, for instance, to love in a complex, ambivalent way—even as he recognizes the need in the current political situation to give up individualism in the interest of a communal Marxist cause. Spender was experiencing the passion and the romance of his relationships with Tony and Muriel and, at the same time, was feeling equally passionate about Dollfuss's suppression of the Socialists. The situation was complicated by Muriel's personal commitment to the Socialist cause, which became Spender's, too. Muriel was working hard as part of a "cell" that was smuggling people and material back and forth between Vienna and Bratislava. She felt that the relationship with Spender was probably doomed because neither she nor he could escape from the fateful political events with which they were both so involved. They were overcome by "fears of a doomed future" for their civilization.[30]

As has been suggested by Sanford Sternlicht and others, *Vienna* is clearly influenced by Spender's reading of T. S. Eliot. Vienna in the poem, "embattled, gutted, and raped of its hope, becomes a 'wasteland' in which the dream of a Socialist civilization perishes."[31] It is as if Spender had chosen to enter one of the great fallen cities listed in *The Waste Land* to experience its fall directly. In Part I, "Arrival at the

City," the persona of the poem takes up residence in a Viennese pension peopled by the culturally dead. The first lines of the poem are those of a poet who clearly has Eliot in mind:

> *Whether the man living or the man dying*
> *Whether this man's dead life, or that man's life dying*

The poet wanders through the city of "floors scrubbed clean of love," which stands for the decay of a whole civilization.

In Part II, "Parade of the Executive," the essential social conflict is established between the power of capitalism linked with that of the political dictatorship, represented by the voice of the executive, and the people, represented by the voice of the unemployed. Into this conflict Spender interjects both Muriel, "With dark eyes neglected," and the boy lovers who had been so much of his earlier German experience, who were now in the Fascist youth movements, and who would in the future be "howitzer fodder."[32] The voice of the unemployed suggests that the listener ask the unemployed why they "stare at us" as if at "the inexplicable irrelevance/of lust? . . ."

Part III, "The Death of Heroes," contains the story of the defeat of the students and workers at the hands of the Fascists at Karl-Marx-Hof. This failure stands for Spender as the symbol of the end of the possibility of heroism in the context of the old European civilization and the rise of a new necessarily communal struggle in which the individual is only an ignorant cog in a larger machine. Those who remained living would have to exchange a life of "tasks fit for heroes" for one of "constructing cells."

In Part IV, "Analysis and Final Statement," the voice of the poem attempts to hold on to objectivity and to understand what he has seen and what Vienna means. But what emerges out of the collective horror is a sense of the importance of the individual love that can bring solace. The poet stands once again as a free individual, free of everything, including his father's and England's own kind of moral imprisonment and the rise of German Fascism, free even of the boys of Weimar Germany and all they represent. And he turns to the woman he had described in Part II, asserting in a manner that is lyrical, optimistic Spenderesque rather than Eliotic, that

> *Our sexes are the valid flowers*
> *Sprinkled across the total world and wet*
> *With night. It surely was my father*
> *His dry love his dry falling*
> *Through dust and death to stamp my feature*
> *That made me ever fear that fortunate posture.*

In some ways *Vienna* is a love poem, and Spender dedicated it to Muriel.

T. S. Eliot read a draft of *Vienna* in September and liked it well enough to agree to a contractual change so that Faber and Faber could publish it before the as-yet-unfinished *Trial of a Judge*.[33] E. M. Forster read it in draft form, too. He found it "modern" and compared it to music—specifically to Debussy. He preferred its emotion to that of *The Waste Land*.[34]

In September Spender and Tony left Vienna, Spender intending to do something about his lover before returning, as he fully intended to do, to Muriel. Back in London there was the usual social whirl. Dinner invitations came from the Woolfs. Could he come with Rosamond Philipps? With Herbert Read? E. M. Forster (now familiarly "Morgan"), Bob Buckingham, William Plomer, and Joe Ackerley were anxious to see him, too. Ottoline Morrell was insistent that he come for tea—often. Yeats wanted to talk with him again—especially after the appearance of "W.B. Yeats as a Realist" in Eliot's *New Criterion*, an essay derived from work done on what would become *The Destructive Element*.[35] Yeats's late, modernist verse, Spender had written, demonstrated that "realism is not inconsistent with a certain romanticism," but "[Yeats] has found . . . no subject of moral significance in the social life of his time."[36] That Spender himself aimed for a poetic voice that could combine the realism of pylons and contemporary concerns with his own tendency toward a lyrical romanticism was no secret to anyone.

The social obligations became so extreme that Spender refused an invitation from T. S. Eliot for an evening occasion by insisting that he did not have proper clothes. Eliot, always somewhat fatherly with Spender, answered in a tone that combined irritation and humour, suggesting that Spender could arrive "in a barrel" if he wished or, if he promised to give it back, in a suit that he would lend him.[37] Spender did as he was told.

When *Vienna* appeared in November, Virginia Woolf, who did not like it, refused the *London Mercury*'s request (suggested by Spender) that she review it. Furthermore, his old friend Geoffrey Grigson called it a "bad poem," and the *Times Literary Supplement* suggested that the poem tried to make us pity the Socialists but led us "to a view of the poet himself in an act of being pitiful."[38] Spender was horrified and asked Eliot to withdraw the poem from Fabers' list. Eliot attempted to soothe his feelings. There were good things in the poem, he said, but it had probably been written too quickly.[39] *Vienna* was better than Spender thought it was, he wrote, and if there were problems because of his personal closeness to the subject, such problems were justifiable given the social climate of the times.[40] In any case, the new edition of his *Poems* came out at the end of the year, with nine new poems added, and the reception was good. And at the beginning of 1935 the story "Burning Cactus" was published in *Best Stories of 1934*. Spender quickly recovered from his disappointment.

In January he returned to Muriel in Vienna. Muriel remembered particularly joyful times spent at the cottage in Sulz that January— "intimate conversations" in front of the fire, skiing on the hills nearby.[41] But Spender still had not settled his "situation." He wrote to Plomer that he missed Tony. Without the Vienna project he sometimes seemed at a loss at Muriel's.[42] In a month Spender was back with Tony at Randolph Crescent, and in less than a month after that he was back in Vienna— this time with Tony—and by then it was clear that the love affair, though not the friendship, with Muriel was over. In fact, Spender had received a letter from her announcing her relationship with Joseph Buttinger (Franz in *World Within World*), the leader of her Socialist cell, news that surprised him but also left him with a feeling of some relief. He would write later to William Plomer that he had waited too long to make up his mind about Muriel but that in any case he needed to be on his own.[43]

In Vienna Spender settled down to work. Eliot agreed in a letter of March 8, in which he addressed Spender familiarly for the first time as "My Dear Stephen" and signed himself "Yours affectionately, Tom," that he should leave poetry for a brief time in order to put together a book of short stories. He had thought of suggesting that Spender review Pound's *Cantos* for *The Criterion*, but was afraid that people would say that *Vienna* had been written under their influence and would look askance at a positive review. In any case, he felt in general that poets should never review poetry.[44]

In April Jonathan Cape published Spender's important book of literary criticism, *The Destructive Element,* dedicated to Rosamond (Lehmann) and Wogan Philipps. This was originally to have been Spender's long-talked-about "James book," and Part I is on James. Sometime in 1934, however, Spender had decided to expand the work to include in a second part three modernist writers he particularly admired—Yeats, Lawrence, and Eliot—who were, like James, "faced by the destructive element, by the experience of an all-pervading Present, which is a world without belief."[45] And finally he added a third section defending the politicization of literature that marked his own generation. For Spender it was urgent that the important writers of the past be reexamined in light of that politicization.

Spender sees Henry James as a writer who turned away from the horrors of the decadent European civilization in which he places his characters, by having those characters develop an inner world of aesthetic morality—an "aestheticism of behaviour."[46] But the reader of *The Destructive Element* is told that below the elegant surfaces of James's premodernist style, in the inner worlds of characters like Maggie Verver of *The Golden Bowl* and Kate Croy of *The Wings of the Dove*, there is the chaotic horror that foreshadows a modern world of war, economic depression, and the rise of Fascism: "Beneath the stretched out compositions there are abysses of despair and disbelief: *Ulysses* and *The Waste Land*."[47]

Eliot, Yeats, and Lawrence are treated by Spender as "individualists," like James, who created artificial if effective means of struggling against the destructive element. Eliot turned to religion and myth for his defence, Yeats to a mixture of myth and mystery. Lawrence turned to psychology and sex. Eliot's failure is that he is isolated within himself, providing only a pessimistic view of existence. Yeats is unable to connect his mythology with the reality of the times. In order to support the cause of antireaction, the writers of Spender's generation have no choice but to struggle against the despairing viewpoint presented by these two great modernists. As for Lawrence, he was at least able to deny the Eliotic waste land vision in favour of a concern with the real problems of the contemporary political world.

In the final section of the work, "In Defence of a Political Subject," Spender asserts that "the greatest art is moral even when the artist has no moral axe to grind." By discussing Joyce, Auden, Rilke, and others, he develops his point of view that while the true artist is always concerned with aesthetic matters and with the examination of the inner self, he must also always be concerned with the moral/political life around him. And, as Spender had discovered in his very real situation with Muriel, there are times—specifically revolutionary times such as the mid-thirties—when "questions of social justice, of liberty, of war or peace, of election . . . become really important . . . [and] questions of private morality . . . become almost insignificant." So it is that Spender, who admires the modernists he discusses, takes a Marxist stand in 1934, arguing that "political conscience" must finally determine the essence of any given work.[48]

The reviews of The Destructive Element were generally good, and his closest friends among the older modernist generation generally approved. In her diary, Virginia Woolf praised the book's "considerable swing and fluency," and although she felt the last section was weak, she admired the author for "grappling" with the problems of morality, politics, and modernism.[49] Woolf wrote to Spender to this effect, adding that she thought writers of Spender's generation preached too much.[50] Ottoline Morrell took the opposite position. She liked the last section of the book better than the sections on James, Eliot, Yeats, and Lawrence. She also informed her friend that Yeats liked Spender's poetry but had little use for his criticism.[51] As for Eliot, he wrote to Spender praising the work. He assured Spender that he was by no means

offended by anything said about him. For him, art and morality were
inseparable. His primary criticism centred on what he saw as misinterpretations of James, which he attributed to Spender's not knowing his
subject well enough. Most important, Eliot agreed with Spender about
the kind of literary criticism that was appropriate for their age.[52]

Eliot seemed most concerned with the fact that *The Destructive
Element* had been published by Jonathan Cape rather than by Fabers. He
was anxious that Spender not leave Fabers, and he received assurances
that he would not.

In June Spender was back in Mlini with Tony. Auden wrote to say he
had married Thomas Mann's daughter Erika so that she might leave
Germany more easily and that he admired *The Destructive Element*.[53] In
July Spender and Hyndman went back to the Tyrol, where Spender
worked hard on the short story collection that would take its title from
"The Burning Cactus."

A story that had been intended for inclusion in the collection and
was, like several of the stories, to be published first in the *London
Mercury* was the catalyst for a personal conflict that had been brewing
for some time. The story involved a character called Landin, a handsome
and highly promiscuous "cruising" English homosexual in Berlin. No
one who knew Spender and John Lehmann could have had any doubts
about the identification of Landin as Lehmann. Spender's treatment
of Lehmann was indiscreet, particularly as they had a working relationship at Hogarth Press and Spender was close to his sister Rosamond.
The indiscretion had its source in a rare dislike that Spender had for
Lehmann, one that had begun as early as 1931 and persisted and exploded
into several disputes in later years.

In September of 1931 Lehmann had written to Spender suggesting
that they discuss their friendship, and Spender had answered in an
uncharacteristically harsh and sarcastic tone, suggesting that if Lehmann
wished to have anything to do with Spender, he had better learn to "be
a hero." That is, he had better learn to be strong enough to stand as
an individual in their friendship without examining its nature.[54] Behind
the somewhat immaturely pompous words of the letter there is a sense

of a genuine disdain. Later Spender would apologize, but without taking back his letter's essential content.[55] Still later he would write to William Plomer, who knew Lehmann well, that although he "adored" Rosamond, he did not like her brother—perhaps because he and Lehmann were all too much like each other.[56] This insight was not altogether accurate. Spender saw in Lehmann, especially when Lehmann visited Isherwood and him in Berlin and cruised the gay bars, a callous use of boys as sex objects that he hoped was not a fault that could be attributed to himself. Christopher Isherwood at first "was suspicious of and on his guard against this tall handsome young personage with his pale narrowed quizzing eyes, measured voice which might have belonged to a Foreign Office expert, and extremely becoming, prematurely grey hair."[57]

In the case of the Landin story, Spender had second thoughts after he showed the manuscript to Isherwood and to Rosamond Philipps. They both considered it improper, and although by the time it got into Lehmann's hands Spender had withdrawn it from the *London Mercury*, the damage had already been done.[58] There was an unpleasant exchange of letters in which Spender rationalizes his use of Lehmann as a mere fictional device and Lehmann expresses his distress at what he sees as a gross indiscretion and invasion of privacy.[59] Near the end of his life Spender would have to face what some would call a similar indiscretion and invasion of his own privacy.[60]

In August of 1935 Spender and Tony visited Christopher Isherwood in Brussels, where he was living with his lover Heinz, who was attempting to avoid being drafted in Germany. Forster and Buckingham went, too. In the next months Spender and Hyndman would take several trips to Brussels, during which they made plans with Christopher and Heinz for an extended trip to Portugal. On December 1 Virginia Woolf, who had recently entertained Spender at dinner, wrote to her nephew Julian Bell that Spender and Isherwood were off to Portugal with two male friends "of the lower orders." She also could not resist an arch remark about Spender, Auden, and Day-Lewis as a "holy trinity."

Before leaving, Spender lectured on modern poetry to what he considered a boring old women's club meeting chaired by T.S. Eliot. Spender, supported by Eliot, argued for the importance of modern poetry and for a public moral stance on the part of contemporary poets.[61]

The record of the Portugal experience was kept jointly by Spender and Isherwood, and sometimes Tony, in a diary book given to Spender by Lady Ottoline. The four men took a Brazilian ship from Antwerp to Sintra, where they rented a house from a "spooky" English landlady and quickly acquired a puppy, a cock, five hens, and a few rabbits.[62] Tony did the accounts, Heinz looked after the animals, and Spender and Isherwood worked on projects, Isherwood on a novel and Spender on two political works, *Forward from Liberalism* and *Trial of a Judge*. Spender kept up a lively correspondence with his older patrons—Lady Ottoline, Virginia Woolf, and Eliot. Woolf loved reading "The Burning Cactus."[63] Lady Ottoline discussed Eliot's *Murder in the Cathedral*, which Spender admired for its poetry but not for what he considered its irrelevant content.[64] Eliot suspected that the diet in Portugal was probably "constipating" and noted that Yeats was in Minorca with a swami translating the Upanishads.[65]

At first things went smoothly enough, and there was a happy visit from Humphrey Spender, but eventually petty domestic tensions overcame what they had all hoped would be a utopian idyll, and Spender and Tony left for Spain just as Wystan Auden was arriving to work with Christopher on a play.

Spender was delighted to be back in Spain. He and Tony spent a few days in Madrid and Barcelona. But Tony was not happy with travelling, and he and Stephen fought a great deal. A trip to Athens did not do much good. As Spender would say later in *World Within World*, their relationship had gone as far as it could go. They had arrived "at a point where they [knew] everything about each other" and it seemed "impossible for the relationship to develop beyond this."[66] In marriage there might be children; with Tony there was merely the prospect of something static. Nevertheless, they kept trying. From Athens they went to Vienna and then back to the Tyrol and to Bonn and Berlin and finally Salzburg. Spender was seeking revitalization in favourite haunts. But in July the Spanish Civil War broke out and soon the lives of both men would change radically.

Spender's return to London at the end of the summer coincided with the publication of his collection of short stories, *The Burning Cactus*. Besides "The Burning Cactus," "The Dead Island," and "Two Deaths," the book included two autobiographical stories. "The Cousins" is essentially a parable about a young Spender-like aesthete who chooses Socialism and art over the life of his superficial bourgeois relatives, one of whom is a boy based on his cousin John Schuster, with whom he had been in love as an adolescent.[67] "By the Lake," the rewriting of the early story Spender had shown to Auden and Isherwood at Oxford, is based on his sojourn in Switzerland before going up to the university. The hero of the story, who falls in love with a younger English companion, is a thinly veiled portrait of the young Spender. *The Burning Cactus* is marked by the psycho-erotic concerns of D. H. Lawrence's work and by the mixture of poetry and prose that Virginia Woolf had suggested to Spender as an appropriate modern approach to fiction. The work is a modernist collection, which embodies something of the "destructive element" discussed by Spender in his book of that name. We confront in all of these stories lives that can best be understood against the background of a waste land world of looming catastrophe. Spender dedicated *The Burning Cactus* to Tony Hyndman and W. H. Auden.

In November the live-in relationship with Tony ended. Spender found his friend a job with the *Left Review* and continued to employ him two days a week as a secretary and also in other ways to assist him.[68] Both he and Spender had moved even further toward Communism now that people were taking sides in the Spanish Civil War. After breaking with Tony, Spender moved alone to a new address in Hammersmith at 11 Queen's Mansions in Brook Green. He decorated the flat in the Bauhaus style reminiscent of his Berlin days, taking pleasure in the metal and bentwood furniture and the modernist lamps.

As soon as his new flat was ready, Spender, saddened by the end of his relationship with Tony, took a nostalgic trip to Skelgill Farm in the Lake District, where he had gone with his parents so many years before and where he had listened to his father read Wordsworth. Isaiah Berlin came to visit, and Hugh Walpole, who was staying nearby, came for lunch from time to time. And he read Wordsworth and the Germans

Hölderlin and Rilke. The relationship with Tony had failed, as had the one with Muriel Gardiner. Now he was about to begin a new life centred on the political realities of his time. It was as if by going to the farm he could start all over again.

Late in November at a Spanish Aid Committee in Oxford, Spender met the twenty-two-year-old Marie Agnes "Inez" Pearn, who was, like him, active in support of the Republican cause and who was studying Spanish poetry at the university. That day he sat next to her at a lunch party. Inez was almost boylike; she "had an oval, child-like face, under fair hair cut almost to an Eton crop," and she was as energetic and as impulsive as Spender.[69] Soon after a flat-warming party at Hammersmith, which Inez attended, Spender took her to lunch at the Café Royal. He asked her to marry him, and she accepted, although they had known each other for less than a month. After the failure of the relationship with Tony and his having waited too long to decide about Muriel, Spender felt driven to try marriage. But he wrote to William Plomer that he still loved Tony, too, and to himself he admitted sometimes feeling an "intense depression" as a result of his ill-considered decision to marry.[70] To a somewhat disapproving Christopher Isherwood he indicated a need to make "an absolute final step."[71]

The step was taken at the Hammersmith Registry Office on the fifteenth of December, 1936, with Spender's grandmother as a witness. Mrs. Schuster had a reception for the couple at her flat. The guests included William Plomer, Lady Ottoline Morrell, Auden, Isherwood, family members—led by the very formal J. A. Spender—and several "rather revolutionary new acquaintances."[72] Tony Hyndman's apparent reaction, which filled Spender with guilt feelings, was to join the Communist Party and the International Brigade and to leave at Christmastime for Spain with Giles Romilly, a nephew of Winston Churchill's and a friend of Spender's. Spender had attempted to win Isherwood's sympathy for his marriage, citing a need for a "permanent and established relationship," but his attempt "didn't placate the implacable Christopher." "Rather a dreary affair and no champagne" was Wystan Auden's verdict.[73]

6

THE CRUSADER

In January of 1937 Victor Gollancz published Spender's *Forward from Liberalism* and named it book of the month for his Left Book Club. Spender's argument in the long essay was that traditional liberals like himself, in the context of events in Europe in the mid-1930s, had to move forward from Liberalism to Communism. Fascism was an extreme movement, the defeat of which required extreme measures. It was clear that the old Liberals were incapable of uniting against the Fascists and that only the Communists had the discipline necessary to defeat them. Although Spender was by instinct a civil libertarian, who, as an individual, had doubts about Communist methods—for example, Stalin's show trials—he argued that even the rights of the individual must now give way to the requirements of the public good.

The poet and critic who had so recently made his mark on literary London had now become a political theorist and a crusader. As such he was immediately taken up by the British Communist Party in the person of its secretary, Harry Pollitt. Pollitt invited Spender to his offices off Charing Cross Road. And although he criticized his guest for doubting the guilt of the defendants in the Moscow trials, he suggested that, as he and the party agreed on the Spanish Civil War, Spender might be of assistance to the International Brigade and the Republican side. When Spender pointed out that he had no experience as a soldier and was, in any case, a pacifist, Pollitt suggested that he could help by joining the party, thus lending his name to the cause. Spender agreed, in return for being allowed to write an article in the *Daily Worker* answering Pollitt's and other Communists' reactions to his lingering doubts about Communism—especially the Moscow trials. Spender also agreed to travel to Spain in a noncombatant capacity if such a trip would be useful.

Almost immediately the *Daily Worker* asked Spender to go to Spain to discover what he could about the Russian crew of the *Comsomol*, which had been sunk recently in the Mediterranean. As the Russian government was behind the request and as Spender did not want to be seen as in any way a spy, he refused payment for his trip but did ask for travel expenses for a companion, Cuthbert Worsley. Worsley would later write a novel, *Fellow Travellers,* based on his trip with Spender. The two Englishmen flew, by way of Marseilles, first to Barcelona and then to Alicante. Unable to find information—or signs of war—in either place, they decided to attempt to obtain information in areas under Franco's influence or control. From Gibraltar, where they went first, they hoped to get to Franco-controlled Cádiz but were refused permission by the rebel frontier guards. In Gibraltar they found little help from the governing English, who sympathized with Franco. In Oran and later Tangiers, through inquiries, they succeeded in discovering that the missing Russian crew was in fact imprisoned in Cádiz. In Tangiers Spender was thrilled to discover that, in spite of rebel propaganda, the people seemed to be adamant in their support of the Republican cause in Spain. On the seventeenth of January he attended a meeting of Popular Front supporters who raised their fists and sang the "Internationale" as a greeting for the Socialist Spanish consul.[1]

Part of Spender's enthusiasm for the Communists and their allies in Spain was his concern for and pride in Tony Hyndman. On a brief excursion he and Worsley took from Tangiers to Marrakesh, Spender found himself "staring at a donkey standing stock-still in front of us . . . it seemed to be carrying the weight of the whole day." Suddenly he was crying, and he realized it was because the burdened donkey reminded him of Tony—his "brush-like" hair and his "unflickering patience under the loads of ideas ... which I forced on to him."[2]

Christopher Isherwood had always felt that Spender's "peculiar kind of strength lay in his emotional flexibility; faced with an emergency he sometimes laughed, sometimes wept.... Stephen was rather proud of his ability to weep, and rightly so." It was a way of eliminating "many of life's poisons."[3]

In his *Daily Worker* article of February 19, 1937, "I Join the Communist Party," Spender had become sufficiently convinced in his support of the Communists that he apparently accepted the possible validity of the Moscow trials, suggesting that when he had written *Forward from Liberalism*, he had not realized the extent of the "gigantic plot against the Soviet government." He argued that, in any case, "the most important political aim of our time should be the United Front" and stated that he had decided to "belong to the party which is most active in working towards this end." But the hard-line British Communists were not satisfied. Spender received his party card but was never contacted by his local cell as Pollitt had said he would be. For most Communists Spender was a bourgeois intellectual whose heart was not with the party.

The Communists were for the most part correct in their assessment. Although he was apt to act impulsively—as most recently in the cases of his marriage to Inez and his joining the party—Spender the liberal intellectual almost always analysed his actions after the fact and expended a great deal of time and energy wondering whether he had done right. To William Plomer he wrote that he was trying hard to be both a literary intellectual and a "good Communist," and it was proving to be a difficult task. In almost the same breath he analysed the reasons for his marriage to Inez, who had, so soon after their marriage, gone off to Brussels to study her Spanish manuscripts. He was coming to the conclusion that she was someone like himself, who was not prepared to become committed to another person. In both the case of Inez and that of the Communists, he decided it was best to accept the fact that he was capable of acting in an ungentlemanly manner.[4]

Yet on the ninth of February Spender joined Inez in Brussels and wrote to Plomer that they were "happy." He also revealed that Pollitt definitely wanted him to go to Spain as a radio propagandist.

On the twelfth, back in London, Spender had lunch with E. M. Forster and Bob Buckingham. At lunch and in a thank-you note two days later, he expressed strong doubts about the "individualist-collectivist position" in the party. Forster gave him a copy of *Das Kapital* to read in Spain. Forster and Buckingham were worried about Tony Hyndman, who was by now fighting there. Spender, too, was worried, even though Isherwood had recently assured him that in conversations in Brussels before he left for Spain, Tony had stated adamantly that he had joined the brigade for political reasons, not in reaction to Spender's marriage.[5] During the very hours of Spender's lunch with Forster, Hyndman was, in fact, fighting in the Battle of Jarama, in which his battalion was reduced by three-fourths. By then Tony was already disillusioned by the war; he "felt no anti-Fascist anger, only overwhelming pity."[6]

On the sixteenth of February, the day he received his party card, Spender had tea with the Woolfs. A few days earlier at dinner he had convinced them to subscribe to the *Left Review*, on the staff of which Tony Hyndman had served before leaving for Spain. They did so in spite of their scepticism about political movements and the effectiveness of the war in Spain. Woolf wrote in her diary that Spender thought the Communists wanted him to go to Spain and be killed so that he could be "another Byron." He had asked her to send her latest books for himself and other "comrades" during what he apparently assumed would be a long absence.[7] At tea, he "opened himself" by discussing his displeasure with Inez's being away at this difficult time for him; he was "confused" about his marriage and wondered why he had gone through with it. Virginia thought the marriage "curious."[8]

On February 19 the writer Elizabeth Bowen, who was close to Spender and Inez and a strong supporter of the Republican cause in Spain, wrote saying how much Harry Pollitt admired *Forward from Liberalism* and encouraging Spender as he prepared to leave again

for Spain. The head of the Socialist Party radio station in Republican
Valencia had offered him the position as English broadcaster and he had
accepted.

He crossed into the little town of Port Bou from France and there, as
recorded in the poem "Port Bou," experienced his first sense of real fear
in connection with the war. Watching a practice firing between troops on
two headlands,

> *I assure myself the shooting is for practice*
> *But fear is all I feel. The machine gun stitches*
> *My intestines with a needle, back and forth:*

In Barcelona Spender met up with Wogan Philipps, who was on his
way to the front as an ambulance volunteer. They travelled together with
some soldiers to Valencia, and narrowly missed entering Franco's lines
by mistake. On this trip there were signs of war and air raids everywhere. Outside of Tortosa the group visited an English doctor who ran a
hospital. When they went outdoors after lunch, there was a Falangist
plane in the skies. Spender "felt a deep hypnotic fear, as though the eyes
in the aeroplane were a stiletto pointed at my heart."[9]

In Valencia Spender found a note on his hotel room door addressed to
"Stephen Darling" from a recently departed Wystan Auden, who had
come briefly to Spain to see for himself what was happening. The next
morning Spender went to the Socialist station only to find that he was
no longer wanted, as the station had been absorbed into a United Front
station. That being the case, Spender continued on with Philipps to
Albacete, where he knew Tony Hyndman was stationed.

The visit with Hyndman was depressing. Albacete itself was drab
and unpleasant. Spender had difficulty locating Tony, and when he did,
he had to face the fact that his friend was totally disillusioned, perhaps on
the verge of a breakdown, and anxious to leave Spain. Spender pointed
out that as a member of the brigade Tony could not leave because of the
damage such a move would cause to morale. All that could be hoped for
was a transfer to a noncombatant role. Spender was able to convince the

English commissars that his friend was ill and should be withdrawn from active combat.

One of the commissars suggested that Spender should visit the front, and he did, hitchhiking to an area near Madrid where the International Brigade faced a battalion of Arab allies of Franco. Spender was impressed by brigade fellowship in a truck in which he found a ride; when he gave a bar of chocolate to a soldier sitting next to him, the soldier broke it into six tiny parts for each of his comrades.[10]

At the front there were corpses everywhere, and in the trenches Spender was warned that he should duck, as his height made him an obvious target. A short Indian writer, also visiting the front, looked up at him and said, "I can see death's great question-mark hovering between the trenches." At a gun emplacement Spender was told to fire some shots at the enemy facing the Republican lines. He did so, "praying that I might not by any chance hit an Arab." The English soldiers he met complained that they had come to Spain to be part of a liberal Republican cause but were now under the control of "Communist bosses of the Brigade."[11]

Frightened and disheartened, Spender left for Madrid with the journalist Denis Campkin, who was a friend of Inez's. They stayed at the grandiose Casa de la Cultura. It was March, and Madrid was still cold. The building was not heated. When journalists around him discussed atrocities committed by the Republican side as well as by the Falangists, Spender was disturbed, but he tried desperately to hold on to his conviction that the Republicans, and especially the Communist-dominated brigade fighters, were still better than the Fascists.

On his way back to Valencia Spender stopped at Albacete only to discover that Tony, who had deserted and been captured, was now in prison barracks. He had fled to Valencia rather than follow orders to return to the front.

On the way to Valencia Spender was preoccupied with the question of what he could do about Tony. As the train pulled into Valencia, his extreme fatigue brought him to "an involuntary awareness of the darkest movements of thought within the mind." And, like Coleridge seeing the

lines of "Kubla Khan" in his opium dream, he watched as "lines suddenly ran into his mind."[12] These were lines that would develop into
"Two Armies," another Wilfred Owen–like poem that would stress the
absurdity of war. The poem reflects the feelings of a man who was
deeply disturbed by the situation of his friend and whose instincts were
pacifist in spite of his intellectual commitment to one side in the conflict.
One stanza especially reflects this point of view:

> *Clean silence drops at night when a little walk*
> *Divides the sleeping armies, each*
> *Huddled in linen woven by remote hands.*
> *When the machines are stilled, a common suffering*
> *Whitens the air with breath and makes both one*
> *As though these enemies slept in each other's arms.*

In Valencia Spender stayed in the Victoria Hotel with other journalists, including Denis Campkin, who introduced him to several Spanish
people, including Hildalgo de Cisneros and his wife, Constanza, who in
turn introduced him to the poet Manuel Altolaguirre. Altolaguirre, who
would become a close friend, amazed Spender by giving him his eleven-
volume 1786 edition of Shakespeare.

Spender also met Ernest Hemingway at the local press bureau. He
was surprised that this man, whose art revealed such "inner sensibility,"
could be so brusque. Hemingway told Spender he was "too squeamish."
Still, the two writers warmed to each other. One evening they wandered
into a taverna where there were gypsies playing guitars. Hemingway
took one of the instruments and sang Spanish songs. Spender was
pleased to find the "inner sensibility" expressed occasionally, as, for
instance, when Hemingway recommended Stendhal's *La Chartreuse de
Parme*, suggesting that the opening section about Fabrice wandering
through the Battle of Waterloo was one of the most accurate of literary
descriptions of war. Spender was also grateful for Hemingway's support
when a man on sick leave from the brigade made "humiliating" remarks
about his friendship with Tony.[13]

The question of Tony was uppermost in Spender's mind during his stay in Valencia. His one wish was to get his friend out of Spain, whatever the political implications. A member of the British Embassy staff offered to help if he could, and through Cisneros, who was commander of the Republican Air Force, and Altolaguirre, Spender was given an audience with the Republican foreign minister, Julio Álvarez del Vayo. After Spender promised to argue the Republican case with a not-so-friendly British government, the minister guaranteed that Hyndman would serve a sentence and then be released.

Spender hoped to see Tony again by joining Cisneros on a car trip back to Albacete. Altolaguirre went, too. In Albacete an absurdist drama developed. At the brigade's British Battalion Office, Peter Kerrigan and others berated Spender for trying to influence Hyndman's case through the "class enemies"—the British Embassy and, although he was in theory an ally, the Republican foreign minister. After Spender argued his position, Kerrigan sent him to discuss matters with the men who would decide Tony's case. The International Brigade judges, who were Yugoslavian, Polish, and/or Russian, were staying outside of the city, and Spender was invited to have dinner with them. During the meal, he was once again "overcome by despair." The judges suggested that he not be distressed about his friend; Hyndman would indeed be convicted and be sent to a prison camp, which would be "good for [his] education."[14]

Spender left Spain a few days later and met Inez in Paris. During his brief stay there, he continued to concentrate on Tony. Sylvia Beach at Shakespeare and Company Bookstore knew many influential people, and Spender enlisted her to write letters on Tony's behalf. In London he pleaded on many occasions with Pollitt and his colleagues for Hyndman's release, pointing out that he had serious stomach ulcers and had had a nervous collapse. He revealed to William Plomer later that it was only after he admitted under pressure that sex was involved in his concern with the case that Pollitt agreed to see that Tony was released.[15] In fact, the release did not take place until June, after numerous letters from Spender and his friends to various people of influence among the

Communists associated with the International Brigade. At E. M. Forster's suggestion, Spender had almost returned to Spain to try to expedite Tony's release. From Paris Spender had written to William Plomer that he was now disillusioned with the Communists.[16]

In London, during the spring of 1937, he was asked to speak on Spain at various meetings. In June he would lead a group of writers— including Hugh Walpole, Elizabeth Bowen, Cecil Day-Lewis, Desmond MacCarthy, and Compton Mackenzie—in a "Writers Declare Against Fascism" meeting at the Queen's Hall. Another writers' declaration was published in the *Left Review*. Also in June there would be a large Spanish relief occasion at the Royal Albert Hall (at which Spender introduced Auden to Virginia Woolf) and a literary luncheon with readings at a Holborn restaurant. The invitation for the latter said the featured talk would be "Mr Spender and Spain."

The literary social life dominated by the older modernists and their concerns continued as well. At an early April dinner Spender told Virginia Woolf that her *Years*, which she had sent him, was the best of her books. In a letter of April 26 he had thanked her for the book, saying he had particularly admired the characterization of people who spend their time "asking themselves, Is this life?" thus undermining the "reality of their own experience." In her diary Virginia admits that Stephen "pleases" her.[17] Later in the spring he would confide in her that he felt oppressed by his shyness—that it undermined his creativity.[18] Eliot invited him for lunch on the twenty-second of April, and on the third of May he had lunch again with Eliot, followed by tea with Rosamond Lehmann, dinner with the novelist and essayist A. P. Herbert, and coffee after dinner with the Woolfs. On May 5 there was a large dinner party at the Woolfs in honour of Hugh Walpole, who had just been knighted. Many old and new friends were there, including most of "Bloomsbury" and "Maida Vale."

The next day Spender left to pick up Inez in Brussels, after which they spent a short vacation in Corsica. From there they travelled to Paris, where Spender and Ernest Hemingway gave readings at Sylvia Beach's Shakespeare and Company library on the twelfth. The Spenders ate several meals with Miss Beach and her friend Adrienne Monnier, of whom Inez later requested some recipes.

A description in the *Herald Tribune* of the reading at Shakespeare and Company captures something of Spender's mood and appearance at the time and of his relationship with Hemingway. The reporter, Francis Smith, notes that James Joyce, "who had been sitting in the shadows of the room," left before Spender's reading, as the applause was dying out for Hemingway's. Then

> ... the tall rumple-haired English poet and critic, who, like Hemingway, has just returned from Spain, read five poems, expressing his opinion about war in general, not "about this war." He read in a peculiarly definite tone: "I have an appointment with a bullet at seventeen hours, minus a split second, and I shall not be late," and many other lines. When he was through, he asked Hemingway for some beer. The latter assented and then the evening came to an end.[19]

On the next day the Spenders, Hemingway, and Martha Gellhorn had lunch together at the Brasserie Lipp. Hemingway called Inez "yellow" because she only drank water. He said he had toughened up Gellhorn years before by taking her to the morgue in Madrid. Finally, he showed Spender photographs of murders in Spain to toughen *him* up.[20]

On June 1 Spender was back in Paris—this time to deliver a lecture on contemporary English poetry. His old friend Gisa Soloweitschik, whom he had once called his "fiancée," was there, now married to André Gide's nephew. Spender was moved by meeting her and was impressed by the happiness she and her husband so obviously shared. It was a happiness that he and Inez just as obviously did not share. Spender also met André Gide that evening.

He would meet Gide again in July, when both men participated in the Second International Writers' Congress in Madrid, which was convened so that the intellectuals could react publicly to the Spanish Civil War. In fact, Gide was the focal point of a major argument between hard-line Communists and disillusioned Liberal-Communists like Spender. Gide, once the darling of the Russians, had travelled to the Soviet Union and had recently published his *Retour de l'U.R.S.S.*, which was critical of the Soviet system. He was denounced by the Russians at the conference as, like Trotsky, a Fascist. His main critic was the *Pravda* correspondent, Michael Koltzof, who himself became a victim of the Stalin purges when he returned from Spain to Russia.

Spender travelled to Spain with André Malraux, whom he had only recently met. As Spender had been unable to obtain a visa to travel to Spain from the British Foreign Office, Malraux arranged a false passport for him as a supposed Spanish citizen named Ramos Ramos, "a name which seemed to involve a minimum of invention." Other participants in the conference with whom Spender spent a good deal of time were Ernest Hemingway and Manuel Altolaguirre, and new friends Octavio Paz and Pablo Neruda. One day, during an excursion to Valencia, the group visited the village of Minglanilla, and some children danced and sang to entertain the famous intellectuals. The irony of a party of well-fed foreigners being entertained by a suffering peasant population so upset Paz's wife that she "burst into hysterical weeping." In the same village, Spender and Neruda visited an impoverished peasant home and were given valuable sausages to sustain them on their journey.[21]

The irony of the conference itself came home to Spender on many occasions. The intellectuals were constantly feasted by the government and were ferried about in large comfortable cars and wagon-lit trains. The conferees were the valuable instruments by which support might be obtained from Western governments, and they were treated as such. The whole congress, in spite of its good intentions, "had something about it of a Spoiled Children's Party."[22]

Spender took note of the fact that he was "secretly offended" at being rarely asked to speak at the conference.[23] One of the few times he was asked to do so was in Barcelona, at the end of the trip, when he caused an argument between various Spanish groups by praising the Catalans for translating Spanish classics into their language to make them available to the people. He was amused at the absurdity of the "separatist spirit" that dominated the situation in Spain as well as the conference itself. It was both funny and disillusioning that before each speech at the Barcelona meeting the national anthem of the speaker's country was played. When Spender rose, the orchestra "burst into God Save the King whilst the audience rose to its feet with clenched fists."[24] By the end of this trip to Spain, he wondered whether there was much for a poet to achieve through political involvement.

Still, several moments stood out in his mind about the summer of 1937 in Spain. Madrid was actually being shelled by the Falangists as the conference met there. On one occasion Spender had visited the university front just outside the city. Here, as they fought, peasant Republican soldiers were taking reading and writing lessons from students: "The whole place looked like a school for children who were dressed up as soldiers, playing at war." In one lecture hall Spender was restrained by a guard as he was about to pass by a window that would make him a target for enemy fire. There was a corpse who had become such a target "on the floor under the blackboard" near the window.[25]

On another occasion he had had a long discussion with Malraux about poetry in the modern age. As Spender later reconstructed the discussion, he thought he had understood Malraux to say that modernist poetry was "over-complicated and obscure" because, in the absence of viable "spiritual symbols" and the use in their place of nonspiritual "symbols derived from machinery, . . . the modern poet was not only preoccupied with his own poetic vision but also with establishing the validity of his symbols."[26] In *The Destructive Element*, Spender had discussed the problem of viable symbolism in the works of the early modernists like Yeats and Eliot. He had, of course, used "symbols derived from machinery" in his own poetry.

Upon entering the luxurious wagon-lit train that was to take the conferees from Port Bou to Paris, Spender watched the irritated famous intellectuals shouting and banging on the cars demanding service, and he "wondered whether the Canterbury pilgrims behaved in this way." He left Spain with a feeling of "deep dissatisfaction."[27]

After a brief stay in Paris, Spender returned to London and, joined by Inez, took a house, Church Farm, Warcham, in Mersham near Ashford on the Kentish coast. It had become clear to both Stephen and Inez that something would need to be done to bring them closer together.

A good part of the time since their wedding had been spent away from each other, and it was time now to see if they could live together. The days in Mersham were happy enough, and the couple took several short trips to Paris, spending time especially with Sylvia Beach and Adrienne Monnier. Auden visited the couple in early August. On the ninth, he and the Spenders were invited to lunch and tea at Sissinghurst Castle by Harold Nicolson and Vita Sackville-West. In his diary Nicolson says the visit was a great success and comments that "Wystan is grubbier than ever and Stephen is as like Shelley as ever."[28]

The summer was marred in late July by the news of Julian Bell's death in Spain. The whole disillusionment associated with the Spanish Civil War and the hypocrisy even of the side he supported came over Spender again. But at least he was able by September to report to various friends that Tony Hyndman was home.[29]

At the end of August Spender was taken ill with appendicitis and had an operation on September 1. For his convalescence, he and Inez went to the village of Salcombe on the Devon coast, where the Spenders had often vacationed during Stephen's childhood. The stay was ruined by a fishing outing during which one of the participants, a businessman, announced to Spender with great glee that his company was providing the Falangists with trucks that would carry guns that would "smash your friends in Madrid to pieces."[30] Spender was so angry that he insisted on getting back to London, where he could continue work for the Popular Front movement, however imperfect it might be.

His sense of that imperfection—especially his dissatisfaction with the Communists—is conveyed in a little article, "Art Treasures and the Spanish War," that he wrote for the *New Republic*.[31] Spender was still torn between the good of the masses and the values of bourgeois individualism and culture. He demonstrated even more dissatisfaction toward his old mentor, T. S. Eliot, and his publisher, Geoffrey Faber, for allowing right wing poet Roy Campbell to slander Jews and those who had suffered in Spain.

There was tension with his other mentor, Virginia Woolf, as well. In her diary, after hosting the Spenders for dinner, Woolf refers to Inez as a "precise horse-headed woman," and she notes that now, since nephew

Julian's death, she somehow "resents" Stephen. The Spenders had last come to dinner together to meet Julian. Part of Woolf's resentment very probably resulted from Spender's tendency at this time to talk less in his private sphere about literary or political issues and to turn "towards an extreme preoccupation with the problems of self."[32] For Woolf, this attitude might well have seemed self-centred and inappropriate in the face of her nephew's death.

In turning inward, Spender was reacting against the kind of "Communist self-righteousness" that had marked his attitude before the Spain experiences and that struck him forcefully upon meeting up with his old Oxford friend Gabriel Carritt (Tristan)—now, as a communist man of the people, "Bill" Carritt. Carritt was refusing to speak to former political allies—including his liberal father, Spender's Oxford tutor—who, in light of the Soviet purges, were moving away from their former sympathy with or support for Communism and the Soviet Union.

As he became less overtly political, Spender wrote poems that attempted to express a modernist—almost existential—sense of personal isolation as a "universal condition of all existence."[33] "Recall me from life's exile," he wrote in "Exiles from Their Land," a poem of the period.

> *let me join*
> *Those who now kneel to kiss their sands,*
> *And let my words restore*
> *Their printed, laurelled, victoried message.*

Spender expressed his inward turn by entering psychoanalysis. Although this process contributed to a disciplined examination of himself, it did not solve any problems, and Spender gave up analysis for painting. He studied for a time at the Euston Art School founded by a group of artists, including his friend William Coldstream, who had painted portraits of him and of Inez. Although Spender continued to enjoy painting, he soon realized that he had no real talent for it. In fact, he came to the conclusion that his more meditative poetry, psychoanalysis, and painting were all means by which he was easing the pain of a realization that his marriage might be a failure.

Soon after Spender's return from Spain, he and Inez had moved from Hammersmith to 6 Landsdowne Terrace in Bloomsbury. They had also bought a seventeenth-century house in Lavenham with Stephen's brother Humphrey and his wife, Margaret. The Great House, as it was called, remained the official Spender residence until it was requisitioned by the army in late 1939. At Lavenham Stephen and Inez "spent some of the happiest months of [their] marriage." But Spender's almost obsessive concern for Tony Hyndman's welfare, even after his release from the brigade prison, and the preoccupation with the Spanish Civil War in general, left little time for the kind of relationship-building that the marriage required. Sometimes it was as if the couple were playing at marriage. Inez would say things like, "I love you and shall love you always, but I might leave you."[34] Later she would do just that.

Spender's return to a more meditative-confessional mode of poetry was in part due to his interest in the *Duino Elegies* of the great German poet Rainer Maria Rilke. He was beginning to work on a translation of the *Elegies* with the Anglo-German scholar J. B. Leishmann for Hogarth and W. W. Norton in New York. The end of 1937 found him in a complicated dispute with Leishmann over the translation. Spender had entered into the arrangement with some enthusiasm, assuming that Leishmann as a Rilke scholar and he as a poet would complement each other positively in the project. As it turned out, Leishmann was disdainful of Spender's poetic concerns and attempted essentially to take over the work. Virginia Woolf and John Lehmann and the Nortons found themselves uncomfortably caught between the two translators, and the *Duino Elegies* were not finally published until 1939.

During this period, Spender also continued to wrestle with the subject of politics in relation to art. On January 26, 1938, he debated his old friend Harold Nicolson at the Cambridge Union. The position for which he argued and from which Nicolson dissented was "Art Must Be Political." Spender's presentation lacked passion—perhaps because of personal problems, his disillusionment with the Communist movement, and his overbearing concern for the situation of friends in the International Brigade rather than with the propagandistic needs of the Popular Front. In any case, Nicolson won the debate handily. At the end of the evening over a drink, Nicolson found Spender "charming as ever," but also "as egotistic and as void of all humour."[35]

Meanwhile in the midst of his work for the Spanish cause, his process of self-examination, and the gradual breakup of his marriage, Spender found time to contribute to a special English issue of the Chicago-based magazine *Poetry*, edited by Wystan Auden and Michael Roberts, and to do more translating. In Spain Spender had become particularly interested in the great Spanish poet and playwright Federico García Lorca, who had been brutally murdered by the Falangists in 1936, and with J. L. Gili, he reworked some of his poems.[36] For Faber and Faber he did a translation with Goronwy Rees of Georg Büchner's *Danton's Death*, and for Random House he translated Ernst Toller's *Pastor Hall* with Hugh Hunt. Toller, a German Socialist who had fled Germany, had become friendly with the Spenders. He committed suicide in London in 1939.

Most important, Spender completed work on his play *Trial of a Judge*, which was performed in late March at the United Theatre in Camden Town by Rupert Doone's London Group Theatre. Doone, a former ballet dancer, was a close friend of Auden's and produced several Auden-Isherwood works. He had asked Spender to serve as literary director of his company.

Spender had seen and read Eliot's *Murder in the Cathedral* three years before and had been greatly impressed by Eliot's command of verse in the service of drama. What he could not accept about Eliot's play was the religious message. Although he approved of the idea of using Becket's dilemma—"spiritual pride vs. the will of God"—as the basis for the agon of the play, he felt that Eliot had used the dilemma to preach too much.[37] What he hoped to do in *Trial of a Judge* was to create a verse play that would speak to real issues, issues he considered to be political rather than religious. As he told his old Hamburg friend Eric Alport, his central character would be a judge who represented "Liberal Justice" caught between Communism and Fascism during a time of "counter-revolution." The play grew out of the Fascist murdering of opponents just before Hitler's coming to power.[38] It also coincided, as it turned out, with the annexation of Austria by Hitler in March.

Spender's goal in writing a play about a Liberal judge—a figure

who reflects something of Spender's own political position between
Communism and Fascism after his falling out with the Stalinists and the
International Brigade—was to guide "complacent middle-class" theatre-
goers to his opinion that they played an unwitting part as "pawns" in a
universal political conflict. Spender outlined this position in a *New
Statesman and Nation* article called "Poetry and Expressionism."[39] The
judge in the play capitulates to certain Fascist demands and is, nevertheless, jailed and executed for his troubles. His situation echoes various
aspects of Spender's situation at the time—his fear that the hopelessness
of the world situation was reflected in what he saw as the failure of his
personal life and of his political action since the Oxford days.

It is perhaps telling in the context of his problems with Inez and the
pain that his continuing obsession with his former lover caused her, that
Spender dedicated the play to Hyndman (T.A.R.H.).

Spender's play, which has been neglected over the years, contains
some of his strongest poetry and worked reasonably well on the stage.
Isherwood called it "the greatest play of our time."[40] Auden liked it
except when he felt Spender used an Audenesque comic style. He suggested that his friend was more like Rilke than Lorca, more comfortable being "philosophic."[41] Virginia Woolf and T. S. Eliot went to the
opening together after dining in Bloomsbury. In her diary Woolf
describes the play as "moving." If there was a bit "too much poetic elo-
quence," she was nevertheless "given the release of poetry." Of
Spender himself she writes, "I like him always," and she praises his
"large generous sensitivity."[42] Perhaps most important to Spender, T.
S. Eliot wrote to him that he found the play moving and admirable.
He complained that the judge wavered too much, but his only serious
criticism echoed Virginia Woolf's. He felt that the play was too con-
sciously poetic. In a postscript to his letter, Eliot, always the critical
"father," could not resist a tiny barb, questioning the poet's scansion.[43]
E. M. Forster was impressed by the play in performance, but after he
read it in its published form, he said he was left with the impression
of a "weak man who was a liberal" rather than of the weakness of
Liberalism.[44]

In 1938 Spender buried past conflicts with John Lehmann—at least for the moment—and worked with him on a collection of poems about the Spanish Civil War called *Poems for Spain*, which was eventually published by the Hogarth Press in 1939. Lehmann had gone into equal partnership with Leonard Woolf at Hogarth in April of 1938, and Virginia Woolf had withdrawn from active participation in the company. In late 1937 Lehmann had discussed with Auden, Isherwood, and Spender the possibility of their buying the press jointly, but they did not have the funds for such a venture.

The friendliness with Lehmann was short-lived. In early October Spender complained to Eliot about his financial arrangements with Faber and Faber and announced that he wished to do a new book of poems for Lehmann at Hogarth. Always patient with his often impulsive protégé, Eliot took Spender to lunch and convinced him to give his poems to Fabers and to allow Hogarth to have a play. Lehmann was not at all pleased with this arrangement and also complained that he had hoped Spender would participate more in his new journal, *New Writing,* which he was publishing at Hogarth and for which he had been assured of Auden's, Isherwood's, and Spender's support.[45] Spender's answer was abrupt. He would do more work for *New Writing* if he was asked. As far as he knew he had not been invited to editorial meetings. As for future contracts, he rather rashly promised all of his future books to Hogarth after current contracts were fulfilled. Somewhat arrogantly, he pointed out to Lehmann that he was extremely busy, simultaneously working on the introduction for the *Poems for Spain* collection that they were coediting, doing a critique of Picasso's *Guernica*, and working on the Rilke and the Toller translations and five reviews.[46]

He was also writing a short book for Hogarth on the connection between social issues and modern poetry that he would entitle *The New Realism: A Discussion* (1939). The point of the book marks a change in Spender's thinking. The poet's job, he said, was to observe and reveal, not to change the world. The poet must "remain true to the standards which he discovers only within himself." Writers who forsake their bourgeois environments for "revolutionary" ones either become victims or politicians.[47] The Marxist experiment was clearly over for Spender.

Meanwhile, the Munich appeasement and the Sudetenland occupation had sent him into another bout of depression, coinciding as they did with marriage problems. The relationship with Inez was now coming to its end. Inez was involved with a mutual friend, the poet and sociologist Charles Madge.

The new life of marriage had failed and the old life as a practising member of a homosexual community was no longer a viable option. In his diary, the painter William Coldstream describes a farewell party given by Benjamin Britten and his friend Peter Pears in January 1939 for Christopher Isherwood and Wystan Auden, who were about to leave England for New York City. The guests, besides Auden and Isherwood and their "boys," were William and Nancy Coldstream, a Britten boyfriend, the singer Hedli Anderson, who announced herself as "Queen of the boys tonight," several "anti-boy women," and Stephen and Inez. The evening was full of tension, as Spender did not much care for Britten's music at the time and Britten did not care for either of the Spenders. Furthermore, the presence of women who were not interested in "camp" behaviour put something of a damper on what was to be a "gay" party for Christopher and Wystan. Stephen felt uncomfortable and several times during the evening sat next to Nancy Coldstream (who would later become his sister-in-law) as if for security. The singing of a Spender poem to a Britten song was greeted with some embarrassment, as the words seemed ironically sentimental in so tense a situation.[48]

Soon after the party, Spender took himself off to Paris alone to get away from the London scene and Inez's love affair. After a short time, however, he returned to London and tried to go on with his literary and social life. He wrote an angry letter to the writer Julian Symons, refusing to contribute a poem to a Marxist number of *Twentieth Century* because of a negative review by Symons of his play,[49] signed a three-book contract with Hogarth, took his grandmother to tea with Virginia Woolf,[50] and wrote an essay, "The Importance of W.H. Auden," for the *London Mercury*.[51]

In May Faber and Faber published a new book of Spender poems called, at Eliot's suggestion, *The Still Centre,* in keeping with the poet's current meditative mood. At first Spender had wanted to call it *Flames of*

Ice. The collection was the first of his post-Marxist period. The title itself indicates the new approach outlined in *The New Realism*. The new poetry in the book would be responsible to "standards only within himself." Poetry, he said in the book's introduction, "does not state truth, it states the conditions within which something felt is true." The poet must start from his "still centre" of being and express that being through his experience in the world.[52]

A. Kingsley Weatherhead has rightly recognized that the dominant theme of *The Still Centre* is "that of the achievement of unity of being or of an image of the integrated self ... attained to, apparently, by those who are dead, those who were (or are) 'truly great.' "[53] Poems such as "Exiles from Their Land" were, said Spender, about "those who after their deaths, obtained for their lives a symbolic significance."[54]

The Still Centre is not made up completely of the new kind of poetry. It is a collection of thirty-nine poems written between 1934 and 1939. The first three sections of the book are mostly didactic works, many concerned with Spain, including such Spender landmark pieces as "Port Bou" and "Ultima Ratio Regnum." One of the best known of Spender's thirties poems is "An Elementary School Classroom in a Slum," which, though political, is centred in personal observation and Spender's sense of isolation in his world. It is found in Part I and contains a depiction of "One unnoted, sweet and young, his eyes live in a dream / Of squirrel's game, in a tree room, other than this." This Spenderesque character is much like the lonely boy we find in the autobiographical novel *The Backward Son* (1940), which grew out of Spender's early school experience and his process of recalling the past in psychoanalysis. The poetry itself, however, is anything but sentimental. Spender had moved beyond the romanticism of his youthful work and had learned well the modernist lesson of concreteness of vision discovered in the late Yeats, Eliot, and W. H. Auden.

It is in the fourth section of *The Still Centre* especially that the poet "turned back to a kind of writing which is more personal."[55] Many of these poems are love poems that reflect his relationship with Inez. But they almost all contain the sense of existential and personal isolation that is so much the essence of modernism. "The Little Coat" is such a poem:

The little coat embroidered with birds
Is irretrievably ruined.
We bought it in the spring.
She stood upon a chair
And raised her arms like branches.
I leaned my head against her breast
Listening to that heavy bird
Thudding at the centre of our happiness.
Everything is dragged away.
The clothes that were so gay
Lie in attics, like the dolls
With which wild children used to play.
The bed where the loved one lies
Is a river bed on which
Enchanting haunting life
Is carried where the current may—
Tangled among blocks of ice,
Nests and singing branches
Were the Springs of yesterday.

Spender dedicated *The Still Centre* to Inez.

On the nineteenth of August Virginia Woolf wrote to Vita Sackville-West announcing that Inez had left Stephen "for Mr. Madge a poet." The breakup of the marriage, while inevitable, left Spender obsessed with what he saw as his guilt and full of anger. Virginia Woolf noted in her diary that Spender was writing a lot "about himself."[56] In fact, he wrote a journal, which he published as "September Journal" in several issues of a literary and political review he would found with Cyril Connolly called *Horizon*. The "Journal" was extremely personal and reflected Spender's misery over the invasion of Czechoslovakia in March, Hitler's nonaggression pact with Stalin in August, the impending war, the victory of Franco in Spain, his separation from Inez, and the incurable cancer that was killing his much-loved sister-in-law Margaret (Lolly).

Spender remained as much as possible in Lavenham, pouring out his pain to the always optimistic Lolly, until one day

Margaret touched my forehead with her skeleton-like hand, and at that moment I realized as I identified my misfortune with hers the egotism of my demand for sympathy and of my claim to be unhappy.[57]

Hitler invaded Poland on September 1, and Britain declared war. London during the "phony war" of 1939 that followed was blacked out at night. Spender wandered the streets wondering what to do with his life. On September 23 Freud died in Hampstead. This seemed to mark the end of more than an individual life. The same day he left for a weekend in the country with the Woolfs at Rodmell near Lewes. The house had a pond with goldfish. Spender would remember that when in later years he would tend his own goldfish pond in the south of France. Virginia wrote in her diary that their guest scribbled in his diary, read Proust, and talked of everything—including Inez, religion, and homosexuality. He was "sensitive," but his mind was "loose-jointed." He had boiled potatoes for lunch. The weekend was "drudgery."[58] Spender remembered it differently. They began the first day by playing bowls on the lawn. Then he and Virginia had the first of several long talks about writing, about keeping a journal, about the importance of not "creating a literary personality for oneself," and about the importance of successful women not trying to imitate men.[59]

On the twenty-sixth he had lunch with Eliot, who was gentle and supportive and encouraged him to work on his poetry. It was important in times such as they were entering for writers to maintain objectivity—a certain detachment from official positions. Yet both men admitted they had recently applied to enter government service. Eliot suggested that the old modernism could not coexist with a war situation. Joyce's *Finnegans Wake* and even Spender's *Trial of a Judge* would have to be treated much differently now. The two poets discussed their approach to their art. They agreed that at all costs the poet must entice the reader to

identify with him "and enter in his subjective mood," but that the threat
to this identification was a later situation change that rendered the subjective mood irrelevant.[60]

To fight his loneliness and unhappiness, Spender stayed for long periods of time with his brother Humphrey and Lolly at their London flat.
One day they went on a nostalgic excursion to pick mushrooms at
Lavenham. He also spent several days at Oxford with Isaiah Berlin,
reading the latter's book on Marx and working on his novel of childhood, *The Backward Son*.[61] In time he was able to convince himself of
certain advantages in living alone. In his journal entry of October 26,
1939, he spoke of increased creative energy and the relief of not having to
reproach "myself for not paying enough attention" to a companion. He
recognized that he attached

> far too much attention to other people's whims and moods, which
> make me feel guilty of inconsiderateness. I feel that pleasures
> which people might, in fact, easily sacrifice, are mysteriously
> important, and this makes any decision, like living in the country
> or demanding that my wife should stop having an "affair," etc.,
> very difficult. In fact altogether there is a lack of confidence in any
> behaviour within a possessive relationship. The effect of this is not
> to lessen but rather increase the egotism which I am trying to
> repress in myself.[62]

These remarks can serve as what might be called a Spender manifesto on
personal relationships.

Spender was now thirty. His country was about to go to war, his
political and literary activities had done nothing to prevent the rise of
Fascism, his primary relationships—homosexual and heterosexual, cul-
minating in his marriage—had failed. Yet, as Eliot and others reminded
him, he had established a reputation as one of the finest poets of his
generation, and was now once again writing the kind of personal, inner-
directed poetry that came naturally to him. And his generous liberalism—

literary, political, and personal—was still very much intact, as was his adherence to modernism.

A few days after the lunch with Eliot, Spender bought a printing press and installed it at the home of Bobby Buhler, a painter friend with whom he often stayed and painted during the lonely days after the breakup with Inez. His intention was to print the works of unknown poets of promise.[63] He was perhaps attempting to return to the purity of those days with the old chemist's press at 10 Frognal, when he had printed his own and Auden's early poems.

7

WAR

For Spender the departure of Auden in 1939 for America marked the end of an era: "The individualist phase was over." As undergraduates, Spender and Auden had epitomized individualism, often to the point of eccentricity. During and after their Oxford years, they had gone to Germany in search of experiences that alienated them still further from the conventional elements of their society. And they had strongly backed a crusade in Spain that did not have the support of their government or the majority of their compatriots. Acting with other radicals, allying themselves with Communism against the rise of Fascism, they had tried, not only through their writing but through their actions, to "influence history." Friends like Julian Bell and John Cornford had paid with their lives in that heroic attempt. Now, ironically, in 1939, facing the combined power of Stalin and Hitler, "two monsters out of the Book of Revelation," individualism among Britons gave way to a stiff-upper-lip community effort in which the idea of individual heroism was submerged in popular national leaders like Churchill and later Roosevelt. For the ordinary person it was not so much a question of good versus evil as it was the fact that Hitler had broken the rules, had, after "reasonable" arrangements at Munich, "gone too far."[1]

As for Communism and the hope it had held out for Spender and other radicals in the mid-thirties, it had, after the purges and the Soviet alliance with Hitler, lost its appeal as a vehicle for individual heroic struggle. Later under attack themselves, the Russians would join the Allies, not as a workers' paradise betrayed, but as part of a de facto community effort in which even democracy and freedom, the rallying ideologies of those who had rushed to the defence of the Spanish Republic, were put aside in the need to stop the man who had "gone too far." This was not a revival of the alliance of idealistic pure Communists and social liberals seeking a new world order. It was an alliance of various powers attempting to hold on to what they had. Those who saw Hitler as the worst of several evils had no choice but to rally around governments that had once made pacts with the Nazis, appeased them, or ignored their most vicious prewar policies. For idealists like Spender, the reality of this situation was upsetting in the extreme.

Given the new mood of the nation and the world and the over-running of Europe by Hitler, it was difficult for intellectual writers to hold fast to old political allegiances, to conceive of writing poetry as usual or of continuing the debate among modernists about the place of politics in literature. Geoffrey Grigson, the editor of the defunct radical *New Verse*, represented what might be called the last gasp of the old Left when he wrote his friend Spender a "fulminating" letter accusing him of "whoring" with such reactionaries as Harold Nicolson and Edith Sitwell.[2]

Spender had, in fact, always been friendly with Nicolson and had now befriended Edith Sitwell and her brothers, Osbert and Sacheverell. He loved Edith's appearance, describing her in his journals as "fantastic . . . a medieval carving of herself, attired with brocades and hung with enormous jewels." Her "manner" was "that of Queen Elizabeth the First," and her conversation was a kind Spender and his circle always enjoyed—"the malicious kind which is redeemed with wit, so that one is able to think that things are said because they are more amusing than spiteful."[3]

Another of these "reactionaries," T. S. Eliot, wrote to Spender for advice about a contemporary poetry series Fabers hoped to publish for the general public in support of the common war effort.[4] The works in this series would be called the Sesame Books and would include volumes by Eliot and those sometime radicals Auden, MacNeice, and Spender (*Selected Poems 1940*), among others.

Eliot continued to meet regularly with his younger friend. He was still Spender's publisher, and the two men shared many interests and maintained a friendly father-son type of relationship, usually marked by good humour. In November of 1939 Spender sent Eliot a Wensleydale cheese, which Eliot, playing the Prufrock role he so enjoyed, compared to Mozart; riper cheeses such as old Cheshire were more like Beethoven.[5]

For Spender, the best choice of activities until he was "called up" to the armed forces, as he expected to be, was to work with his friends Cyril Connolly and Peter Watson on the new journal *Horizon*. Unlike *New Verse* or the old *Left Review*, and in keeping with the views of Connolly, whose opinions dominated the journal's editorial policy and its choice of articles throughout its existence, *Horizon* would not take a particular ideological stand. It was in general loyal to the war effort, but it was not to be a vehicle for individual heroism or for national propaganda. In his first editorial "Comment" in *Horizon*, Connolly declared, "Our standards are aesthetic, and our politics are in abeyance."[6] *Horizon*'s purpose, as Spender would later write, was to show that "civilization, literature and art could be sustained at a time when everything seemed shrouded by the austerities and exigencies of war."[7]

Cyril Connolly was a complex character. A product of Eton and Oxford, he was, nevertheless, anything but conventional. Christopher Isherwood describes his appearance:

His big face—flat blue eyes, tiny nose, and double chin—looked as ageless as a Buddha's; but he was more of a pope than a Buddha, for he spoke with a conscious authority, implying that he knew you, as a writer, better than you knew yourself—knew you historically in relation to the entire hierarchy of letters, past and present, and could assign you a place in it. You might lose that place later, of course. If you ever did, he would tell you so, blandly but brutally. He had a terrible phrase for such outcasts: "Those whom the God has forsaken."[8]

Christopher Isherwood admired "the brilliant artifice of . . . [Connolly's] wit and the genuineness of his passions—for landscape, architecture, classical and Romantic languages, food, wine, lemurs, and literature." Although he loved his friends, Connolly was capable of extreme disloyalty to them—including his several women friends, and colleagues such as Watson and Spender—in the pursuit of his need to "tell a good story" or to practise one of his favourite activities, parody.[9]

It was Peter Watson who provided the money for *Horizon*. Watson, a wealthy and extremely handsome man who collected art and difficult young men, had left Paris and a lover for London at the beginning of the war and had reluctantly gone along with Connolly's project. It was he who suggested Spender as an associate editor. The two men had known each other for some time and had even taken a trip together through Switzerland in 1938. Spender liked Watson—for his dislike of "priggishness, pomposity and almost everything to do with public life" and for his having educated himself "through love of beautiful works and through love of people in whom he saw beauty."[10]

Spender was an excellent choice as an associate editor, not only because of his journalistic talents but because of his reputation in the literary-artistic world and his willingness to use that reputation to attract major and potentially major writers and artists to *Horizon*. He also allowed the journal the use of his Landsdowne Terrace flat as an office. The large front sitting room was where Connolly worked. In the middle room, Spender placed the long black-topped modernist inlaid desk that he had had built for the Hammersmith flat. This desk was used by the secretarial and business staff: Bill Makins and Connolly's friend "Diana," and after her departure Lys Lubbock (Connolly's mistress), managed the business; Sonia Brownell, who later would marry George Orwell, was in charge of sorting manuscripts. The back bedroom remained Spender's private space until he moved to another flat in 1942.

There was, however, a sour note for Spender in the founding of

Horizon. Sometime before the first discussions with Watson and Connolly about the new journal, he had agreed to be on the editorial advisory board of John Lehmann's *New Writing* at the Hogarth Press. Realizing that Lehmann might be upset by his connections with a rival publication, he had asked that his name not be on the masthead of *Horizon*. Somewhat naively, Spender apparently felt that, in spite of earlier tiffs with Lehmann, this would be a sufficient precaution. It was not. The "deadly feud," as Lehmann called it, between the sometimes friends had unfortunate repercussions. Virginia Woolf was particularly concerned, as Lehmann was associated with Hogarth and Spender was a close friend. She felt, as Lehmann did, that inevitably through Spender *Horizon* would "steal" young writers of promise away from *New Writing*. She asked Spender to dinner to discuss the issue and wrote that she sincerely hoped an understanding could be reached.[11] Claiming she had nothing new at the moment, she avoided contributing any of her own work to *Horizon*, as did E. M. Forster.[12] In her diary Woolf went so far as to say that she and Hugh Walpole "condemned" Spender for what they saw as a betrayal of Lehmann and Hogarth.[13] Even the always loyal T. S. Eliot at first said he had nothing to contribute, though he was one of the first of the old guard to relent, with a brief note on Joyce in the March 1941 issue, followed in the May 1941 number by a comment on Virginia Woolf and the December 1944 issue with an essay, "The Man of Letters and the Future of Europe."

Lehmann tried to remain professionally cordial, particularly as he was Spender's editor at Hogarth for other contracted works, most notably the novel *The Backward Son*. After several inconclusive and unpleasant exchanges, Spender, too, made an attempt to carry on the professional relationship as if nothing had happened, and in the Christmas 1939 edition of *New Writing* there were two Spender poems.

In January of 1940, after the appearance of the first issues of *Horizon*, Spender tried to reestablish personal relations as well. As continued to be the case over the years to come, years that would be marked by further disputes, the two men needed each other professionally and were inevitably thrown together by common interests and pursuits and, most of all, by mutual friends, including William Plomer, Christopher Isherwood,

Joe Ackerley, E. M. Forster, Virginia Woolf, and T. S. Eliot, not to mention Lehmann's sister Rosamond.

On January 15, Spender wrote a very personal letter to Lehmann from North Wales, where he was working on *The Backward Son*—at that time entitled *Tissellote House*. He confided in Lehmann in the tone of a close old friend. He was with two art students, he said—Lucian Freud and David Kentish. Freud he considered the "cleverest person" he had met since Auden at Oxford. He was devastated by continuing bad news about the health of his sister-in-law Lolly. Yet for the first time since the separation from Inez, the outbreak of war, and Lolly's illness, he was putting up "a real fight," seeing lots of people, and even enjoying "getting tight." He could not resist noting also that the first numbers of *Horizon* were a "great success."

Lehmann's answer on the eighteenth was much cooler. In spite of the "quarrel," he wanted Spender to be happy, and he believed in his "destiny as a writer." The "wound" dealt by the *Horizon* business, however, would change their relationship forever. And he complained with some bitterness about what he saw as Spender's having allowed Connolly to make negative editorial remarks about Auden's and Isherwood's departure for America in the face of war.[14] He continued by faulting Spender for publishing the "September Journal"—among other things an intimate record of aspects of his breakup with Inez— and by suggesting that "in spite of your denials," *Horizon* would undermine *New Writing*.

Both of Spender's literary parents agreed with much of what Lehmann said. Eliot shared Lehmann's distaste in regard both to the remarks about Auden and Isherwood and to the question of the publication of intimate journals.[15] Virginia Woolf, always more bitter than the mild-mannered Eliot, complained that Spender, in the wake of his marriage, had "fallen into vice" again and that he was "sentimentalizing" with Lucian Freud. In fact, she decided for the moment, he was a "bleeding heart."[16]

But by spring matters had calmed down. Woolf had recognized the success of *Horizon* to the extent that she was even considering contributing something[17]—partly, however, because she was irritated by a Connolly "Comment" referring to her as an "Ivory Tower Dweller."[18] Eliot liked the numbers that followed the one with the Auden-Isherwood remark and felt that Connolly's "Comments" were improving.[19] E. M. Forster enjoyed the journal, too, but found Connolly's "carping" at Christopher and Wystan "decivilizing."[20] Even John Lehmann had to admit that *Horizon* was a success and that it had had no apparent effect on *New Writing*. He was also greatly pleased when Spender, as a peace offering, gave him a leather ledger containing the original manuscript of *Trial of a Judge* and various poems.[21]

Horizon was, in fact, an immense success. The first number sold out in a week and required a second printing. It included contributions by Walter de la Mare, W. H. Auden, John Betjeman, Louis MacNeice, J. B. Priestley, Herbert Read, H. E. Bates, and Geoffrey Grigson, mostly solicited by Spender. There was a review article by Spender himself called "How Shall We Be Saved?" which began with a claim that the German-Soviet pact completed "the return of our civilization . . . to the game of power politics." Thinking people were left in "comparative isolation."[22] In short, in the wake of the union of Fascism and Communism and the consequent throwing together of old liberals and conservatives, socialists and capitalists, there was no longer room for intellectual "heroes." Among other things, the article was a review of Eliot's *The Idea of a Christian Society*. Spender is unusually harsh with his mentor. With his call for a Christian society Eliot betrays the fact that he is both "impressed and confused by the European tradition." In his best poetry and in his admiration for Joyce, Eliot implicitly recognizes the "outrageous and even revolutionary" in that tradition, but he fails to see that the " 'tradition' today might be the Waste Land rather than the chapel among the ruins." Spender ends with a rather Woolf-like remark: "I feel that 'The awful daring of a moment's surrender' forsook him at some moment, and that now he's left looking for the beatific vision amongst the obituary notices of the *Times*. But I hope I may be wrong."[23] Eliot, as always, took Spender's criticism well and soon invited his critic to lunch.

The second and third numbers of *Horizon* sold even better than the

first. They included works by George Barker, Cecil Day-Lewis, George
Orwell, Philip Toynbee, W. H. Auden, William Plomer, John Betjeman,
and Hugh Walpole, who, in spite of his recent condemnation of Spender,
apparently decided he could write for a journal that was now the hit of
literary London. He was not alone. Over the next few years *Horizon* con-
tributors, many recruited by Spender, included, among many others,
Edouard Roditi, Alex Comfort, Roy Fuller, E. M. Bowra, Béla Bartók,
Henry Miller, Louis Aragon, Barbara Ward, Joe Ackerley, Stuart
Gilbert, Augustus John, Dylan Thomas, Rose Macaulay, Kathleen
Raine, Edith Sitwell, Edwin Muir, Howard Nemerov, Eudora Welty,
T. S. Eliot, soldiers at the front, and even John Lehmann.

Spender's "September Journal" dominated several early issues and
created something of a sensation as well as the disapproval already noted.
In fact, the publication of the journal was distinctly un-English and very
much in conflict with the anti-individualistic, antiromantic mood of the
times. Like *World Within World*, which would come much later, the journal represented something of that "outrageous and even revolutionary"
aspect of modernism, the lack of which Spender mourned in the atmosphere of England at war. Here, as in much of his poetry, he was trying
to express his sense of the universal loss in terms of his personal life.

In one segment of the journal he expresses a sense of despair by way
of an intimate image of his relationship with Inez. On a particularly
depressing and lonely afternoon he came home to his empty flat and

> lay down. I couldn't help imagining the comfort of her when her
> legs are drawn up against her breasts, her hands clasp her ankles,
> and her head rests on her knees with the hair falling over them.

He speaks of memories like this as "self-pity," as "weakness" leading to
isolation and a loss of energy. But we need domesticity, he writes.

> Everything should be rooted. This is the simplest thing in life, it is
> the cocoon that surrounds childhood, it is the simple security of
> the flesh and the kiss and the fireplace and the setting sun which

brings him home. The hands that destroy this homeliness whether in children or grown up people are ripping the child in all of us that never leaves the womb away from the womb, and tearing the belly of the mother into ribbons. No one should want anything except to find his place in life, the centre of his potentiality to love and be loved.[24]

The most controversial article in the early *Horizon*s was Connolly's February 1940 "Comment." The "departure of Auden and Isherwood to America a year ago," he wrote, "is the most important literary event since the outbreak of the Spanish War." Auden was "our best poet, Isherwood our most promising novelist." Both had sought and obtained publicity in England, both had an "instinct for self-preservation," and both had gone to America, where they could "gain most." It was also in this comment that Connolly referred to Joyce, Proust, and Woolf as "Ivory Tower Dwellers."[25]

Inevitably, Spender was blamed for what were seen as Connolly's inappropriate remarks, and it is somewhat surprising that he apparently did little to prevent their being published. In fact, Connolly had nothing against Auden and Isherwood for their departure and by letters was able to explain his remarks to their satisfaction. But when Harold Nicolson wrote in the *Spectator* that Auden and Isherwood should have stayed in England, he also said of Spender, "Siren calls which reach him from America may induce even that great bird to wing silently away."[26] Spender's answer to this undeserved barb came in the next issue of the *Spectator*: "This great bird," he wrote, "has every intention of remaining where he is put, and helping, to the best of his ability, and until he is called up, Mr. Cyril Connolly with *Horizon*." As to Auden and Isherwood, he suggested that "arguments which apply to political actions do not apply to artists."[27] If his friends could do better work in America, they were justified in staying there. Louis MacNeice would say something similar in the February 1941 issue of *Horizon*, and E. M. Forster suggested that those who were attacking Auden and Isherwood were simply jealous of their lives in America.[28] Auden himself wrote to his friend E. R. Dodds echoing Spender's remarks in the first *Horizon* essay and in the "September Journal." During the thirties, he said, intellectuals all talked about the isolation of the artist in a repressive English society. "You may speak of England as roots," he wrote, "but after all what is my England? My childhood and my English friends."[29] Like Spender, Auden believed that true roots were to be found in the domesticity of loving and being loved.

Isherwood wrote to Spender defending his and Auden's decision to remain in America—in his case in California. He suggested to his old friend that "this is where you also should be." Auden would make the same suggestion.[30] Spender's reply to Isherwood, in which he clearly dissociates himself "from those writers who have accused their English colleagues in America of running away," was published in the *New Statesman and Nation* in November 1940.[31] In January of 1941 it was republished in *Living Age* as "Escapists Live on Borrowed Time," a title that served to emphasize Spender's one condition to his approval of the Auden-Isherwood decision. Writers must be "the interpreters of life around them." Those who removed themselves from the "time" that was England in 1940—the England of the Battle of Britain—must beware of failing to preserve the "sense" of that time from the perspective of what was, in effect, a prewar, pre-Munich America.

Auden read Spender's article and wrote to say that if he thought he could serve well in some wartime capacity, he would return to England, but that he felt he could best pursue in America "the intellectual warfare" that goes on "always and everywhere" regardless of physical wars. Apparently Auden assumed some negative feeling on Spender's part as far as the immigration to America was concerned. He went so far as to suggest that Spender had turned against him for his decision and attributed this to an essential difference between them. He was a "thinking-intuitive" type who acted and thought realistically, while Spender was a "feeling-sensation" type who acted and spoke impulsively. He also chided Spender for an implied criticism of Isherwood's turn toward yoga and spiritualism.[32]

The fourth number of *Horizon*, in April 1940, contained a predictably conservative solicited article, on modern poetry by Spender's uncle, the formidable J. A. Spender. "Letter to a Nephew" argued that poetry should provide "comfort," that the modern poets (presumably including his nephew) were too theoretical and too misanthropic. The April issue also published works by Laurie Lee, Lucian Freud, and V. S. Pritchett, as well as an essay on A. E. Housman by Spender. Housman's poetry, he said, was the beautiful work of a repressed but eternal boy. Connolly's April "Comment" pointed to the fact that writers seemed to be increasingly "preoccupied" not with politics but with "the investigation of spiritual possibilities."[33] This applied to H. G. Wells, Somerset Maugham, Virginia Woolf, Aldous Huxley, Gerald Heard, J. B. Priestley, T. S. Eliot, and also to the "recent poetry" of Auden and Spender.

Readers of Spender's *Selected Poems* (1940), one of Fabers' Sesame Books meant to popularize modern British poetry, could without difficulty agree with Connolly. The volume was dominated by nineteen poems from the most "spiritual" of Spender's books, *The Still Centre*. It also contained twelve earlier poems and selections from *Trial of a Judge*.

The May *Horizon* contained works by William Empson, Laurie Lee, Dylan Thomas, for whom Spender was attempting to raise money, and Auden and Spender's old Oxford friend Richard Crossman, now the editor of the *New Statesman and Nation*. In his "Comment" Connolly recognized Eliot's "East Coker"—later one of the *Four Quartets*—as "one of the finest long poems of the century." And in the final instalment of his "September Journal" Spender tells of a lunch of beer and cheese with Eliot at his club. They had discussed, among other things, poetry and Beethoven. Spender tells how after that lunch he had gone out to Lavenham alone and played on the gramophone Beethoven's Opus 127 Quartet and the last movement of Opus 130 in A Minor, containing "the most mysterious and religious of all Beethoven's ideas."[34] These were ideas that perhaps represented hope in a dark time. They would permeate Eliot's *Four Quartets* and Spender's own postwar "Spiritual Explorations."

In the spring of 1940 Hogarth published Spender's autobiographical novel of his childhood school experience, *The Backward Son*. On May 5 Spender visited the Woolfs, and Virginia pronounced that she liked the novel very much.[35] With this visit the chill that had been generated by the *Horizon–New Writing* conflict came to an end.

The Backward Son is the story of sensitive young Geoffrey Brand, child of an overbearing rhetorical father and an ineffectual mother. Geoffrey is sent to boarding school at an early age. He hates the school for its arbitrariness, its pomposity, and its cruelty. It stands for everything Spender hated in British culture. *The Backward Son* is also about roots that, given a situation of existential alienation, can only be found within the self: "It would be terrifying to be another. Being I is home," says the miserable child as he cries himself to sleep in the school dormitory.[36] In this scene there is an expression of Spender's own search for the individual way in the face of what he saw as an unnatural upbringing in a repressive, child-suffocating culture. Sanford Sternlicht accurately describes the novel as an "allegory of man's inhumanity to man and to child."[37] In a general sense, the child (at any age) in question is the one described by Spender in his "September Journal," the one ripped by "hands that destroy" from the domestic "womb"—from the "homeliness" or "security of the flesh," which is true "roots."

The "hands that destroy this homeliness" were now at work not only in Spender's past and present domestic life but on the world stage. On April 9 the Germans invaded Denmark and Norway, and a month later they took Holland and Belgium. On May 10 Churchill replaced Chamberlain as prime minister, but that did not prevent the severe losses between May 27 and June 4 as British troops who had been sent to support France were evacuated from Dunkirk. On June 14 the Germans took Paris. The "homeliness" of European culture was shattered. The assumption was that England's turn was coming.

Immediately after Dunkirk Peter Watson evacuated *Horizon*'s office, with Connolly, Spender, and Diana to a thatched cottage he rented in Thurlstone, Devonshire, near Salcombe, where Spender had spent many childhood vacations as well as a brief time with Inez. If Connolly was bored by life in the country, Spender was not; when not working on *Horizon*, he took up his childhood pursuits of bicycling in the narrow lanes, and rowing and fishing in the bay.

But all was by no means well. There was no escape from war.

Whatever Spender felt about the forces of evil embodied in Nazism, he was at heart a pacifist who could not believe in war as a viable solution to national disagreements. It was victory in the first war that had led to the policies against the defeated Germany that had in turn led to the rise of Hitler and the Nazis. During the summer, he worked at a *Horizon* essay entitled "A Look at the Worst," stressing the importance of learning from past mistakes.[38] If the anti-Nazi forces were to be truly victorious, they must reform democracy; they must recognize that the rise of Fascism could be traced in part to capitalism and the isolation of individualist intellectuals in so-called free societies.

Nowhere is Spender's scepticism about the new war more forcefully expressed than in a poem written at Thurlstone, a poem with slight Prufrockian overtones. "June 1940" begins in the idyllic garden of the little thatched cottage:

> *The early summer prepares its green feasts*
> *In the garden, hot on the blossom of the peach,*
> *Pressed close by bird song, crossed by bees,*
> *Electrified with lizards; and the voices each to each*
> *Speak, afloat on deck chairs.*

But the poet envisions, in the language of his machine-dominated imagery of the "pylon" days, the reality of the approaching armour-clad ideology of Fascism—"caterpillared-wheeled dreams"—lurching through France, destroying "homeliness" and the Wordsworthian nature-dominated world he so loves. Voices who remember the last war speak of "the dragon's teeth of the past."

> *But the voice of one who was young and died*
> *In a great battle, in the light leaves sighed . . .*
>
> *". . . I lay down dead like a world alone*
> *In a sky without faith or aim*
> *And nothing to believe in,*
> *Yet an endless empty need to atone."*

The voice is not only that of the Wilfred Owen World War I soldier but also that of the "child within" Stephen Spender—the child who from an early age had longed for the "security of the flesh," and later for political and personal justice and heroism in Germany, in Spain, and at home.

By early July the war was coming ever closer. Air attacks on coastal shipping and ports became frequent. "From the cliffs at night," Spender said, "we could see air raids on Plymouth" only a few miles away.[39] In the poem "The Air Raid Across the Bay," "Searchlights probe the centre of the sky,/Their ends fusing in cones of light."

By late August Connolly was bored with his Devonshire hideaway and Watson had had enough of entertaining his guests. *Horizon* was moved back to Spender's London flat in time for the Battle of Britain, the daytime bombing, followed by terrifying nighttime "blitz" raids, which, though particularly frequent during September and October, continued throughout the war. Much of Spender's world was crumbling around him. The offices of Hogarth Press were bombed, as was the Woolf house on Tavistock Square. The *Horizon* offices, too, suffered damage. In *The Thirties and After* Spender describes the peculiar combination of bombing and life-as-usual that characterized the period and made England into "a little island of civilization in our lives":

> . . . a dinner party at Elizabeth Bowen's house in Regents Park and walking out into the street afterwards to find it lit whiter than daylight by dropped flares; but also concerts at the National Gallery with programmes played by Myra Hess, Clifford Curzon, or some famous quartet, magical Shakespearean performances with John Gielgud and Peggy Ashcroft, the series of Shelter Drawings by Henry Moore, paintings of burning buildings by Graham Sutherland and John Piper, poetry readings and lectures at the famous Churchill Club at Westminster, T.S. Eliot's poignant *Four Quartets*, the grim and realistic poems of Roy Fuller, the apocalyptic ones of Dylan Thomas and the unaccountable, weirdly inspired ones of Edith Sitwell. A little island of civilization surrounded by burning churches . . .[40]

while the bombs exploded outside. Spender remembered a noonday performance of an early Beethoven quartet at the National Gallery during which there was a "tremendous explosion ... in the middle of the
minuet." Some of the listeners raised their heads for an instant; a bomb
had exploded in Trafalgar Square, but the musicians "did not lift the
bows from their strings."[41]

A combination of circumstances led to Spender's separating himself
to some extent from *Horizon* in the autumn of 1940. Although he
remained friendly with his *Horizon* friends, there was always tension
around Connolly and Watson, and the daily editorial work was not satisfying. Furthermore, the time in Devon had awakened old memories of
childhood, and, still suffering from the separation from Inez and the
realities of divorce proceedings, he had found a certain solace during the
summer months there. *The Backward Son* had been a revisitation of
childhood, too, and he had for several months been preoccupied with the
question of the betrayed child within the man, as indicated in the "September Journal" entries discussed above. When it was suggested to him
that he might take a teaching job at Blundell's School in Devon, he
impulsively accepted a position there.

Almost immediately he realized that, unlike Auden, he was not a natural schoolteacher. He wrote to John Lehmann, with whom, especially
now that he was no longer officially associated with *Horizon*, he had
resumed friendly relations, that he had no desire to teach. Being in a
school left him as isolated as he had been at school as a child in a place
that symbolized everything he hated about English culture. The only
solution was to write, because it was the only thing that expressed who he
was. He could as easily have repeated the thoughts of the child hero
of *The Backward Son*: "Being I is home." Life had become a seemingly "endless vista." Yet there was a spark of humour in the letters to
Lehmann. Some of the boys were nice enough. One had "got tame" and
lived "in a basket in my room." And there was another reason to hope.
One day there was a visit from a young woman he had met recently
in London at a *Horizon* lunch. Her name was Natasha Litvin. She
was a pianist, and Spender liked her.[42] Her father was the musicolo-
gist Edwin Evins, her mother the actress Ray Litvin. Natasha's back-

ground was what Ian Hamilton called "the fringes of the nineteen-thirties left-wing intellectual scene."[43] Later, in January, Spender would write to Cyril Connolly that he was having a "swing" in the direction of girls.[44]

On November 10, less than two months into the term, Spender explained in a letter to his headmaster, Neville Gorton, that he had decided he must return to London to help with *Horizon*, which was suddenly having a difficult time. It was particularly important that he return now because Connolly was leaving temporarily and required that Spender take his place. He would also work with John Lehmann on a Penguin-sponsored new series of *New Writing*. He would be willing to lecture occasionally at Blundell's in return only for expense money. This arrangement was approved by Gorton, and Spender returned to London at Christmastime.

In London he courted Natasha. Coming out of restaurants, they would find workers shovelling up bomb debris. At a party during an air raid, Erika Mann and Brian Howard hid under a piano that Natasha was playing.[45]

On January 13, 1941, James Joyce died in Zurich, leading Spender to reexamine the whole question of the modernist movement. His obituary essay in the *Listener* is at once an overview of Joyce's career and a comment on the nature of high modernism.[46] Inevitably Spender begins with the picture of his subject, remaining in high modernist fashion aloof from current events—like Beethoven writing his music as Vienna was being bombarded. He wonders if in the current era the artist has other responsibilities. The audience of Beethoven was a "cultured minority." Today's educated minority is "sick, rootless and self-centred" and perhaps requires more direction from the artist.

Leaving his question essentially unanswered, Spender discusses Joyce's work in terms of the development of modernism from introspection to fragmentation, to the use of a disintegrating process as the subject of art itself:

> The *Portrait of the Artist as a Young Man* is the first volume of a great self-absorbed autobiographic work, which is treated objectively in

Ulysses, and which, finally, in *Finnegans Wake* transcends itself and passes into the universal, disintegrating in the process.

In *Ulysses* the "interior monologue" method provides, says Spender, "a truer picture of the human mind than has ever been achieved before." But the problem with this method is that when carried out to its logical extreme, it leaves us unable to communicate. Without the support of the conventional abstracting of "certain qualities . . . our picture of life would break into meaningless fragments. Perhaps the world is fragmentary and meaningless," as the works of the great modernist painters and composers would suggest, but art "which becomes meaningless," in demonstrating this possibility, "defeats its own ends." *Finnegans Wake* approaches this problem by creating a story about "everything" in what amounts to the beginnings of "a universal language." Joyce's works as a whole "undermine our picture of life by pointing out that our conception of individuals," for example, "is only a tiny approximation of the truth that we have deduced in order to be able to form rough charts of living for ourselves."

T. S. Eliot praised Spender for his obituary but was bitter about the limited one in the London *Times* and wrote a letter to say so. When the *Times* neglected to publish his remarks, he offered them to Spender at *Horizon*, who published them in the March issue. In the February issue, in "The Year's Poetry, 1940," Spender had discussed Eliot's current approach to modernism, suggesting that although he had in the past argued—like Joyce—that the poet must not be concerned with "aims outside poetry," "Burnt Norton" and "East Coker" represented poetry that "shows a tendency to move outside itself and question its own use."[47] In short, Spender seems to be saying, Eliot's movement parallels Joyce's from *Portrait* to *Finnegans Wake*.

March brought the death of another great modernist, Virginia Woolf. On the seventh (the letter is misdated 1940 in the *Collected Letters*) she had written to Spender referring to both her own situation and England's: "Here we exist on our little plot of ground," she had complained. She demanded of her friend an "immense long letter," something to keep her connected. On the twenty-eighth, having been deeply depressed for some time, she walked into the River Ouse. Spender observed this "personal tragedy" as a reflection of a "vast transparent impersonal one" in which he and Virginia and all who suffered in England admitted "spiritual defeat," opposed "despair with despair" by hoping that the bombers "swinging over us, should swing back again over Germany." In the quest for victory and revenge, much of what Virginia Woolf's work had celebrated was now being "surrendered." With all-out war went "the only true hope for civilization—the conviction of the individual that his inner life can affect outward events and that, whether or not he does so, he is responsible for them." It was "perverted love in the form of nationalism" and "class solidarity" (whether upper or lower) that produced "the forces of destruction in our time."[48]

Spender wrote a sympathy letter to Leonard Woolf on April 4, the day after an obituary appeared in the *Times*. He was thankful for the achievements "of Virginia and yourself." Later he would offer Leonard a place to stay in the *Horizon* flat in Bloomsbury, an offer that Woolf accepted. To his close friend Julian Huxley, Spender wrote that although the suicide was "appalling," it was understandable when one considered that Virginia could not face the idea of another bout of insanity. He went on to say that she had been among his favourite people—the one, in fact, he valued being with above all others.[49]

For the May number of *Horizon*, Spender arranged for a series of comments on Virginia Woolf. Contributors included William Plomer, Rose Macaulay, Vita Sackville-West, and T. S. Eliot. For Eliot, as for Spender, "with the death of Virginia Woolf a whole pattern of culture [was] . . . broken."[50]

In the letter to Huxley, Spender spoke of his impending marriage to Natasha, which was to be on April 9. He was "thrilled" at the prospect in a way that he had not been by his first marriage. This was because to Natasha, who was a "remarkable" person, "being married" meant more than just living together. The effect on Spender of this sense that someone expected "something real from me" was "revolutionary."

The wedding took place at the St. Pancras Register Office with Peter Watson as witness. After a luncheon party at the Étoile Restaurant in Soho, there were drinks at the studio of Mamaine Paget (later Mrs.

Arthur Koestler). Guests at the various festivities included Cecil Beaton, who took pictures; Cyril Connolly with Lys Lubbock; Cecil Day-Lewis; Tambimuttu, the editor of *Poetry London*; Rose Macaulay; Julian and Juliette Huxley; John Lehmann; Janetta Sinclair-Loutit (later Palarde); Sonia Brownell; the philosopher A. J. ("Freddy") Ayer, who brought along the future spy Guy Burgess; the architect Erno Goldfinger and his wife Ursula; Louis MacNeice; Nancy Coldstream; and William Plomer and Joe Ackerley, who, according to John Lehmann, provided a "satiric chorus in undertones."[51] Lehmann also noted the "painfully marked absence" of Auden and Isherwood, who were in America.

The Spenders spent their honeymoon at Carbis Bay in Cornwall near painter friends Ben Nicolson and Adrian Stokes. After the honeymoon they moved to Oxford, during which period the Germans invaded the Soviet Union. "Tod und das Madchen," a poem about the suffering of his sister-in-law, reflected the suffering and death of war: "the sorrowful golden flesh,/Scorched on by disease."

Later in the summer the Spenders visited their friends Julian and Juliette Huxley in the country, and then stayed at the home of friends in Wintersham on the Romney Marsh in Kent, near Rye, where they had visits from Leonard Woolf and John Lehmann and others. After a brief trip to Devon and then to Bristol, where Spender gave a talk for a socialist clergyman,[52] the couple moved, by invitation, into 33 Chiltern Gardens, Cricklewood, as paying guests of "Berthella," the sisters who had "brought up" the Spender children at 10 Frognal: "Natasha's piano almost filled the living-room, and my books and papers flooded the rest of the tiny house." Once again Spender was reliving his childhood by placing himself under the protection of Berthella. Their house "seemed like a raft bearing a few belongings from the shipwreck of our world."[53]

On Christmas Day, 1941, Ella's postman husband Frank presided over a reunion luncheon of Spenders. Michael, now an RAF flight lieutenant, came and so did Humphrey, who was a photographer in the army, and Christine, who was working for a Catholic charity.

As for the newly married couple, Stephen at first lived under the shadow of his earlier failed marriage and tended to blame himself and others for past problems. Then one day Natasha said: "From now on there is no question of blame. There is only us." Spender would write later, "This was the faith, the search for a unity which was ourselves belonging to one another, on which our marriage was founded."[54] It was a faith that was to last, through many rough places, until his death fifty-four years later.

In October Spender wrote to William Plomer that he had more or less given up *Horizon* and was ladder-climbing instead.[55] He referred to his new wartime job as a fireman. Having been called up for service and having failed the medical exam for military duty because of a recurring colitis problem, he was able to obtain a posting to an auxiliary fire service (AFS) branch of the National Fire Service (NFS) in Cricklewood. Auden wrote to Spender suggesting that it was a pity firefighters probably no longer wore "those lovely brass helmets. . . . You would look such a camp in one."[56]

The blitz subsided radically during the German preoccupation with Russia, and Spender's main concern as a firefighter was an education programme for the service. In a *Partisan Review* letter-article entitled "From England: War and the Writer," dated October 25, 1941, he wrote that the working classes had no sense of the possibility of a change in their condition that could result from the war. He saw this fact as a "disillusionment at the basis of society."[57] The AFS education programme consisted of discussion groups that were primarily concerned with postwar planning. For Spender this was an opportunity to impress on ordinary people his views on learning from past mistakes and on creating an educated public that could see the importance of reforming democracy itself as well as defeating the enemy. He felt that he and others who worked on the education programmes contributed to the eventual victory of the Labour Party in 1945 and the development of a welfare state thereafter.

Spender's days with the fire service were a surprise. He had expected to be resented by his mostly working-class colleagues but found that they were cordial and supportive. At an evening Christmas party at the station in 1941 Spender was struck by the decorations that had turned the station recreation room into "a classic example of something the writers of the left had spent so much time discussing in the 1930's: proletarian art, folk art even." Finally Spender was among the working classes as, at least for the moment, a fellow worker. He was happy to find himself in an atmosphere that reminded him of Rabelais's free Abbey of Thélème, in which the inhabitants "observed a natural restraint and discipline, which grew out of a loyalty to one another."[58] In *Citizens in War—and After* (1945) Spender would praise the civil defence workers and emphasize their importance to the welfare of society.

After a few weeks at the Cricklewood station Spender was moved to one in the familiar ground of Hampstead. The Spenders moved to an attic flat at 2 Maresfield Gardens, very close to the Maresfield fire station. Downstairs was Sigmund Freud's son, the architect Ernst Freud, and his family, and just along the street was Anna Freud, who ran a nursery for war victims. The Spenders helped raise money for the nursery, and later Miss Freud offered Natasha baby-care lessons at the nursery.[59] Lucian Freud had a studio full of dead birds in the Spender flat.[60]

The fire station at Hampstead was not as convivial as the one at Cricklewood, but his friend the writer William Sansom was there, and together they wrote a book about the fire service called *Jim Braidy: The Story of Britain's Firemen* (1943), a book illustrated by several of the firemen. Near the end of his time in the fire service Spender was transferred to the Holland Park Avenue station. It was there that he had most of his experience as an actual firefighter.

Life in the fire service during the general bombing lull that marked the period of Spender's tenure there was time-consuming and essentially dull. Still, he managed to produce a significant amount of work, and as much as possible he and Natasha continued to see their old friends and to make new ones. There were weekend visits to the Nicolsons, the Huxleys, and Robert Graves in the country.[61] Dinner parties in London, given the war shortages, were not elaborate but were an important diversion. Benjamin Britten, Elizabeth Bowen, T. S. Eliot, the Sitwells, the Huxleys, and Morgan Forster were all guests at various times, as were Lehmann, Plomer, Ackerley, and other old friends.[62] Sometimes people brought delicacies they had in one way or another procured. Forster once accepted a Spender dinner invitation and asked whether he could bring "tinned fish or Algerian wine."[63]

In February 1942 *Horizon* published Spender's annual review of the poetry of the previous year.[64] He particularly admired Eliot's "East Coker" and "Dry Salvages" and Edith Sitwell's *Street Songs*. He now recognized and accepted the fact that Eliot's "mission was to interpret the integrated past within the fragmentary present, relating himself to both." For Eliot—as indicated in the poems that would become the *Four Quartets*—"however much the individual might be committed to social tasks, he belonged to an eternal order of events where he was not product and victim of his time."[65]

Yet Spender still had reservations about Eliot's philosophy of life and poetry. In a letter to Alex Comfort discussing Comfort's poetry, he advised avoiding the sententious quality of Eliot. It was important to be precise, clear, and concrete. As great as Eliot's poetry could be, his philosophy so dominated it that he could begin a poem by saying he had once read a D. H. Lawrence story and everyone would think, "How kind of Tom," and then move on only to learn that ends and beginnings were the same.[66]

As for Sitwell, her greatness lay in her "beautiful objectivity . . . derived from a profoundly personal existence." The Spenders had become close to this woman whose "own well-being was bound up with that of her friends."[67] Spender's letters to her were always to "My Dearest Edith." In the July 1943 issue of *Horizon* he published a poem, "Lines for Edith Sitwell."

Spender's major critical work of the war years was his *Life and the Poet* (1942), which argues that poetry cannot be cause-oriented. This work marks, therefore, the final break with a poetic value system based on Marxism. Sounding much more like his literary parents, Virginia Woolf and T. S. Eliot, he proposes that even in times of great political and social stress a poet must be true to his sense of "satisfactory living." Spender is even willing now to accept the value of religion—at least in a general humanistic sense. Sounding like Auden, he suggests that the artist need not live in turmoil to succeed in his art, that he has "sufficient experience of his own mind and body and social environment" to do so. The artist's proper task is to concern himself "with being, and being is infinite."[68]

In 1942 and '43 Spender wrote several other reviews and articles for *Horizon*, the *Spectator*, the *New Statesman and Nation*, and the *Fortnightly*; his "A Stopwatch and an Ordnance Map" was put to music by Samuel Barber; he did a translation with J. L. Gili of *Selected Poems by Federico García Lorca* for John Lehmann at Hogarth[69]; he wrote *Spiritual Exercises*, which he printed privately and dedicated to Cecil Day-Lewis; and he published *Ruins and Visions*, a book of poems for Fabers.

Spiritual Exercises, which would later be included in *Poems of Dedication* as "Spiritual Explorations," marks the completion in the gradual turn in Spender's poetry toward what he called "subjective contemplation."[70] The exercises are essentially a prologue and conclusion and seven sonnets, each of which explores the universal question of life's meaning. In each of the sonnets there is something of a modernistic, almost existential, sense of alienation combined with the humanistic religiosity that Spender had recently allowed as a possibility in his life. There is, in fact, a mood and sound of Eliot's *Four Quartets* in the poems, as in the fifth sonnet:

> *The immortal spirit is that single ghost*
> *Of all times past incarnate in each time*
> *Which through the breathing skeleton must climb*
> *To be within our living minds engrossed.*
> *Without that spirit within, our selves are lost,*
> *But shadows haunting the earth's rim.*
> *Unless we will it live, that spirit dims,*
> *Dies in our lives, its death, our death, the cost.*
> *One sacred past, present, futurity*
> *Seeks within our many-headed wills*
> *To carve in stone the dove, the flame-winged city.*
> *Shut in himself, each blinded subject kills*
> *His neighbour and himself, and shuts out pity*
> *For that sole making spirit which fulfils.*

Ruins and Visions is twenty-eight poems arranged in four sections. The first, "Separation," refers back to the "ruin" that was Spender's marriage to Inez. In "No Orpheus, No Eurydice" he succeeds in completing the separation. Inez has gone with another to experience "pleasures of the sun."

The "ruin" of Part II, "Ironies of War," is that of war itself. Here we find "The Air Raid Across the Bay" and "June 1940" and "Winter and Summer," describing "the perpetual winter/Of this violent time, where pleasures freeze."

Part III is the "ruin" associated with particular "Deaths." "The Ambitious Son" is a poem about the death of his father and the spiritual death of himself in a "grave of fame." "Tod und das Madchen" is here, too—the poem about the gradual dying of Lolly. "Wings of the Dove" is also about Lolly's suffering. Both poems would later be included as part of the poet's "Elegy for Margaret" in *Poems of Dedication*. "Of what use is my weeping?" the poet asks, given "The granite facts around your bed."

Part IV contains Spender's "Visions," which culminates in one of his wife, who represents in "To Natasha" the possibility of peace emerging from a personally fragmented world and a larger world at war:

> *Darling, this kiss of great serenity*
> *Has cast no sheet anchor of security*
> *But balances upon faith that lies*
> *In the timeless loving of your eyes*

Spender had sent Auden an advance copy of *Ruins and Visions* in late April and received a reply dated May 12. After praising the work as an "advance" on *The Still Centre*, Auden admonishes his friend for a certain dishonesty in his life and work—specifically for hiding behind what he sees as a facade of meekness. Perhaps with perceived slights to himself in connection with his removal to America in mind, Auden launches into an analysis of Spender's character—one with which John Lehmann, for instance, might well have agreed—in which he suggests that when Spender behaves "badly," it is not because of "weakness of will but excess of will." When Auden—or Cyril Connolly, for example—behaves badly, he does so "out of fright." Auden wonders if Spender's preoccupation with death in several of the poems in *Ruins* is based not on the "pity" that the poems attempt to convey but rather on a feeling of "Goody. He's dead and I'm alive." Spender, he says, is a "hypertense" person, while he, Auden, is a "hypotense." Thus Auden depends on various addictions to survive, while Spender wears the mask of sensitivity to protect him from a sense of guilt about being "destructive" to people "weaker" than himself—people such as Inez and, presumably, Tony Hyndman. Auden goes on to say with characteristic facetiousness that whereas Spender can become jealous over someone else's good poem, what he, Auden, envies are strengths he "cannot make use of as support, eg. your prick." In terms of poetry, Auden says his own work is too much that of the directive "scoutmaster," while Spender's needs to drop its "whiff of the yearning school-girl." In a sense, Auden was extending his Oxford period criticism of Spender's tendency to be overly "romantic" and undisciplined. He ends his letter with a suggestion that Spender cannot lead both the contemplative and the political life. Auden's criticism was a typical attempt to dominate his friend, but Spender seems to have taken it without rancour.

Meanwhile, the war continued, but the tide had turned. America had entered the war in December of 1941; in November of 1942 the Anglo-American forces had invaded North Africa, and in October 1943 they landed in Italy.

On February 28, 1944, Spender turned thirty-five. Natasha wrote to Edith Sitwell saying that Stephen was walking around intoning the opening lines of Dante's *Divine Comedy*.[71]

Spender continued his reviews of poetry for *Horizon*. In the March 1944 number he ranked the poets of 1943, recommending in order the recent work of David Gascoyne, Kathleen Raine, Lawrence Durrell, Roy Fuller, Peter Yates, Cecil Day-Lewis, Edwin Muir (an old and close friend), Geoffrey Grigson, and Terrence Tiller, and making special note of the latest poetry of Osbert Sitwell, John Lehmann, Dunstan Thompson, and Robert Frost.

In June Natasha Spender played some highly successful concerts, Rome fell to the Allies, the Normandy landings took place, and Natasha became pregnant. At a fire near St. Mary Abbots Church in Kensington High Street Spender was almost trapped by flames in the back of a build-

ing and was surprised at his own reaction, one very much in tune with
Eliot's "Little Gidding":

> There was a rustling and crackling all around me, and in my heart
> I felt the peace which I had always longed to know before I went
> out on a fire, the knowledge that we were going to have a child. It
> was as though a cycle of living was completed, and in the fire I
> stood in the centre of a wheel of my own life where childhood and
> middle age and death were the same.[72]

One night, soon after Spender had been released from the AFS, a
buzz bomb, the sound of which was "like that of a train emerging from a
tunnel," landed on a house nearby. The bedroom ceiling collapsed, but
"Natasha, who [seemed] without fear, was scarcely affected by this," but
through Spender's mind went what he supposed was his last thought:
"This is something I have all my life been waiting for." When he told
Auden this later, Auden said, "What an old solipsist you are!"[73] Solipsist
or not, soon after the bombing Spender wrote up a will and asked John
Lehmann and Edith Sitwell to be his literary executors.[74]

It seemed best, given Natasha's condition and that of the flat, to move
to Oxford. Spender worked there for several weeks, and Natasha went off
to a friend's home in Wiltshire, where there was a piano but no room for
Stephen as well. Spender wrote to Julian Huxley that he was happy to be
away from the bombing, and he confided that he was involved platoni-
cally and in a minor way with an intelligent Oxford student. As with age
his feelings were becoming somewhat illusory and sentimental, the
thirty-five-year-old Spender suggested that he could be happy enough
with dreams. A canoe ride with a handsome and intelligent young man
could cheer him up at least for a short time.[75] There were to be many
such young men in the years to come.

Back in London in the autumn, Spender took up a position in the
intelligence branch of the Foreign Office. His group compiled material
about Italian Fascism for the occupying British forces in Italy.

On December 16 the Battle of the Bulge began, and despite setbacks,
the end of the war was now in sight. The December 1944 *Horizon*

contained a "Christmas Anthology" compiled by Spender. It included poems by Edmund Blunden, whom Spender had known from his Oxford days, and by Edith Sitwell, Cecil Day-Lewis, John Lehmann, Howard Nemerov, Roy Fuller, Frances Cornford, and several others. It was an optimistic collection in tone. There was also an essay by Eliot on writers and the future of Europe.

Matthew Spender was born to Natasha and Stephen in March "during one of the worst nights of V2 missiles."[76] A week later the family moved to 15 Loudoun Road in St. John's Wood in London. Stephen and Natasha would live there for the rest of Spender's life. On May 7 the Germans surrendered. Soon afterward Stephen's brother Michael was killed in a plane crash in Germany. Spender wrote to Edith Sitwell, "We never got over a certain embarrassment with each other."[77] He attended the funeral in Munich.

Later in May, Wystan Auden visited London in his capacity as part of an American group studying the effect of bombing on German cities. Spender, with Natasha and Matthew, answered the doorbell one evening to find Auden standing on the doorstep in an "American officer's uniform, which, since he was not built for uniforms, could not but look bizarre on him." Spender burst out laughing, partly at the uniform but also because he was so happy to see his old friend. Auden was not amused. "You have a son," he said as he crossed the threshold. "All babies look like Winston Churchill," he pronounced, and left it at that.[78]

1. Stephen Spender

2. Hampstead

3. Auden, Spender, and Isherwood

4. In Germany 1929

5. In the early thirties

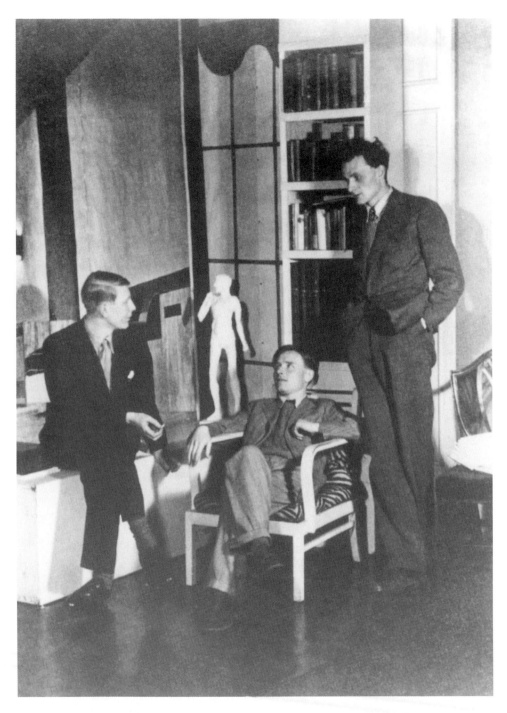

6. Auden, Isherwood, and Spender

7. Spender by Henry Moore

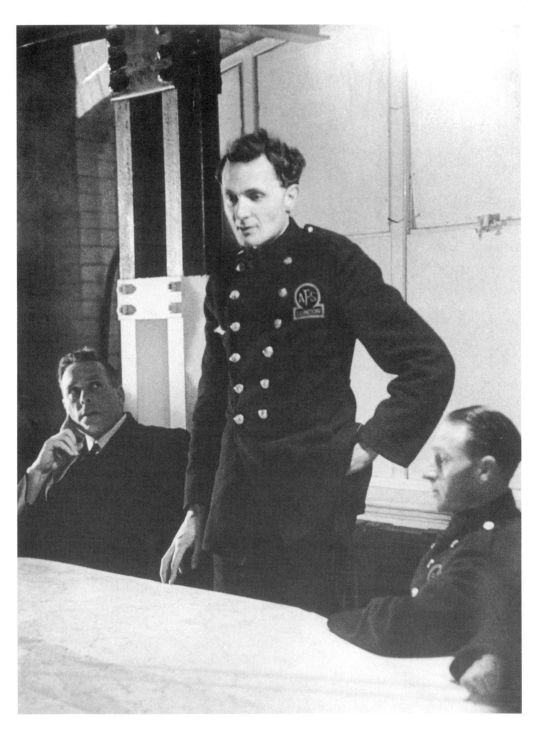

8. A member of the Fire Service

9. MacNeice, Auden, Hughes, Eliot, and Spender

10. Auden, Day-Lewis, and Spender

11. With Lizzie

12. Paris, 1986

8

NEW WORLDS

The environment in which Stephen Spender found himself in mid-1945 was a very different one from that of the prewar years during which he had made his name as a literary figure. Virginia Woolf and Ottoline Morrell were dead, and Auden and Isherwood were established in the United States. As for European civilization, so important to Spender's cosmopolitan tastes and views, it lay in spiritual and physical ruin. The Germany that had once been central to a new sense of personal freedom in his life, in effect, no longer existed. The political radicalism that had provided a base for his rebellion against what he saw as a stultifying economic and moral system in Britain had been undermined by the corruption of the Marxist movement as directed by Soviet Communism. Furthermore, his former homosexual lifestyle had now been superseded to a great extent by his role as a husband and father, though this was a role to which he was committed and one that he genuinely enjoyed. Any deviations from the generally accepted responsibilities and expectations of that role he would, for the most part, treat with the kind of discretion he had witnessed among reasonable people like the Nicolsons and Virginia Woolf, who had also led somewhat unconventional private lives

outside of their generally successful marriages. As for politics and international issues, there seemed to be nowhere to turn but back to the tolerance and generosity of the broad liberalism that came naturally to him.
In Britain the victory of the Labour Party was no revolution, but it
marked a move to a sense of social responsibility and class equality that
had not characterized British governments in the past. In any case,
Spender had never concerned himself much with political parties, and
since his Communist experiment, he had become disillusioned with ideologies. But for the rest of his life he was deeply committed, through
organizations like PEN (International Association of Poets, Playwrights,
Editors, Essayists and Novelists) and *Index on Censorship*, to the struggle
against the psychological and physical oppression of people—particularly
intellectuals—by totalitarian regimes. As far as his wanderlust was concerned, there were still worlds to explore. First there would be war-torn
Europe, then the new superpower, America, and, as always, the complex
world life within himself. Spender's life was necessarily more subdued
and less dramatic than it had been before the war, but the old curiosity
was still there, and the need to express himself in words.

In 1945 alone Spender managed to write several major essays of literary
criticism, a number of shorter pieces on problems for European writers
and other intellectuals after the war, and a book on his visits to Germany
and France in the summer and fall. He also completed a novel for John
Lehmann at Hogarth. It was called *Instead of Death* and was a reworking
of his Oxford-days novel. Spender is represented by a character called
Benjamin and Auden is Vernon. Marston appears by that name. The
work is lifeless, and Lehmann and Leonard Woolf were wise to refuse it.

"The Realist Novel and Poetic Imagination" and "Two Landscapes
of Novel" were written for Lehmann's Penguin *New Writing* Series.[1]
These essays are studies of modernism in the novel. In the first Spender
suggests that the great realist novelists of the past took as their task
the "liberation of ideas in events"; they were analytic historians of
the manners of their times. While not at all denigrating the achievements of the classic realists such as Dickens and Balzac, Spender is
clearly most interested in the more poetic, introspective achievements
of the premodernist Henry James and his favourite modernist novel-

ists, Virginia Woolf and James Joyce. These writers had made use of the techniques of stream of consciousness or interior monologue, in which "the external scene is identified more and more closely with the internal processes of feeling and sensibility in the minds of characters."[2] They took various approaches to the problem of natural distortion, fragmentation, and complexity that attends any attempt to re-create the workings of the mind. James tended to turn his late characters into symbols of aspects of his own sensibility. Woolf achieved "wonderful flights of lyricism" in which characters became symbols in an "intimate poetic narrative of drama." As for Joyce, he more than the other modernists was "aware of the logical implications" of his method. He understood that the interior monologues of *Ulysses*, in which inner ideas are always related to external incidents in order to make them understandable, do not take into account the actual language of the mind. In *Finnegans Wake*, therefore, Joyce "invented a new language of the dreams of the human race," which, he admitted, would require a lifetime to understand.[3]

The discussion is continued in "Two Landscapes of Novel." The first landscape is dominated by Tolstoy, Dickens, and Balzac, the second by Proust, the late James, Woolf, Joyce, and sometimes Forster and Lawrence. In the realist novels well-defined characters—good or bad—travel through a recognizable, historical landscape to which they react according to their situations and personalities. In the modernist landscape the characters see their surroundings in individual ways according to their particular sensibilities. The realists grow naturally out of societies that are defined. The modernists reflect "the specialization of modern knowledge and culture, the disintegration of middle class society, the breakdown of the family," and a general fragmentation.

Finally, Spender associates the modernist aesthetic with the position of people like himself who have the "sensibility to insist on the reality of [the] subjective ego" in a world organized on the basis of vast capitalism and power politics "too large to be related to the scale of the human individual or even of the human group." There seemed to be few options but the modernist one: to "revolt against the systematised organisation of aims and ideas outside himself."[4]

In "Moods and Reactions" Spender provides a sketch of contemporary British poetry for the American magazine *Poetry*.[5] "Modern" English poetry reflected a rebellion after World War I against the "diluted kind of poetry written about the countryside and literary subjects" by poets referred to as the "Georgians." The best of these older poets, in Spender's opinion, were Walter de la Mare, W. H. Davies, Edmund Blunden, and Frances Cornford.[6] The modernists, who turned against the methods of the past, aimed for a more "concentrated" style and greatly broadened the subject matter suitable to poetry. Spender points to Yeats as, "in his old age, the greatest modern English poet," to Eliot as perhaps the most influential. Neither, of course, was actually English. The poetry of D. H. Lawrence was an attempt to "center a whole system of values around personal experiences." Dylan Thomas, George Barker, and David Gascoyne are mentioned as being important, and MacNeice, Day-Lewis, Spender, and Auden are noted as being, "in the public mind," a group because of their awareness of the "same problems" and the treatment of the "same subject matter." Auden is held up as "the greatest talent of his generation" with a brilliant ability to express ideas and enter into "intellectual attitudes" and with a real facility for "psychological penetration."[7] About his own work Spender writes that he is "too near . . . to be able to judge it."[8]

All of Spender's literary criticism of the immediate postwar period, as well as of the years that followed, stresses liberal humanistic values. In a *Partisan Review* article, "Modern Writers in the World of Necessity," written just after the German surrender, he refers to the "curse of a necessity" for ruthless governmental power that is the "sinister inheritance" of Fascism.[9] It is urgent, he says, that writers and intellectuals keep before the world the idea that besides organization and national interests there is the fact that "we are humans, with all the grandeur, the full social responsibility and the necessity of freedom, which this implies."[10]

In late May Spender returned to France for the first time since the outbreak of war. Under the auspices of the British Council, he was invited to deliver a lecture in Paris entitled "The Crisis of Symbols in Poetry." In that lecture Spender discussed the problem facing modern artists of having to develop alternatives to symbols that had taken their strength from now weakened institutions.[11] In the audience were several friends he had not seen or heard from since before the war. Sylvia Beach of Shakespeare and Company, who had been imprisoned for refusing to participate in anti-Semitic activities, was there and so was his old friend and onetime "fiancée," Gisa Soloweitschik Drouin, who, as a Jew, had suffered the agonies of negotiating survival for herself and her family wearing the Star of David in occupied Paris. Spender had feared that Gisa had not survived.

During the days and evenings after his lecture, Spender spent time with the Drouins. He also took a trip to Montpellier and Toulouse for British Council–sponsored discussions with French intellectuals. Back in Paris in late May and again in August and October, he saw modern icons of culture in France. He met with Gertrude Stein, André Malraux, Jean-Paul Sartre, Albert Camus, Jean Cocteau, Louis and Ilse Aragon, André Gide, and Pablo Picasso. At a restaurant with the great painter there was a conversation about the "re-education of Germany" in which Picasso suggested "if everyone would paint, political re-education would not be necessary." Spender assumed Picasso meant that people needed to achieve "a sane and healthy relationship to objects around them." He admired Picasso's paintings because of their modernism: "His pictures are of the moment when the experience is in process of being transformed into the poem."[12]

Spender visited Gide in his flat on the Rue Vaneau. The writer sat in his book-lined study "wearing an Arab cloak and cap which resembles the long sleeve cap I have seen in the portraits of mediaeval money-lenders."[13] Again the conversation was about Germany and specifically about their mutual friend Professor Ernst Robert Curtius.

During a walk with Jean Cocteau through the gardens of the Palais-Royal, Cocteau pointed to the toy cannon that had always been fired at noontime and that had "been stopped ever since the real guns began to fire."[14]

At the end of the European war Spender had volunteered for and was eventually accepted into the civilian military forces that would participate in the occupation of the zone assigned to Great Britain in Germany. His specific assignment as a representative of the Foreign Office's Political Intelligence Division (PID) was to "de-Nazify and then reopen public libraries." One librarian in Germany was quick to announce that she understood what was expected of her. "I understand exactly what you want, Herr Spender," she said. "I must take all the books by Nazis off the shelves and put them in the cellars, and bring up from the cellars all the books by Jews and put them on the shelves."[15]

Another of Spender's jobs was to interview professors and other intellectuals about the war and the occupation. For this he had to be granted a special dispensation, as there was at first an official Allied policy against "fraternization" with Germans during the occupation. Armed with that dispensation, as well as a uniform giving him the status of an officer, Spender began his work in July. It was ironic that when he had first visited the Rhineland as an undergraduate seventeen years before, Germany had stood in his mind for fraternization in every sense—for naked bodies proudly revealed in public, for sensuality, and for intimate conversations about everything. Now the beautiful countryside was still there, but the people were broken, aloof and resentful, and their cities were marred by bomb craters, rubble, a plague of midges and flies, and the smell of death and decay.

The record of Spender's two official trips to Germany, the first in July and August, the second in September and October, and several visits to France during the same period was originally called "Rhineland Journal" and was written for *Horizon*. It was included in *European Witness* (1946) as "Rhineland Journey" and "Journeys Through the British Zone," in part in *The Thirties and After* as "Rhineland Journey," and in a long *Journals, 1939–1983* entry entitled "German Diary."[16]

In his *Journals*, Spender admits that his "private reason" for volunteering for the occupation forces was to be reunited with his old German mentor and friend Ernst Robert Curtius in Bonn. In fact, Spender would see a great deal of Professor Curtius and his wife. The reunion was warm, and Curtius spoke freely about his negative impressions of Germany, Germans, and the war. Spender told him he would in all likelihood publish these impressions, and Curtius agreed on the condition that he be allowed to see Spender's manuscript before publication. The fact that Spender, with somewhat characteristic carelessness, published Curtius's chastisement of his own people in his *Horizon* "Rhineland Journal" without obtaining the promised approval caused a break between the two men. Enraged by what he saw as a betrayal, Curtius sent letters of protest to T. S. Eliot and the archbishop of Canterbury, among others.[17] Eliot, in fact, took Spender to task for his treatment of Curtius, saying that the impression of him in the *Horizon* piece was unfavourable and that it should not have been published without the subject's permission.[18] Always willing to accept reasonable criticism—especially from Eliot— Spender removed the Curtius passages from *European Witness*. But the row with his old friend was not settled until 1955, when Spender visited him again in Germany.[19]

What interested Spender most about the July-August German visit was the people he met. Besides the professors he was expected to interview, there was a student who refused to believe what was said to have happened at Belsen and Buchenwald and who argued for the superiority of the Nordic races; there were Polish refugees who discounted the "myth" that the German people were at heart anti-Nazi; there was a concentration camp inmate who detailed his experiences in the camps and a sick child whom Spender saved by having penicillin delivered to him. He also met Konrad Adenauer, the future leader of the new West German Republic. Adenauer emphasized one point in his conversations with Spender—that "the Germans were really starving spiritually, and that it was, therefore, of the utmost importance to give their minds and souls some food."[20] Schools, theatres, cinemas, books, concerts, and newspapers were at least as important as rebuilding cities. And Germany must not be isolated from the rest of the world. Spender agreed and would argue in the coming months and years for exactly that point of view.

A few days after the Adenauer visit, Spender experienced something like a minor breakdown, which he referred to as a general nausea resulting from the "sense of hopelessness which is bred of the relationship of Occupiers and Occupied." He felt that the ruin of Germany and what had led to it had been predictable in a world that insisted on choosing power politics and war over other solutions that were clearly available to it. The symptoms of his depression were "violent home-sickness accompanied by a sensation of panic that I would never get out of Germany."[21] How different this feeling from those of his late 1920s and early 1930s German visits.

After an August French interlude and a brief vacation in London, Spender returned to Germany. On this tour of duty, during September and October, his assignment was to concentrate on the reestablishment of libraries, but he did continue to meet with intellectuals, such as the novelist Ernst Jünger and Jünger's friend Klaus von Bismarck. There were also concerts and dinner parties in the company of British officers and officials, many of whom he knew well. In Berlin he ran into Richard Crossman, his and Auden's close friend in Oxford days, now a Labour member of Parliament. But much of his time was spent waiting for the repair of the car he had been assigned. In his *Journals* Spender describes how on one occasion in October his car broke down on the autobahn outside of Berlin. A car stopped to help, and in it was Natasha Spender, who was herself on a concert tour of Germany.[22] Together they travelled to Berlin, where they visited Hitler's bunker and walked in the ruins of the old streets. Not much was left of the city in which the young Spender, Auden, and Isherwood had experienced so much personal liberation not so many years before.

In late October, after another brief stay in Paris, Spender returned to London and almost immediately accepted his friend Julian Huxley's invitation to serve as counsellor to the Section of Letters under Polish poet Anton Slonimsky in the newly formed UNESCO. Huxley, a renowned biologist and the brother of novelist Aldous Huxley, was the first general secretary of UNESCO. When the organization was moved from London to Paris, Spender essentially commuted between the two cities. But Huxley eventually was forced out by the militantly anti-Communist American delegation, which accused him of being left-wing, and Spender ended his UNESCO association but for the occasional meeting.

Meanwhile, at the end of 1945, Lolly Spender's condition had become much worse, and on Christmas Day she died. After the funeral Humphrey stayed with Natasha in London while Spender went to Humphrey and Lolly's home in Sutton Veny to take care of details.[23] Some months before her death Lolly had convinced Spender to destroy the charred fragments of Hitler's desk that he had taken from the bombed bunker in Berlin. They were evil, she said—not something to keep.

The depth of Spender's feelings for his sister-in-law are revealed in one of his greatest poems, the six-part "Elegy for Margaret." In keeping with the tradition of the classical elegy in this poem, Spender assimilates and accepts the death of a loved one by a spiritual process of transformation. The Margaret of the poem, like Lycidas before her, drowns—"Darling of our hearts, drowning/In the thick night of ultimate sea"—and is passionately mourned by "The deprived fanatic lover."[24]

But the loved one merges with the universe through nature, "In an infinite landscape among tribal bones."[25] And in the last section, dedicated to Humphrey Spender, the poet reminds his brother that death can mean a marriage, an eternal marriage, a sealing of love between the bereaved and the one lost, and an Adonis-like resurrection:

> As she will live who, candle-lit,
> Floats upon her final breath,
> The ceiling of the frosty night
> And her high room beneath,
> Wearing not like destruction, but
> Like a white dress, her death.[26]

Spender included the elegy as Part I in a book of poems entitled *Poems of Dedication* (1947), perhaps the most spiritual of his collections. The works in *Poems of Dedication* are examples of what he called, in a British Council–supported booklet, *Poetry Since 1939* (1946), "introspective poems in search of universal experience through subjective contemplation"[27]; they are essentially concerned with the poet's brooding on the great questions of life and death and the meaning of existence during and in the aftermath of a power politics war that has left him disillusioned with the political and "public" poetry of the thirties. The best British poetry of the war years, he tells his reader, was introspective poems written by Auden, whose "American freedom enabled him to improve his technique" to the point that he was "now the most accomplished technician writing poetry in the English language," and Eliot, whose *Four Quartets* was the greatest poetic achievement of the war years by "the greatest poetic influence in the world today."[28] Spender also praises the work of Edith Sitwell, Robert Graves, Edwin Muir, William Empson, George Barker, David Gascoyne, and especially Dylan Thomas. And he outlines the development of his poetry and that of MacNeice and Day-Lewis in the direction of introspection. *Poetry Since 1939* is essentially the same essay as the *Poetry* article entitled "Moods and Reactions" (see above).

Part II of *Poems of Dedication*, "Love, Birth, and Absence," was dedicated to Natasha Spender; Part III, "Spiritual Explorations" (a later version of the 1943 "Spiritual Exercises"), to Cecil Day-Lewis; and Part IV, "Seascape and Landscape," like Part I, to Margaret Spender, with a single poem dedicated to Edith Sitwell and another to Michael Spender. Early in the new year he sent a copy of the complete manuscript for this book to Sitwell "with love from Stephen Spender, Feb 4, 1946."

Following the elegy, the poems of Part II celebrate intimacies—especially the mysterious ones of love and childbirth—and reflect the poet's delight in and fascination with his role as a husband and father. In "The Dream" Spender writes:

> *"You dream," he said, "because of the child*
> *Asleep in the nest of your body, who dreams."*
>
> *He smiled.*
>
> *He put his head weighed with a thought*
> *Against her lips. Thus locked*
>
> *They felt the life their lives had wrought*
> *Moving within her flesh: complete*
>
> *Between their cradling bodies rocked.*
> *The future folded crowing street.*

Part III of *Poems of Dedication* is discussed earlier (Chapter Seven). Part IV contains "Seascape," a much-anthologized Spender poem that was written in memory of Michael Spender, the poet's brother, who loved sailing. The sea stands as a symbol of a cruel but beautiful life by which "heroes" are inevitably swallowed and then blended into a harmony of eternity, "While, far above, that harp assumes their sighs."

In spite of the spiritual nature of his poetry, Spender still concerned himself with the affairs of the world. He wrote to his prewar friend

Hermann Broch, German author of *The Death of Virgil* (1945), announcing, in a manner that seemed to echo Thomas Mann, that he hoped to travel in Europe during the next few years and, as a writer, to represent a European rather than merely a British consciousness.[29] In keeping with this desire, Spender had written and would continue to write several journal articles on such topics as "The Intellectuals and Europe's Future" and "Europe's Thinkers."[30] He would also write to Edith Sitwell, saying he wanted to keep his poetry separate from his life as a public figure.[31]

In March, after Natasha had more or less recovered from a somewhat serious illness in February, the Spenders travelled to Brussels and to Italy, and in April Spender went to Paris to work on UNESCO with the embattled Julian Huxley.[32] Then after a summer at Lavenham, before the house was finally sold, the Spenders attended a conference of intellectuals in Geneva called "Rencontres Internationales de Genève." Several of the most important "representatives of European consciousness" were there, including the French existentialist Maurice Merleau-Ponty, with whom Spender became friendly, the German Christian existentialist Karl Jaspers, the Hungarian Marxist critic Gyorgy Lukacs, and many others. This was only the first of many such conferences attended by Spender. Not only did they serve to satisfy his craving to be a part of the European intellectual recovery, but they satisfied his continuing fascination with the actual or spiritual nobility of his age. After the Geneva conference, he and Natasha were taken by a new friend, Dominique de Grunne, to visit the chalet in Gstaad of La Baronne Hansi Lambert, who would become a particularly close friend.[33]

Early 1947 was tainted by illness. T. S. Eliot was hospitalized in February with severe bronchitis. Spender dutifully bought him a bottle of good brandy, and Natasha delivered it to him.[34] A bright spot was an overnight visit from Christopher Isherwood for Stephen's birthday. In March Natasha was taken sick, and the Spenders went to Switzerland in search of better air and better health. Later they would stop in Italy where in Florence they would briefly meet up with Dylan Thomas.[35] In July Eliot was ill again and underwent an operation, after which the Spenders visited him in the hospital.

By 1947 Spender had become well known in American in addition
to British intellectual circles. He was writing regularly for *Partisan Review*
and occasionally for *Commentary*, and in June an American
company, Dial Press, published his anthology *A Choice of English
Romantic Poetry*, including poems by Blake, Wordsworth, Coleridge,
Byron, Shelley, Keats, and, perhaps more surprisingly, George Darley,
Thomas Lovell Beddoes, Tennyson, and Emily Brontë. Spender's
renewed interest in the romantics—it was Wordsworth, after all, who
had first stimulated his interest in poetry—follows logically from his
more spiritual, emotional, and one could even say "romantic" approach
to his own poetry in the mid-forties. A poem like "Lost Days," for example, which is Spender's answer to Wordsworth's "Prelude" as a reminiscence of childhood, could not have been written by the political or
"pylon" poet of the thirties. The poem begins with a segment called
"Chalk Blue," in which the butterfly

> *Opens now, now shuts its wings,*
> *Opening, closing like a hinge,*
> *Sprung at touch of sun or shadow.*

This is not exactly romanticism, as the poet's eye is more that of the
scientific Darwin he once wanted to emulate than that of the nature-
worshipping early Wordsworth. But it is the interest in nature for its own
sake and the intimate tone of the observation that indicates Spender's tendency as a modernist to return to something that the romantics admired
and the "pylon poets" did not. In his introduction to his anthology
Spender suggests that romanticism is "irremediably vague by reason of the
vagueness of the experience it describes." When he says that the romantic
setting is an "inhabited . . . civilized . . . communicable solitude" and that
"the romantic solitude is a vision of nature which reflects the solitude of
the poet," he could be describing the context for much of the poetry in
Poems of Dedication. It is clear from the introduction that Spender, like the
romantics, is preoccupied now by nature and by the Keatsian idea that
"poetry can create a world truer than the world of reality."[36]

The first visit to the United States was at the invitation of Harold

Taylor, president of Sarah Lawrence College in Bronxville, New York. This was to be the beginning of what was, in effect, a secondary career for Spender. Until the mid-eighties he would take frequent teaching positions—usually for a semester at a time—at American colleges and universities. One reason for his acceptance of these positions as well as extensive American lecture tours, in spite of a continuing dislike of classroom teaching and public speaking, was a need for money. The payments from the old trust fund were no longer sufficient to meet the requirements of a family such as the Spenders in the postwar economy, and Spender's writing was never of the high-advance-, high-royalty-producing sort.

The Sarah Lawrence experience was at least stimulating. Spender arrived in late summer of 1947 and spent time on Fire Island with Auden and Isherwood. Natasha and Matthew and a mother's helper followed in the late fall, and the family settled at 8 Stratford Road in Scarsdale. Spender's Sarah Lawrence colleagues included such notables as Mary McCarthy, translators and poets Robert Fitzgerald and Horace Gregory, poet Randall Jarrell, mythologist Joseph Campbell, and scholars Rudolf Arnheim, Mark Slonim, and Robert and Helen Lynd. Also nearby was Spender's friend from prewar days, the composer Samuel Barber, who had composed a setting for the poet's "A Stopwatch and an Ordnance Map" (1942). Through Barber he met composer-conductors Gian Carlo Menotti and Leonard Bernstein. He also met a young poet, William Jay Smith, for whom he felt an immediate affection. Smith was about to leave for Oxford and Spender liked him so much that he was happy to rearrange his schedule so as to spend as much time as possible with him.[37] In New York he met Lincoln Kirstein and Diana and Lionel Trilling, ran into Aldous Huxley on their way to the same dentist, and, most important for Spender, was able to visit W. H. Auden often in his Greenwich Village apartment on Cornelia Street.

Auden seemed in some ways the same—dishevelled, living sparsely—in others much changed. One morning Spender, who was staying with his old friend for a few days, tried to open the living room curtains, causing them to crash with the curtain rod onto the floor. Auden woke up, called Spender an "idiot," and proclaimed, "In any case, there is no daylight in New York."[38] Auden was now an Anglo-Catholic and committed to a life in America. Yet the old closeness remained. On one occasion Auden criticized Spender for being too emotional about things. When Spender agreed and said he would work to change, Auden, characteristically, "buried his head in his hands and exclaimed: 'But don't you realize that I don't want you to change? Why do you take me so seriously?' "[39]

In October Spender met Claude Fredericks, who had founded the Banyan Press and contracted to print a limited edition of Spender's *Returning to Vienna, 1947: Nine Sketches*, later reduced to seven sections when it was included in *The Edge of Being* (1949). Not only was the poem the result of an actual visit to Vienna earlier in the year, but it represented a return to the subject of the long poem *Vienna* written during the Muriel Gardiner days in Vienna in the 1930s. The poet now recalls the struggles of the thirties—the "burning bodies"—and the city of his first real heterosexual love affair.

Spender, in fact, had reestablished contact with Muriel, now married to Joseph Buttinger and living near Princeton, working in a state hospital for the insane.[40] Muriel and Joseph had escaped from Austria after the Anschluss and settled in France, where Joseph had been interned as an "enemy alien." Eventually Joseph had been released and the couple had married and after the war moved to the United States. Spender and Muriel would see each other regularly until Muriel's death in 1985, and he would dedicate his *Journals, 1939–1983* (1985) to her.

In spite of the pleasure he experienced with old and new friends, Spender at first was not comfortable in the United States. On December 24 he wrote to Rose Macaulay saying America was in some ways relaxing but, as he had expected, more exaggerated prose than poetry. Gradually his attitude would change.

In June he and Natasha took a trip together to the American West. After visits to Seattle, Portland, and San Francisco, where Spender delivered lectures, they visited Christopher Isherwood, now a devotee of Vedanta—along with Aldous Huxley and Gerald Heard—in Los Angeles. They then accepted an invitation to visit Taos, New Mexico, where Auden and Chester Kallman had spent their "honeymoon" in 1939. There they established contact with Frieda Lawrence and her future husband, Angelino, as well as with Lawrence's disciple Lady Dorothy Brett, and with the heiress Mabel Dodge, who was married to Tony Luhan, a Taos Indian. They also met writer William Goyen and his friend Walter Berns. Spender developed one of his many "crushes" on Goyen and enthusiastically accepted Frieda Lawrence's invitation to return to the Lawrence ranch later in the summer.

Natasha left for London in mid-July and Matthew and "Nanny" followed shortly afterward. After a short visit with Claude Fredericks and his friend in Vermont, Spender left New York for Taos in a car with Leonard Bernstein and his seventeen-year-old brother, Bertie. When Spender had told Bernstein he intended to spend his time in Taos in solitude writing an autobiography *(World Within World)*, Bernstein asked if he could go along to write his ballet based on the Auden work *The Age of Anxiety*. The journey was difficult. The Bernsteins insisted on making the trip in three days; there were frequent flat tyres, during which, according to Bertie, Spender sat by the road contemplating poetry; the weather was impossibly hot; and one night the only room they could find was in a brothel. More pleasant highlights of the trip were Lenny and Bertie's keeping themselves awake to drive by singing the complete score of Britten's opera *Peter Grimes*; Stephen and Lenny pretending to be T. S. Eliot and Serge Koussevitzky; and the trio's listening to a recording of Bernstein's recently released recording of Gershwin's *An American in Paris* in a Santa Fe music shop. As the record played, Bernstein stood near a photograph of himself, but no one recognized him, even though his brother and Stephen addressed him loudly several times as "Lenny." A week after arriving in Taos the Bernsteins left for New York, finding the solitude unbearable. Their departure was a great relief to Spender, as they rarely stopped talking and he was having difficulty working.[41]

Once he was alone, Spender found that he actually enjoyed working from early morning until late at night, cooking for himself, chopping wood for the fire, and hauling water from the pump. Although America had not yet made any "impression" on him, he appreciated the spectacular beauty of his surroundings.[42]

But for exchanging visits with Bill Goyen and Walter Berns—the "boys"—and sometimes with Frieda, Spender spent his days on the Lawrence ranch writing what would be published in part in *Partisan Review*[43] as "The Life of Literature" and later by Hamish Hamilton and by Harcourt Brace (1951) as *World Within World*, a working title of which had been *Autobiography and Truth*.

As he wrote, telling the story of, among other things, his relationship with Tony Hyndman, he found himself drifting into a condition of fascination with Goyen. Near the end of his life Spender would write an afterword to Goyen's *Selected Letters from a Writer's Life* (1995) describing the peculiar but enviable relationship between the bisexual Goyen and the "straight" Berns, who "were inseparable . . . loved one another, but . . . were not lovers." Goyen was a "romantic" with an "idiosyncratic" view of life.[44] There were similarities between Goyen's life and attitudes and those Spender was describing in *World*, and in a minor sense, at least, he fell in love. When it came time for him to take the train back East, he told Dorothy Brett that he hated to leave and would return as soon as possible. After a visit with the Buttingers in Princeton, Spender returned to the West, stopping to see Isherwood in Los Angeles and visiting the "boys," who were now at Goyen's home in Portland.[45] He wrote to Dorothy Brett in what can only be called a sentimental tone describing his weekend alone with Goyen in Port Townsend.[46] Back in New York he attended a Gotham Book Mart reception on November 8 for Edith and Osbert Sitwell. Pictured with him in the now famous postcard photograph of the event are many literary luminaries, including the Sitwells, W. H. Auden, Elizabeth Bishop, Marianne Moore, Delmore Schwartz, Randall Jarrell, Charles Henry Ford, Marya Zaturenska, Horace Gregory, Tennessee Williams, Richard Eberhart, Gore Vidal, and José García Villa. Spender, perched on a table, seems to be surveying the collection of poets with pleasure.

On his way home on the *Queen Elizabeth* he wrote to Lady Dorothy saying he would have stayed in the United States had it not been for his family,[47] and early in January he wrote again saying that he liked being in America now, that he was no longer at ease in England, and he could say he was now living partly in America—with Auden, Isherwood, and "new friends."[48] To Margaret Marshall at the *Nation* magazine, he said he felt one quarter American.[49] On January 11, as Matthew, sitting on his lap, typed repeated *A*'s on the paper, Spender wrote to Saxe Commins at Random House begging him to be supportive of William Goyen's work.

In the winter of 1949 Natasha had several concerts and Spender spent a great deal of time at home, in part tending to Matthew, who had scarlet fever. He did give lectures, the most notable of which involved a direct confrontation with poet and translator Roy Campbell. For several years Campbell and Spender had been enemies. Spender resented Campbell's negative attitude toward the Spanish Republic and those who had fought for it. In his collection of poems *Talking Bronco*, Campbell had created a character called MacSpaundy, who, in spite of Campbell's denial, probably referred to MacNeice, Auden, Day-Lewis, and Spender. He implied that MacSpaundy and other poets had profited financially from the Spanish Civil War. Spender responded in a letter of June 2, 1946, by calling his adversary "a liar, a gross slanderer, an empty-headed boaster, a coward, a bully, and a Fascist." Campbell replied sarcastically on June 11 displaying real anger, given his war record in the infantry and Secret Service, about having been called a coward and Fascist. Spender had written to Geoffrey Faber and T. S. Eliot complaining about Faber and Faber's publishing Campbell's slanderous remarks about Spain and about Jews,[50] and on June 6 Faber had written Spender a letter of apology.

On March 14, 1949, Spender gave a poetry reading at the Ethical Church in London, during which he was heckled by a person who at first disguised his voice as a woman's, said "she" had met Spender in Spain, then revealed "herself" as a quite drunk Roy Campbell. He called Spender a "fucking cunt and a fucking Lesbian," among other things, climbed up to the podium, and punched Spender in the face before being dragged off by his wife and daughter and a friend.[51] Spender continued his reading with a bloody nose.[52]

In April Spender returned to the States for a lecture tour. A visit with President Taylor of Sarah Lawrence College was unpleasant. Taylor revealed that several faculty members had resented Spender's presence at

Sarah Lawrence, accusing him of merely using his position as a stepping-off point for money-making lectures.[53] This kind of accusation would haunt Spender for the rest of his teaching career. The fact is, he was in need of money and did make use of his time in America for lecture tours as well as teaching. In 1949, after visiting the Buttingers and delivering a lecture at Hunter College, he travelled to Wells College and Syracuse University in upstate New York, where all the talk was about Communism and Spender's part in the movement in the thirties. On his way to Johnson City, Tennessee, he stopped to visit his friends Samuel Barber and Gian Carlo Menotti at Capricorn, their home in Mount Kisco, New York. There they discussed Beethoven—"Beethoven must have realized on his deathbed the significance of being Beethoven," said Menotti.[54] On a brief side trip to Princeton, he met with critic R. P. Blackmur, who impressed him with the early deconstructionist remark that any mechanism used by critics to explain poetry should contain the capability of destroying the mechanism itself.[55] In Johnson City and Lexington, Kentucky, he was exposed to his first direct doses of Southern racism. In Chicago in early May he met another sort of Southerner in Allen Tate, who with his wife, Caroline Gordon, became a Spender friend. The Tates introduced him to their "adopted son," Robert Lowell, with whom he also became close. In a light tone Tate expressed some of the American resentment against apparently mercenary visiting Englishmen that Spender had experienced in his recent conversation with Harold Taylor at Sarah Lawrence. Tate told Spender that Auden had asked him how one went about winning a Pulitzer Prize. Tate had replied that one had first of all to be an American. So Auden became an American, said Tate, and won the prize. Later in May Spender also reestablished contact in Seattle with Theodore Roethke, whom he had met earlier and with whom he developed a bantering, friendly sort of correspondence that lasted until Roethke's death. The Roethkes and Spenders would visit one another in London and Seattle. Spender would publish several of Roethke's poems in *Encounter* in the mid-fifties. Roethke especially admired Spender's autobiography, *World Within World,* if not his poetry.[56]

But in spite of the presence of friends, the American tour, which also included Kansas City, Minneapolis, a lecture on Goethe at Northwestern University in Evanston, Illinois, and a brief vist to Boston, was exhausting. From Terre Haute, Indiana, he wrote, "This is Hell."[57] On the whole, Spender was disappointed in the America he discovered on this visit. He spoke of the "high price" of American liberty—that of "having the standards and the standard of living that are American." America clearly did not "speak for the world at present" and was in its own way isolated and marred by racism and McCarthyism.[58]

He ended his tour with Goyen and Berns. They met in Portland, visited Christopher Isherwood in Los Angeles, and then returned to Taos for several weeks before Spender attended a writers' conference at the University of Indiana, visited the Buttingers, now in New York, and returned to London.[59] Early the next year, Goyen, Berns, and a female friend of Goyen's would visit London, and Spender would become quickly fed up with Goyen's egocentric demands. In a letter to Dorothy Brett he vowed never to get "involved" again.[60] Christopher Isherwood noted Natasha Spender's "understandable resentment" toward Goyen, whom she called a "man-eating orchid."[61] Spender saw Goyen in New York in August 1950, but there was no longer the intimacy or deep feeling that had marked the earlier stages of the relationship.

After Spender's 1949 American tour he and Natasha travelled together to Portofino in July and then to Florence, where they spent time with William and Barbara Smith and their baby, and to Venice for a September PEN conference, at which Auden, Day-Lewis, and he were delegates. Also, the *New York Times* had asked Spender to do an article on European intellectuals for its magazine section.[62] This gave Spender an opportunity to visit old friends and make new ones in France and Italy on this trip and another one in the spring of 1950. He interviewed André Malraux at his home in the Avenue Victor Hugo in Boulogne-sur-Seine, where he admired the Picassos and Dubuffets on the vast white walls. At I Tatti in Florence he dined with Bernard Berenson, whom he had met before the war with Roger Sessions, and who "in extreme old age" had "something of the spirituality of certain El Greco portraits."[63] He met Eudora Welty at a later dinner with Berenson and a few days later the poet Eugenio Montale, and he attended a Nancy

Mitford party in Paris.[64] During an evening with Arthur Koestler, Koestler, whom Spender had met in London during the war, described his break with Jean-Paul Sartre and Simone de Beauvoir. Spender loved spending time with old literary friends such as these, and he loved listening to their gossip. He especially appreciated being in Italy and wrote to William Smith to say he and his family hoped to live there.[65]

In November 1949, although the State Department at first had refused him a visa because of his former Communist affiliation, Spender was back in New York for a series of lectures. In early 1950, after a brief trip to Dublin, where he delivered a lecture and met W. B. Yeats's wife, George, and brother Jack, he visited William and Barbara Smith in Florence and worked more on the *New York Times* project.[66]

On May 30, the day he finished *World Within World*, Elizabeth ("Lizzie") was born, and Spender vowed to give her a decent upbringing since so many girls in his family had been unhappy.[67] In August of 1950 Spender went still again to the United States for lectures to bolster his income. With two children, the family was feeling still more financial strain. But Natasha's concert career was progressing well and *World Within World* was scheduled to be published in April 1951, when it was to be honoured as Book of the Month by the Book Society in England.

With so much travelling and so many personal and public issues on his mind, Spender managed to be extraordinarily productive as a writer between his first trip to America and the publication of *World Within World*.

For *Saturday Review*, *Partisan Review*, the *New York Times Book Review* and *Magazine*, the *Nation*, the *New Statesman and Nation*, *Horizon*, and several other major journals, he wrote about the problems facing modern poets, about the European situation, about Bernard Shaw, Edith Sitwell, and T. S. Eliot, about London as opposed to New York, about UNESCO, and about the literary situation in America. And in 1949 he joined Arthur Koestler, Ignazio Silone, Richard Wright, André Gide, and Louis Fisher in "a confession" of past affiliations with the Communist Party and reasons for having rejected it. The collection, entitled *The God That Failed*, was edited by Richard Crossman, and in

the Communist scare days of the late forties and early fifties, when people who admitted having once been Communists were losing their repu-
tations and jobs, it caused almost as much of a stir in England and
America as did that other "confession," *World Within World*. Spender's
final comment on Communism in his contribution to the book seems
tame enough now, but in 1949 it was somewhat provocative. Communism as then organized concentrated too much power "in the hands of
too few," he said, leaving the masses open to the depravities of totalitarian leaders and depriving artists of the freedom to witness "the
human condition" as they saw it. But, he added, "neither side, in the
present alignment of the world represents what I believe to be the only
solution of the world's problems." It was urgent that the democracies
concern themselves more with "the millions of people who care more for
bread than for freedom."[68] During a visit to George Orwell at University
College Hospital in January 1950, Orwell told Spender that it was useless
to argue with the Communists—"There are certain people like vegetari-
ans and Communists whom one cannot answer."[69]

In spite of the increasingly private and inner-directed nature of his
poetry, then, Spender never stopped having his say on the public world
stage. In 1949 he became forty and was a much-sought-after lecturer,
journalist, and teacher. In that year he also published a new, very introspective book of poetry, *The Edge of Being*.

Sanford Sternlicht suggests that the poems of this small volume
"move Spender closer to positions of both faith and existentialism."[70]
Poems with titles such as "O Omega, Invocation," "The Angel,"
"Madonna," and "Judas Iscariot" certainly do suggest the use of traditional religious symbols and stories. The omega is the end of the beginning, which is the alpha, the existential nonbeing—"black/Hoop circling
on white." The Madonna in the poem of that title will produce a son who
will demand of humanity the existential choice. All of the "religious"
poems point to the continuing failure of human society, to the place of
humans on "the edge of " rather than in the unity of "being."[71]

A shortened version of "Returning to Vienna, 1947" is included in
The Edge of Being, as are several dramatic monologues, a few love poems,
and poems growing out of the war experience, the most important of

which is perhaps "Rejoice in the Abyss." Here Spender seems to corrobo-
rate Auden's suggestion as to his real feelings about death in war—relief
that he is not among the unlucky. Walking through the London streets
after a bombing attack, he sees in the houses a prayer that is his prayer,
too: " 'Oh God,/Spare me the lot that is my neighbour's.' " And from the
rooftops cockney prophets call, "In the midst of life is Death." The poet,
like them, reaches an existential conclusion about accepting "the empti-
ness/Within the bells of foxgloves and cathedrals," having learned that
"each life must feed upon the deaths of others." The dominant image in
The Edge of Being is dust, the central symbol in what is perhaps the most
existential of Christian sayings: "Remember O Man that thou art dust
and unto dust thou shalt return."

But it was the autobiography *World Within World* (1951) that was the
culmination of the first half of Spender's career and the most thorough
attempt to explore the inner world. By nearly all accounts, it is one of the
most honest and moving autobiographies of our time. It treats Spender's
childhood, his development as a modernist, and his friendships with
such icons as Auden, Isherwood, Eliot, Ottoline Morrell, and Virginia
Woolf. And it reveals his bisexuality and his relationship with the Communist Party—two subjects guaranteed to cause controversy in the early
1950s, especially in McCarthy-dominated America. "I believe obstinately
that if I am able to write with truth about what has happened to me, this
can help others who have lived through the same sort of thing," he
wrote. "In this belief I have risked being indiscreet."[72] He also risked
being "modern" in terms of the chronology of the work. He wrote to
Saxe Commins that the chronology changed the conventional time
sequence of autobiographies.[73] The arrangement of events was determined by theme and the course of Spender's inner exploration rather
than by external chronology. The work remains, with Spender's journals
and correspondence, the primary source for any Spender biographer. He
dedicated his work to his old friend Isaiah Berlin.

In *Twentieth Century*, Christopher Isherwood wrote a perceptive
review entitled "Autobiography of an Individualist."[74] *World Within
World* was a "very important book; an outstandingly clear and coura-
geous statement of certain personal and social problems which concern

us all." Good autobiography, he argued, depended on its author's having "qualities which would make him a suitable hero for a novel." Spender had such qualities. He was a "liberal individualist hesitating before the false options of a totalitarian world," a "victim of a 'puritan decadence' torn between indoctrinated sex guilt and the lure of neo-Freudian licence." Furthermore, he was and always had been a "comic character," whom one mutual friend lovingly called "the right kind of idiot"—in a sense still the awkward, bumbling, but strangely open, intelligent, and talented young man Isherwood and Auden had met at Oxford. *World* was finally a "joyful book full of profound delight in human experience. A book which gives you fresh courage to live your own life and new eyes with which to examine its meaning." Isherwood had already written to Spender praising *World* for its wisdom and humour.[75]

The Freudian Ernest Jones wrote in the *Nation* that the book "never spares its central subject. Out of chaos, private and public, Spender has arrived finally at some private order, at a few affirmations, a tentative knowledge, offered up in humility, which must be taken seriously. . . ."[76]

In the *New Statesman and Nation*, V. S. Pritchett praised *World Within World*, especially for its "remarkable sureness in evoking the phases and idioms of difficult love."[77]

Other reactions included favourable reviews by Leonard Woolf,[78] Harold Nicolson,[79] Cyril Connolly,[80] and Mark Shorer.[81] Frieda Lawrence wrote to say she loved the book and that Lady Dorothy did, too.[82]

There were, of course, those who wondered why a man of Spender's young age needed to write an autobiography.[83] This was to miss the point. Spender did not write *World* to expose the details of his life or to tell his whole life's story. His intention was to make honest use of aspects of his experience to confront political and sexual issues that faced a whole culture.

A more telling reservation was W. H. Auden's. Auden wrote to say that he had read *World* several times with admiration. But he could not resist returning to a familiar theme. While stressing his weaknesses, Spender had ignored his "sins of strengths"—i.e., of "calculation and coldness of heart." In Auden's view such qualities, however veiled, were necessarily present in a man as professionally and socially "successful" as Stephen Spender.[84]

9

SPENDER I AND SPENDER II

In his review of *World Within World*, Cyril Connolly painted a portrait of two Stephen Spenders.[1] Spender I was the

> youthful poet . . . an inspired simpleton, a great big silly goose, a holy Russian idiot, large, generous, gullible, affectionate, idealistic—living for friendship and beauty, writing miraculous poems, expecting too much from everybody and from himself, on whom he laid charges and responsibilities which he could never carry out.

Spender II was a version of the man Auden always accused his friend of concealing beneath the mask of Spender I. He was

> shrewd, ambitious, aggressive and ruthless, a publicity-seeking intellectual full of administrative energy and rentier asperity, a young tiger sharpening his claws on the platforms of peace.

Connolly's two-sided Spender was "both lovable and formidable" and, like Gide and Goethe, an artist who combined "sensuality with Puritanism."

Although the man most of his acquaintances experienced was Spender I, Spender II had always made himself known, and he continued to do so during the years between the publication of *World Within World* and his appointment as poetry consultant at the Library of Congress in Washington, D.C.

This period was not marked by a large body of new poetry, but there were some significant poems and no lack of other activity. During most of the years in question, Spender was preoccupied with journalism, primarily as an editor of *Encounter* but also as a writer of social commentary and some literary criticism for *Partisan Review, Twentieth Century, Saturday Review*, the *New York Times*, the *Listener*, the *Spectator*, the *New Statesman and Nation*, the *New Republic*, the *Kenyon Review*, the *Nation*, the *Atlantic Monthly*, and other journals. In addition, he found time to write a libretto with Nicholas Nabokov called *Rasputin's End*, a three-act opera, and with Donald Hall he edited an encyclopedia of English and American poetry. He also edited a collection of German stories, wrote a short novel, a children's story, and a short book on Shelley, did some travel writing and art criticism, lectured extensively in England, continental Europe, the Middle East, Asia, and especially the United States, where he also held several teaching positions, and participated in UNESCO and PEN activities. His two most important works of the post–*World Within World* fifties were a book of literary criticism entitled *The Creative Element* and the *Collected Poems, 1928–1953*. In the early sixties his lectures and published articles were concerned for the most part with the poetic imagination in the context of modernism. A *Partisan Review* article was entitled "Modern as Vision of a Whole Situation"[2] and three lectures at the Library of Congress were collected under the title "The Imagination in the Modern World"[3] and were an important element in *The Struggle of the Modern* (1963).

In his forties and fifties Spender was also very much the loving husband and father and sometimes the lover of young men met on various lonely income-enhancing excursions abroad. Finally, as he grew older, he seemed to be increasingly concerned about his reputation among his peers and driven by what at times seemed a sycophantic need to be among the "stars" of politics and the arts. Stephen Spender in his middle age was at once ambivalent, ambiguous, and determined to succeed in both his personal and public life. And he was often plagued by a sense of disillusionment and a fear that he was sacrificing his vocation as a poet to his avocation as a journalist, lecturer, and teacher.

In the spring of 1951 after the publication of *World Within World*, Spender went on a speaking tour to Greece, Egypt, and India sponsored by the Congress for Cultural Freedom, a liberal anti-Communist organization that had been developed during the time of the Berlin airlift, was directed by Nicholas Nabokov, and included among its honorary founders Benedetto Croce, Reinhold Niebuhr, Karl Jaspers, Jacques Maritain, and Bertrand Russell. More important than the business aspect of the tour was the chance it gave to the Spenders to be alone together, and to visit Greece—particularly Athens and Delphi—before Spender went on to Egypt and India. For Spender this was a happier version of the visit to Greece he had made with Tony Hyndman before the war. It was, however, a preface to more difficult times.

Almost immediately upon returning to London, Spender found himself embroiled in another argument with John Lehmann, arising out of what turned out to be one of the major events of the Cold War. As he always did when he came to England, Wystan Auden spent a few days that spring with the Spenders on Loudoun Road. On the evening of May 24, Natasha Spender answered an urgent phone call for their guest from Guy Burgess. Auden and Spender had known Burgess and his friend Donald Maclean as part of the Cambridge and London homosexual and left-wing set since undergraduate days. In fact, Burgess had been brought—uninvited—to the Spenders' wedding by Oxford philosopher A. J. ("Freddy") Ayer. In recent years Spender had "avoided seeing" Burgess, who tended to drink too much and to be socially difficult.[4] As Auden was out on the twenty-fourth, Natasha Spender offered to take a message, and Burgess asked that Auden return his call. When he called later, Auden was still out, and again Burgess declined to leave a specific message. He did speak to Spender, however, to congratulate him on *World Within World*, especially for its treatment of the poet's rejection of Communism. This was odd considering the fact that on the twenty-fifth Burgess and Maclean, warned by arch-spy Kim Philby that they had been discovered as spies themselves, fled England. The Spenders had told Auden about the phone calls, but he had declined to do anything about them. "Do I *have* to ring him back?" he asked. "He's always drunk." Apparently Burgess had wanted to stay in Auden's house in Ischia after dropping off Maclean in Prague.[5]

Two weeks later the Foreign Office announced the defection of the two spies, and Auden wrote to Spender saying that because of "some lady who thought she saw la B [Burgess]" on the train heading for Ischia, he was now plagued by reporters.[6] A visiting friend had even been arrested briefly on the mistaken assumption that he was Burgess.[7] The *Daily Express* published an interview with Auden on the subject on January 13. Auden mentioned the phone calls made to the home of Spender—referred to by the reporter as "the poet and former Communist"—and wrongly said he had never been given the messages.[8] Auden did not believe Burgess was a spy, assuming he was a "victim" who had been kidnapped by the Soviets because of his knowledge of atomic secrets. Spender, too, doubted that Burgess was a Communist and suggested to a *Daily Telegraph* reporter that Burgess would not have praised him for his anti-Communism in *World* if he were himself a party member or sympathizer.[9]

On June 15 the Spenders, using proceeds from *World*, began a holiday at a small hotel in the little fishing port of Torre del Benaco near Verona. There, after being bothered by reporters for days and continuing to assume that Burgess was innocent, Spender received a letter from John Lehmann saying that if he "knew what he [Lehmann] knew on the authority of a lady we both knew," Spender would never have made that assumption.[10] Naively hoping to rectify an apparent mistake, Spender showed the Lehmann letter to Owen Seaman, the *Daily Express* reporter who had interviewed Auden. The next day a photocopy of the letter appeared in the London paper, and Lehmann was furious that Spender had shared confidential information that could implicate him and the mutual "lady" friend informant—in fact, Rosamond Lehmann—in the Burgess-Maclean scandal. At one point Lehmann, who always felt Spender's action was based more on maliciousness than naïveté, even threatened a lawsuit.[11] Spender claimed to Lehmann that he had exacted a promise from Seaman not to quote from the letter, but the fact is, he had let him borrow it for a time (he did receive an apology later from the *Daily Express*). Publicly Spender agreed that Lehmann's anger was "reasonable" and his own action "stupid."[12] In any case, the incident added to what was always a cloud over the Spender-Lehmann relationship, and more than ten years later the two men were still exchanging somewhat bitter remarks over it.[13] Lehmann spoke of the incident and his profound anger in the final book of his autobiography, *The Ample Proposition* (1966).[14]

In Torre del Benaco, on the banks of the Lago di Garda, the Spenders rented a wing of the Albergo Gardesana that had once been rented by André Gide. Spender confided to Julian Huxley that he could write an "interesting illustrated monograph" on the memories of "local fisher boys" on the subject of Gide. As for himself, the village children ran after him calling "poeta, poeta." He suggested that the tradition might have been started by Catullus, on translations of whom he was working.[15]

Beneath the lightheartedness of the Catullus remark Spender was not altogether happy. He was beginning to face the fact that whereas he had once been among the young generation of poets in relation to the canonized modernists, he was now considered by the "angry young men" generation as a "thirties poet" past his prime. When a friend, Lynette Roberts, wrote to complain of a malicious review, Spender responded almost enthusiastically. Admitting that he had sometimes been an "unfair reviewer," he revealed an uncharacteristic bitterness as he sympathized with Roberts. He referred to her reviewer, Peter Russell, as a bearded hippy of the new generation, who had recently published a worthless book of his own.[16]

In London in the fall, Spender participated in the usual social rounds. On November 30 he attended a Covent Garden dress rehearsal of Britten's opera *Billy Budd*, the libretto of which was by Morgan Forster. Britten conducted, and his friend Peter Pears was the narrator. In the stalls were many literary "stars," most of them old friends. William Plomer, Somerset Maugham, Joe Ackerley, Rose Macaulay, and John Piper were among them. In the interval Plomer pointed to "Willie" Maugham, "the world's number one exhibitionist." During the second act, Spender sat with Forster, who was "wrapped in a greatcoat . . . with a satchel at his feet, like a warming pad." Forster admitted that he was "deeply moved by my own words." Spender had just seen the Stravinsky-Auden *Rake's Progress*, which he felt had "more originality, more purity, more courage perhaps," but he admired the "gloomy but exhilarating *Billy Budd*, which has the quality of a great white snowy night shining through a mist."[17] Later, in answer to some Spender reservations about the Melville story itself, Forster wrote explaining the beautiful triumph of Billy over evil.[18]

On the fifth of December the Spenders had William Plomer, Rose Macaulay, historian Veronica Wedgwood, and T. S. Eliot for dinner. The conversation was lively and amusing. When it turned to early memories, Eliot said he could remember being bottle-fed. "In that case you must have been weaned very late," said Macaulay. Eliot's reply was characteristic: "Now, now, Rose, you're making me look ridiculous, in public." He also noted, with some glee, that the Russian press had called him "a reactionary, anti-Semitic, pornographic hyena." He left early "on doctor's orders" but in a "very good mood."[19]

The next day Spender left for Paris on UNESCO business. There he attended a dinner party at which Sonia Orwell became drunk and verbally abusive. Recently Spender had visited her husband in the hospital, and they had discussed D. H. Lawrence's death. Lawrence died, said Orwell, when his "philosophy of life had become absolutely untenable."[20]

At Christmastime Christopher Isherwood came to London, and he and Stephen went bookshopping. But Christmas had become a chore: "This part of winter becomes every year more like a dark tunnel one enters about 15 December."[21]

Increasingly Spender was feeling bored by his social and literary life in England. Only the children were a great joy. Matthew was now six and very clever. One day Spender went with him to a gym class at the Hall School, where he himself had once been enrolled. On the way home on the bus, one of Matthew's schoolmates asked if "that old white-haired man with spectacles" was his "daddy." Matthew said, "No," and when Spender asked him later why he had done so, the child answered,

"Because ... you aren't like what he said you were."[22] Matthew's god-father was William Plomer, to whom Spender frequently wrote to report on things the child had said or done. One night when Matthew was ill and Spender was sitting at his bedside, Matthew looked out of the window and announced that no star was more beautiful than his sister Elizabeth.[23] Much later Spender would tell Plomer that Matthew had many talents and was a something of a neo-Elizabethan.[24]

Early in 1952 Spender travelled on a ship that was carrying Jewish orphans from Marseilles to Haifa. While in Israel between March 12 and April 4 he kept a diary of visits to kibbutzim and various children's centres as well as to holy places. He also sketched out a book that would be published later in the year by Weidenfeld and Nicolson in London. *Learning Laughter* is a comment by a man of some Jewish background on the beauty of community sense in Israel—a sense that evolved from Socialist revolutionary ideals that he had admired so much in the 1930s. It is also a prophetic book about the potential for trouble arising from the chasm between Western and "Oriental" Jews in Israel.

In April and May and early June the Spenders attended events at the Festival of Modern Arts sponsored by the Congress for Cultural Freedom in Paris. Among other delegates were William Faulkner, Katherine Anne Porter, Glenway Wescott, Louis MacNeice, and Wystan Auden. Allen Tate was there, too, and a friendship developed between him and Natasha Spender. After the conference Spender left for a lecture tour in Japan.[25] Tate visited Natasha in England, and then told friends, including Katherine Anne Porter and W. H. Auden, that he was in love with her.[26] Auden archly warned friends to protect their wives from Tate.[27] Natasha was clearly not interested in a life with a man who was on one hand an alcoholic and on the other a Catholic plagued by guilt because of his desire for women other than his wife.

Meanwhile when he returned from Japan, Spender was depending on Tate to make arrangements for another lecture tour of America. In the long correspondence between the American poet and Spender between 1951 and 1965 there is, among many other things, a good deal of discussion about contemporary poetry. Spender complained of the academic formality in the kind of poetry often published in the Chicago-based *Poetry*. He admired poets who had never succumbed to that tendency—poets like Richard Wilbur and Vernon Watkins— and those who had managed to work their way through it—poets like Lowell, Tate, Auden, and Eliot and Pound and their followers. Spender felt that there had been an unfortunate shift in poetry from a modernist individualism to a Catholic collectivism.[28]

The correspondence with Tate was always warm. Spender invited Tate and the Robert Lowells to visit Natasha and him in Torre del Benaco during September, painting a comic word-picture of the suggested visit. He suggested that Allen and Natasha might like to travel a bit in Italy together while he stayed with the children.[29] It is evident from this suggestion that Spender had no doubts about his own relationship with Natasha.[30] Once when Natasha was ill, Spender would say to his old friend Stuart Hampshire "on record" that "his life would be quite unimaginable, unreal, not to be contemplated, without Natasha at its centre."[31]

Beginning in 1952 the Spenders had two young Italian women— Idelma and Francesca—to help with the children. At various times in the summer one or more Spenders, with either or both of the women, were at Torre or at Gstaad with their great friend Hansi Lambert. The Lowells and Allen Tate did come to Italy and the group spent time in Venice in October. Spender enclosed a copy of a new poem about Natasha—originally entitled "One Flesh," later simply "One"—in a letter to Tate after the Italian visit:[32]

> *Here then*
> *She lies*
> *Her hair a scroll along*
> *Her neck the grooved warm nape*
> *Her lips half-meeting on a smile*
> *Breath almost unbreathing*
> *A word this word my love upon the white*
> *Linen*
> *As though I wrote her name out on this page.*

> *Here we*
> *Are one*
> *Here where my dreaming wakes upon her sleep*
> *One within one*
> *And a third hidden meeting in the child.*

The child was Lizzie, a poem about whom—"To My Daughter"—Spender also attached to the letter to Tate:

> *Bright clasp of her whole hand around my finger*
> *My daughter, as we walk together now.*
> *All my life I'll feel a ring invisibly*
> *Circle this bone with shining: when she is grown*
> *Far from today as her eyes are far already.*

On a tour to Brazil in November, during which he lectured on Eliot and Rilke, Spender read Tate's translation of *La vita nuova*. Later he depended on his friend to help convince university and government authorities in the United States that he was, in fact, not a Communist. The government was refusing to give him a visa for a planned stay at the University of Cincinnati in 1953. He also shared particularly intimate thoughts on religion with Tate. He possessed, he said, a respectful disbelief, refusing to believe that Christianity was the only path. He had once heard T. S. Eliot tell an Indian woman that although he had passed through a Buddhist period, he now knew that Buddhism was incompatible with the European mind. Spender had been deeply disturbed by the lack of Christian sensibility in this point of view. But he felt that in spite of a personally practised orthodoxy, Eliot had moved beyond it to the truly visionary in his *Four Quartets*.[33]

Spender strongly conveyed his opinion of the importance of individualism as opposed to collective orthodoxy in a short book on Shelley that he wrote for the British Council in 1952. The book emphasizes Shelley as a visionary and a freethinker, and it is clear that the writer is inspired by him.

The winter of 1952–53 in London was particularly gloomy, not only because of bad weather but because it seemed unlikely Spender would be able to obtain his American visa.[34] During a walk with Herbert Read in January, he noted Read's "overwhelming sense of decay" in England and he, too, felt this "rotting away."[35] Even a roomful of old friends and important people at a luncheon for John Lehmann at the Trocadero did not cheer him up. As the guest list included Rosamond Lehmann, Rose Macaulay, T. S. Eliot, E. M. Forster, William Plomer, Joe Ackerley, Laurie Lee, Cyril Connolly, Alan Ross, Arthur Koestler, Louis MacNeice, and William Sansom, it seems likely that the conversation was at least engaging. But the food and wine were bad; the speeches were tedious and inappropriate—especially Lehmann's. In any case, Spender and Lehmann were still ill at ease together because of the Burgess affair.

Finally, with the help of Tate, Senator Eugene McCarthy, and the conservative but reasonable Senator Robert Taft, Spender received his American visa, and in early February he took up his position in the Elliston Chair of Poetry at the University of Cincinnati. This was a prestigious appointment, in which Spender followed John Berryman and was succeeded by Robert Lowell, John Betjeman, and Robert Frost. Spender's primary responsibility, other than to teach creative writing, was to deliver a series of nine lectures between February 10 and April 9 on the general topic "Poetic Vision and Modern Literature." His stated thesis was that the great "writers of the twentieth century have been preoccupied with the endeavor to organize experience, or to interpret contemporary life, in visionary patterns." Obviously Spender referred to the writers he considered the true modernists rather than those who were undermining the movement by turning away from an "individualist consciousness" in favour of a "collectivist" one.[36] These lectures, centring for illustration on the works of Rimbaud, Rilke, Forster, Lawrence, Yeats, Eliot, Orwell, and Auden, fully articulated Spender's critical thought as it had developed since the Spanish Civil War and as it had been tentatively outlined in his correspondence and conversations with Allen Tate. He collected and polished his lectures in his book *The Creative Element*, a work he dedicated to Tate.

The Creative Element is, in effect, a sequel to *The Destructive Element* (1935) and marks a change in the writer's view from that of a Marxist collectivist stressing the social obligations of literature, to a writer "who realizes in his work the decline of modern values while isolating his own individual values from the context of society." At the basis of this modernism is the fact that the writer "never forgets the modern context, in fact he is always stating it, but he does so only to create the more forcibly the visions of his own isolation." The "destructive element" had not been made up of forces such as capitalism and Fascism after all, but was "simply society itself" or any threat to the "unique vision" of "individual isolation."[37] Of utmost importance was a humanistic tolerance of various views and the support of the visionaries who would consider answers to the world's problems by inner rather than political or ideological searchings. In *The Creative Element* Spender clearly expresses his allegiance not to any ideology but to the creative element itself as expressed by the true inner visionaries—Shelley, James, Blake, Rilke, Yeats. In so doing, in spite of disagreements over religion and other issues, he throws his support to Tate and Lowell, and to his old mentor, T. S. Eliot, and his friend W. H. Auden, as the contemporary modernists of his sort.

On February 15 Spender noted in his journal that he had not heard from home in some time. He was homesick—"Being away so long is to miss one-sixth of Lizzie's life and one-fourteenth of Matthew's"—and he was always worried about Natasha's health. Furthermore, he was feeling at odds with America, where mindless anti-Communism was threatening creativity itself and where "everything is questioned and explained, with the result that there is a kind of low-level rationalization or intellectualization of every kind of behaviour. No one is happy until the whole of life has been translated into pseudo-scientific jargon."[38]

One evening Spender was taken to a dinner party which went on until 3 A.M. At one point late in the evening the psychiatrist hostess made all the guests lie down on the floor and pretend they were babies. This would make them feel secure and happy, she said. She put soft music on the phonograph while someone "crooned . . . Mother loves Baby, etc." By the end of the session "white-haired millionaires" murmured "ghoulishly." The seance did nothing to alleviate Spender's malaise. In fact, it made him feel that "World War III" or some other major catastrophe was about to occur.[39]

Early during his stay in Cincinnati Spender was visited by the writer and social scientist Irving Kristol to discuss *Encounter*, which would be a liberal/anti-Communist political and literary journal sponsored by the Congress for Cultural Freedom and funded by Julius Fleischmann's Farfield Foundation. Fleischmann, an Ohio millionaire, and Spender had become friends, and it was arranged that Spender and Kristol would coedit the journal.[40] Spender had hoped for Allen Tate's participation.[41] Later, when Kristol left to work for the *Reporter*, Dwight MacDonald took his place for a while and then was himself replaced by Melvin Lasky. *Encounter* was one of several journals supported by the Congress. Others were *Preuves* in Paris, *Der Monat* in Germany, and *Tempe Presente* in Italy. Spender accepted the editorship because he felt it would mean he would be able to spend more time in London with his family.[42] *Encounter* would occupy much of his life for more than ten years until its surprising demise.

In May, after a visit from Natasha, Spender was visiting the Tates and then the Buttingers in New York when he received several letters concerning his former lover Tony Hyndman, who was creating difficulties in London. Spender wrote to John Lehmann and Morgan Forster, both of whom knew Tony well, indicating that Natasha was upset because Tony had said he planned to write a book denigrating Stephen. Forster wrote to Natasha saying he would try to do something; he had already given Tony money.[43] Spender claimed not to be upset and wrote to Lehmann saying he would be glad to help Tony in his writing in any way he could. It might be good if Tony could think he was a writer. With a little help he could be patched together "like Humpty Dumpty."[44] Forster wrote later in May to say he was sorry Tony was an "anxiety to you both" but that he could do nothing more about the situation. When Tony invaded Peter Watson's flat, Spender did become more concerned. He worried about his own house and the children there and the two young women taking care of them, one of whom was already terrified of Hyndman.[45] After some stern letters from various friends and some problems with the police and the courts, Tony was hospitalized and treated with electric shock therapy. E. M. Forster was both surprised and pleased by the "generosity and responsibility" demonstrated by Natasha Spender in connection with the Hyndman episode.[46]

The early summer of 1953 for Spender was one of finance-building in America. A reading at the Corcoran Gallery in Washington, D.C., was followed by a writers' conference in Salt Lake City and several lectures and readings elsewhere. A bad moment came when his name did not appear on the *Kenyon Review*'s list of the thirty or forty significant modern poets. Spender was sufficiently bothered by this sign of neglect that he wrote a letter of mild protest to John Crowe Ransom, saying the apparent snub made him "sad."[47]

In late July Allen Tate came to London and took Natasha to lunch.[48] It seems apparent that Natasha made it clear to him that their relationship was, in spite of his assumptions, only a friendship.[49] Several years later Tate, who, according to Robert Lowell, still spoke often of loving Natasha, would divorce Caroline and marry three-times-divorced poet Isabella Gardner.[50]

In the fall Spender threw himself into work at *Encounter*. Although at first the Congress for Cultural Freedom attempted to make the magazine a mouthpiece for its own activities, Kristol and Spender insisted that it become an independent publication "partly of literature and the arts, partly of politics." *Encounter* was a joint British-American project, with the primary responsibility for politics being that of the American editor. Spender was essentially in charge of the literature and arts aspect. The strong American presence in a London magazine in the anti-American fifties opened Spender and *Encounter* to the charge that they were merely vehicles for American ideas. In the *Sunday Times* the journal was referred to in February 1954 as a "police-review of American-occupied countries."[51] Nevertheless, *Encounter* proved to be a success and developed a reputation for being lively and honest. The most famous article published in the early years was Nancy Mitford's September 1955 piece, "The English Aristocracy"—*Encounter* was particularly concerned with class distinctions and problems in England—in which Mitford quoted from Alan Ross's pamphlet on "U and Non-U" English usage.[52]

Spender was a highly successful and extremely efficient literary editor.

With his many connections, he was able to produce important contributions for nearly every issue. There were articles, poems, and fiction by most of the major American and British and European literary figures of the day. Few people could match Spender's stable of celebrated friends. On any given day he could communicate by letter, telegraph, or telephone or over a meal with T. S. Eliot, e. e. cummings, Augustus John, Dom Moraes, Lucian Freud, Theodore Roethke, Marianne Moore, Wystan Auden, Hannah Arendt, Samuel Barber, E. M. Forster, Denis de Rougemont, Ignazio Silone, Edmund Wilson, Igor Stravinsky, Ezra Pound, Jean-Paul Sartre, Simone de Beauvoir, Edith Sitwell, or Francis Bacon, to mention only a few. And he made good use of these friendships for *Encounter*, often almost badgering his acquaintances to write for his magazine.

Spender devoted much of 1953 to travel and lecturing abroad. April found him lecturing and reading at Harvard, Princeton, and Yale while, fortunately, Wystan Auden stayed with Natasha and the children in London.[53] And late that fall after his *Encounter* appointment, he did a two-month tour for the Congress for Cultural Freedom that took him to Paris, Rome, Athens, Beirut, Karachi, Singapore, Darwin, Kandy, Madras, Cochin, Trivandrum, Bangalore, and Bombay.

Spender's journal remarks on India are sometimes amusing, sometimes surprisingly unfeeling and patronizing. During one meal in Madras, he felt "conventional feelings of disgust about Indians and India." In the house of the minister of education in which there was a stone floor, a large clock on one wall, and photos of Gandhi and Nehru on the other, he decided, "The only thing I liked was the stone floor." When he and his party of two boarded a train in Madras to go to Chidambaram, two Tamil poets suddenly decided to join them, so that five were in a sleeping compartment meant for three. As soon as they were settled, one of the Tamil poets "with a relaxed feminine face, and with jewelled ear-rings studded in each ear ... produced from his pocket a version in Tamil" of Spender's poem "Ultima Ratio Regum," "which he proceeded to chant in the voice of a watchman from a muezzin tower."[54]

An appointment Spender found more memorable than most during the trip was with the boy poet Dom Moraes—aged sixteen, "dark, thin, silent, absorbed, with long lean hands clutched together over his bony knees, cutting into the arms like knives, a sudden frank, luminous, most excellent smile."[55] Moraes would become a friend, whom Spender would see later in England.

In India he bought a Christmas present of an inlaid silver cigarette case to replace a modern plastic one he had given T. S. Eliot some years earlier. Eliot wrote to Spender thanking him, saying he had placed the case on his mantelpiece but that he had decided he would be happier if he admitted that he could not use the case; the doctor had, in fact, forbidden him to smoke. Still, the present served as a reminder of a long friendship that had been of great importance to him.[56]

The Spenders spent much of the early part of 1955 in California and New York. Natasha particularly enjoyed the California climate, as she had had serious bouts with pneumonia and bronchitis the year before. But back in London Spender came home one day to find the writer Raymond Chandler, whom they had met in California, "carrying on a rather drunken conversation with Natasha," saying that she was a genius and that Stephen had not encouraged her enough in her career.[57] Spender tended to agree with this assessment, and was beginning to see that the combination of lecture tours and editing had infringed upon his own artistic life as well. In his journal he wrote,

> At present, my life seems to me very wasted. This simply means that I am not writing, and that I am even beginning to think of my writing as a kind of withered faculty, a muscle that has become atrophied. This is made worse by the fact that I am perfectly aware that the muscle was never in the first place fully developed. But things I do other than writing seem to take up a larger and larger place in my life.[58]

It was travelling and an extremely active social life both at home and abroad that took most of the time. In late April the Spenders entertained Clarissa Eden, Charlie Chaplin and his wife, Harold Nicolson, James Pope-Hennessy, and Jane Howard at a new dinner table they bought for the occasion. Chaplin was "always amusing." It was clear that his sympathies were with small men like himself who had become "enormously powerful big men" who still cared for the "little men and the poor." A few days later the Spenders were in Henry Moore's studio in the country, and a week later Spender was having supper in Stratford with Vivien Leigh and Laurence Olivier, having already had conversations earlier, during an intermission of *Macbeth*, with Douglas Fairbanks and Danny Kaye.[59] In June Auden wrote Spender from Ischia saying that the whole family could pay him a visit.[60] And later when plans were clearer, he wrote to say that he had hired a "whore" to take care of the children— whores are "good with children," he said.[61]

As it turned out, Spender took a holiday alone with Matthew. Hansi Lambert invited them to join her for a yachting trip on the Mediterranean—a trip that included stops at Corfu, Corsica, Ischia, and Capri, where the party lunched with Gian Carlo Menotti, Samuel Barber, and Thomas Schippers. Spender read Wordsworth on the trip, meditating on the romantic's use of "self" as the "door that opens into the collective I." In Ischia Spender visited Auden, whose dog Moses "started making love" with Spender's "trouser leg." Earlier Hansi with Stephen and Natasha had visited Auden from Positano. Auden lived in the kind of messy environment with which he had always surrounded himself. He irritated Spender by accusing him of smoking up all his cigarettes. When Spender suggested he would buy some of his own if Auden would change a pound into lira for him, Auden checked the rates in the newspaper and made the exchange at the lowest rate possible. If Isherwood had been there, thought Spender, he would have said, "Come off it, Wystan," but Spender, to avoid bickering, said nothing.[62] He remained, as always, apparently in awe of Auden.

In the fall, during part of which Natasha was on a concert tour in the United States, Spender attended an *Encounter* party for William Faulkner in London, met and was impressed by American diplomat George Kennan, visited his old friend Ernst Curtius in Berlin, lectured on Lawrence and Orwell in several German cities, and argued with old Oxford acquaintance Tom Driberg about the Polish poet Czeslaw Milosz. At the *Encounter* party Faulkner claimed he had no literary friends and never read books.[63] Curtius was still angry at Spender's quoting him without permission in the 'Rhineland Journal', but after a long conversation their disagreement was patched up.[64] Driberg infuriated Spender by repeating a Communist ambassador's negative remarks about Milosz and by suggesting that Milosz was supported by the CIA in his flight from Poland.[65]

In 1955 Spender published *The Making of a Poem*, a collection of essays on writing. In the essays he stresses the importance of the poet's relating his writing to the "life of his time," as Auden and Dylan Thomas in their own ways had managed to do. He also emphasizes the importance of work and concentration as opposed to inspiration. At the centre of the poet's craft is the use of memory. Some of the best writing in this book concerns Spender's personal method:

> Sometimes, when I lie in a state of half-waking and half-sleeping, I am conscious of a stream of words which seem to pass through my mind, without their having a meaning, but they have a sound, a sound of passion, or a sound recalling poetry that I know. Again sometimes when I am writing, the music of the words I am trying to shape takes me far beyond the words, I am aware of a rhythm, a dance, a fury, which is as yet empty of words.[66]

A more significant publication was the *Collected Poems, 1928–1953*. This collection of 111 poems was the first version of the *Collected Poems* and would serve as the "definitive Spender" for some years to come. The book is dominated by the poetry of the 1930s, works originally included in *Poems* (1933) and *The Still Centre* (1939). There are some wartime poems as well but only seven new works. Three, including "To My Daughter," "Missing My Daughter," and "Nocturne," are about Lizzie and indicate Spender's preoccupation with individual consciousness as opposed to collective issues. There is a new poem commemorating the poet's friend Dylan Thomas, "this roaring ranter, man and boy,"[67] who had died in 1953, a love poem entitled "Sirmione Peninsula," which Faber and Faber had published separately with illustrations by Lynton Lamb in 1954, and two poems—"In Attica" and "Messenger"—based on memories of Greece. "In Attica" is an example of Spender's ability to paint symbolic landscape, a landscape made

> *Human, like Greek steles, where the dying*
> *Are changed to stone on a gesture of curved air*
> *Lingering in their infinite departure.*

In January of 1956 Christopher Isherwood and his lover Don Bacardy visited London. There was tension, because Bacardy felt that Spender did not like him. On one occasion Bacardy refused to join Christopher, Natasha, Spender, and Peter Watson for lunch.[68] At that lunch Spender noted his dislike of John Lehmann—about the Lehmann family in general he said, "They think they're the Brontës when actually they're the Marx brothers."[69] At this and other meetings Christopher felt that Stephen was "thick-skinned" for not recognizing that Bacardy was uncomfortable with him.[70] It was not until the middle of March that Spender and Bacardy had a "showdown" and became good friends.[71]

During the Isherwood visit, Spender complained frequently about his life in England: "There's nothing here but personal relationships and manoeuvres," he said.[72] Perhaps he would go to Canada or Brazil.[73] At a gay stag party hosted by Spender for Isherwood, Joe Ackerley, William Plomer, Angus Wilson and his friend Tony Garrett, and several others, Isherwood noted Spender's "shiny surface manner" and decided that there could be few things worse than "being shut up on this island and having to ring the changes on this handful of personalities and talents."[74]

Even a potentially exhilarating meeting in Venice, sponsored by the European Cultural Association—a meeting that included Russian and other "Iron Curtain" delegates, marking the new period of de-Stalinization—did not essentially change Spender's mood. He managed to offend J. D. Bernal by suggesting that there should be anti-Communist as well as Communist delegates representing the Iron Curtain countries.[75] He found the conference, in general, irritating and hypocritical. In fact, what he considered to be petty arguments between Jean-Paul Sartre and Maurice Merleau-Ponty—both of whom

he admired—and the total failure of communication between the ideo-
logues of "proletarian" culture and those, like himself, of bourgeois culture led to his writing a satirical novella on the conference. *Engaged in
Writing,* dedicated to Hansi Lambert, would be published in 1958 by
Hamish Hamilton and Farrar Straus.

The main character of *Engaged in Writing* is Olin Asphalt, a fifty-
year-old English LITUNO (read UNESCO) delegate to an East-West
conference the main purpose of which seems to be to discuss what to discuss at the next such conference. Disillusioned, Asphalt resigns from
LITUNO, as Spender would resign from UNESCO.

It was during the Venice conference that an American graduate student at Oxford, Reynolds Price, passed Stephen Spender and Jean-Paul
Sartre crossing a bridge—"One was well over six feet tall, capped with a
head of snow-white hair above a young and splendid face; the other was
short, walleyed and froglike."[76] Without knowing it Spender had just
missed meeting a man who was to become a great writer and one of his
closest friends. It was also in Venice that Spender insulted Morgan
Forster by interrupting a conversation the older man was having with
Rose Macaulay and, from Forster's point of view, by spiriting Macaulay
away for his own entertainment.[77]

Not many weeks later, after what was to him a tedious Congress for
Cultural Freedom meeting in Paris, Spender received bad news. His old
Horizon associate and intimate friend Peter Watson had been found in his
bathtub dead at the age of forty-eight on May 3. On the twenty-eighth of
May Spender was told by Watson's solicitor that Watson had made
bequests to both Cyril Connolly and Sonia Orwell but had not even mentioned him in his will, and Spender was concerned: "I had a quite childish
feeling of being hurt, and left out."[78] For a time he became almost
obsessed by what he saw as a slight from someone he genuinely loved.
One night in July, for instance, he "dreamed all night" about Watson, who
told him he had wanted to leave him something and then gave him an oil
painting by Jean Cocteau, although Cocteau did not do oil paintings.[79]

In late May of 1956 Auden visited on his way to Oxford to succeed
Cecil Day-Lewis in the Oxford Poetry Chair. He would hold the position

for four years, having won it in an election over Harold Nicolson. Spender drove with him to Oxford for the inaugural lecture. It was strange being with his old friend again in rooms at Christ Church, and Auden seemed to revert there to his old arbitrary but amusing Oxford ways. A month later Spender was in Oxford again to be a guest with Auden at the Mermaid Club. Jean Cocteau, in Oxford for an honorary degree, was also present during the evening. One person who sat near the famous trio was "a tiresomely effeminate young undergraduate who wore a cloak lined with red satin and carried a cane" and "talked in a camp way about his fiancée."[80] One wonders whether Auden and Spender were reminded of some of their own undergraduate poses. Spender was well aware that Auden was posing as he spoke in his categorical way to their undergraduate hosts. And in his journal he thought about his own role-playing—specifically his apparent "weakness of behaviour," a characteristic he found convenient, especially around apparently confident people such as Auden.[81]

In mid-June Spender was in Rome for a meeting of congress editors, and early in July he worked with Nicholas Nabokov in Bologna on the libretto for *Rasputin's End*, had lunch in London with critic I. A. Richards, and missed an appointment with old friend Gerald Hamilton because he was giving the children a bath.[82] In early August he attended a performance of Eliot's *Family Reunion* with Lucian Freud and then left with his own family for a vacation in Le Zoute and then Gstaad with the Lamberts. The holiday was not altogether satisfactory because Cyril Connolly insisted on tagging along and then became bored as Spender had known he would.[83]

After a September operation for varicose veins, Spender left for a month of lectures in the States. While there he stayed as usual with the Buttingers near Princeton. Highlights of the visit were dinner with George Kennan, a Robert Frost reading, and lunch with J. Robert Oppenheimer. Oppenheimer, whom Spender had thought of primarily as one of the inventors of the atomic bomb, was surprisingly cultivated and interesting. He showed Spender his paintings, especially a van Gogh he prized. He criticized the recent English-French-Israeli action in Suez, unlike Kennan, who had approved of it. Spender "had the impression that Oppenheimer examined whatever was said to him, and condemned what was superficial."[84]

Soon after his return to London he arranged a meeting between two old friends, T. S. Eliot and Igor Stravinsky. Spender later told William Plomer that the old men had "nothing to say."[85] They talked mostly about their health and the therapeutic value of alcohol. Stravinsky said he "suffered from an excessive thickness of the blood," while Eliot remembered that once in Heidelberg a doctor had told him, "Mr Eliot, you have the thinnest blood I've ever tested." Stravinsky said he never sent people photographs when they asked him to do so "because the postage cost money." Eliot had recently addressed over thirteen thousand people at a stadium in Minneapolis and said that as he walked onto the platform he "felt like a very small bull walking into an enormous arena."[86] Spender was not sure the meeting of these two giants of the arts had been particularly fruitful.

In 1957 Reynolds Price came to London at Spender's invitation. Price had sent short stories to *Encounter* that Spender had liked. As Price would say later, the two "took to one another quickly," sharing a love of the arts and a "commitment to self-exploration and self-repair" in their writing.[87] Spender introduced Price to his world—to his family, Cyril Connolly, Isaiah Berlin, Auden, and even to Laurence Olivier and Vivien Leigh. He not only admired his young friend's work but found him extremely handsome and appealing on a personal level. Over the years the two men would spend time together, and when Price fell prey to a debilitating illness, Spender continued to visit him whenever possible, even giving him his first Walkman to help him through the early stages of his convalescence. He would dedicate his 1985 *Collected Poems* to Price and the two would carry on an energetic correspondence. The Duke University Library claims to have some three hundred restricted letters between Spender and Price.

An important event for *Encounter* and Spender was a June 6 dinner for Robert Frost at Spender's club, the Savile (through Eliot he also joined the prestigious Garrick Club the next year). Other guests were Graham Greene, Cecil Day-Lewis, E. M. Forster, and William Coldstream. The group was asked to be informal, as Morgan Forster preferred "no dressing."[88] T. S. Eliot declined to come because he and Valerie had already invited Frost to lunch on the ninth. He suggested that seeing the same people at every party would make Frost think the literary world of London was tiny and insignificant.[89] Frost seems to have enjoyed the depleted army, such as it was.

Nineteen fifty-seven and 1958 were years during which Spender was preoccupied with Japan and with a new relationship he formed there. Spender and his good friend Angus Wilson went to Tokyo as members of the British delegation to the Twenty-ninth Annual PEN Conference during the late summer and fall of 1957. From the beginning in Japan, Spender seemed to allow free rein to pent-up emotions, no doubt partly in reaction to the disillusionment and boredom that had plagued him in recent years. According to Wilson's biographer, Margaret Drabble, a good relationship developed between Wilson and Spender: "Each found the other amiably dotty. There was to be much giggling, and some weeping." On one occasion Spender "pinched a very pretty boy" from under Wilson's "nose."[90] The pretty boy was named Masao, and after the conference he joined Spender, Wilson, the American scholar Donald Richie, and a particularly melancholy Alberto Moravia for a tour of Japan. Later the party was joined also by Shozo Tokunaga, who would become Spender's Japanese translator.

During the trip through Japan, a profound intimacy developed between Stephen and Masao, who was eighteen but who, according to Wilson, "seemed like a little boy."[91] Spender realized very quickly that, given their age difference and the geographic distance that would soon reestablish itself between them, a love relationship with Masao could only be painful and, for the boy, even tragic. Spender's unhappiness was made even greater when a visit to a "boy brothel" demonstrated a possibly horrifying future for his friend. Several days before it was time for Wilson and Spender to leave for Bangkok, Masao was already in "great distress" and so was Spender.[92]

Once he was back in London, Spender was determined to return to Japan and Masao as soon as possible. But this could not be arranged until the spring of 1958, and before then there were the ordinary demands of life.

There was the vacuum caused by Irving Kristol's leaving *Encounter*, work to be done on *Mary Stuart*, his translation of Schiller's play, *Maria Stuart*, which the Old Vic planned to perform, the drumming up of support for the Homosexual Reform Bill, getting Lizzie settled at her boarding school in the country and Matthew at Westminster, and a lecture tour in America in the early spring. Spender also joined Eliot, Hemingway, and many other writers in a serious and eventually successful attempt to free Ezra Pound from St. Elizabeth's Hospital for the insane in Washington, D.C., where, with Robert Lowell, he had visited him.[93]

In March Spender took a six-month leave of absence from *Encounter* and soon after left for America, having also negotiated a lecture tour of Japan for the Congress for Cultural Freedom through his friend Nicholas Nabokov. On April 17 after lectures in Louisville and San Francisco, Spender was with Isherwood and Don Bacardy in Santa Monica. His friends "felt in him . . . quite a considerable [sense of difficulty in his marriage]." He was "restless" but "charming."[94] On the twentieth Spender was in Honolulu and then, a few days later, in Tokyo. After having missed Masao at the airport, he learned from his friend Donald Richie that some weeks earlier Masao had tried to commit suicide in the apartment of an American lover. Clearly the situation for the boy was as distressing as Spender had feared it might be: "He left me feeling that more than anything else I would like to try to get him out of the rut of humiliation which he has got into on account of his suicide attempt."[95]

Characteristically, Spender confused sexual intimacy with the need to "cure." He was placing himself in the kind of paternalistic position in relation to a lover that had marked and eventually destroyed his earlier relationships with Helmutt, Tony, and perhaps even Inez.

What followed was a tour of Japan, nearly always in the company of Masao. Spender and his friend were sometimes accompanied by Shozo who saw Masao's presence as an undermining of his professional work. There were important cultural occasions as well—particularly meetings with novelists Kawabata Yasunari and Yukio Mishima. Mishima was "extremely frank about being homosexual" and the group went to several gay bars one evening, bars that reminded Spender of similar places in Berlin in the thirties.[96]

In June, in London, Spender wrote to Plomer that he could not forget Masao and that it was his full intention to do something about him. He quoted the last lines of a poem not about Masao but his translator, Shozo, although the lines perhaps convey a sense of the erotic as well as the literary: "Their crossing tongues exchange identities/And when one is the other, both are one."[97] To his friend the Scottish poet James Burns Singer, Spender spoke of a "personal crisis" that had to do with Japan.[98]

In January of 1959 Spender was again in California, this time with Natasha and the children. He had received an appointment as Beckmann Professor of English at the University of California at Berkeley for a semester. In February the family visited Isherwood in Santa Monica. For Isherwood it was "embarrassing, having both Spenders as guests," because "Stephen obviously longed to talk about forbidden subjects."[99] He was bored with his colleagues in Berkeley and was still restless. According to Isherwood, a mutual friend with whom Natasha communicated felt that she was "very seriously worried" about Stephen. She had told the friend that Stephen had "for the first time [been] unpleasant to her." She felt that "the [Masao] business in Japan" was "more serious than anything in Stephen's life previously."[100]

Spender visited Isherwood several times alone after the February stay. On one such occasion, he played Bizet's *Carmen* over and over again on the record player. It was apparently a way of working through the Masao problem. Eventually, the strength of his relationship with his wife and children took precedence over the one with Masao, as it had before in the case of other less powerful attachments. Spender felt the power of the family relationship especially when he was with his children. Once, driving across the Yorkshire moors with the now teenage Matthew on their way to a performance of *Mary Stuart* at the 1961 Edinburgh International Festival of Music and Drama, Matthew surprised him by reacting negatively to his preoccupied expression: "Don't look like that, Dad," he said. "I simply can't bear it." Spender "felt grieved for the burden one inadvertently puts on children." Just before the play in Edinburgh, "Matthew said encouragingly: 'Remember, Dad, whatever happens it can't be as boring as *Hamlet*.' "[101]

At the end of 1959 Spender presented a reading at the Library of Congress and a lecture at Yale on English as opposed to American poetry. America was producing the "great poetry of the 20th Century," he said, while Great Britain was holding on to a traditional poetry that is a "kind of private game amongst the more neurotic and sensitive members of an unneurotic and insensitive kind of society." And in a telling remark, given his own position as an English poet lecturing for money in America, he stated, "The whole of British literature is really part of the American economy."[102]

The turbulent 1960s began for Spender with a visit to Moscow with Muriel Gardiner Buttinger and one of her friends. For the former Marxists this was a significant journey. Their goal was to visit with Muriel's old friend from Vienna cell days, the finally much-honoured sculptor Konienkov. For Spender the most interesting part of the Moscow trip was a long lunch and afternoon with Guy Burgess. It was like lunching with a ghost. Spender sensed in Burgess's agreeable manner a certain pleasure at seeing someone from England, especially someone of the "old group." They talked about religion, Burgess calling it an "intellectual betrayal." He asked Spender not to publish anything about their interview. He opened a copy of Winston Churchill's memoirs and pointed to the inscription from predefection days. It read, "To Guy Burgess, in agreement with his views, Winston Churchill." Spender felt that Burgess thought his crime was negligible and that he ought to be allowed to return to England to see his mother and to "have some kind of a new start."[103]

In April the Spenders met Ted Hughes and Sylvia Plath at dinner at the Eliots. Hughes had "a craggy Yorkshire handsomeness combined with a certain elongated refinement; . . . his wife, who talked more, was a very pretty, intelligent girl from Boston." The conversation lagged at dinner, Mrs. Eliot giving her husband "an encouraging look across the table which positively radiated help." To take up the slack Spender began to talk more—too much, according to Natasha, who had hoped to hear more from Eliot.[104] Spender liked both Hughes and Plath and wrote to them to apologize for talking too much and to suggest that they get together again.[105] He was to maintain a friendship with Hughes and Plath after that.

In June Auden was again in town, and the Eliots hosted a party for him at Faber and Faber. Spender was there, as well as Isaiah Berlin, A. L. Rowse, Louis MacNeice, Tom Driberg, Ted Hughes, and Sylvia Plath. Auden told one person that being professor of poetry at Oxford was "rather like being a Kentucky Colonel."[106]

Spender was now at an age when old friends began to die. Hansi Lambert and Frances Cornford both did so in 1960. Vita Sackville-West would follow in 1962 and Louis MacNeice, Theodore Roethke, and Sylvia Plath in 1963.

In the summer the Spenders toured southern France and were particularly attracted to the Alpilles region around Les Baux. After France and a conference in Berlin, Spender left to teach a summer course at Brandeis University near Boston. There he spent enjoyable weekends with Allen and Isabella Tate, but he disliked his classes at Brandeis. He spoke disparagingly of his students, and he wrote to the Tates that Brandeis was beginning to make him anti-Semitic.[107]

The Spenders did a British Council tour of Turkey, Lebanon, Egypt, and Greece in early 1961, after a week with Matthew in Florence. On April 10 the Tates arrived in London. Spender had a party for them. Natasha was away. Later she wrote saying how sorry she was to have missed Isabella.[108]

In September a successful performance of *Mary Stuart* took place at the Edinburgh festival and then the play had a decent run at the Old Vic. Spender was much buoyed by this success.

Nineteen sixty-two began with a long British Council lecture tour of South America, Trinidad, Jamaica, and Mexico. The lectures in Venezuela were cancelled because of a series of bomb explosions. Otherwise, the trip was uneventful and in February both Spenders went to Berkeley before travelling to Washington for a three-lecture series entitled "The Imagination in the Modern World" at the Library of Congress, lectures that would be incorporated later into *The Struggle of the Modern* (1963).

After a stint as writer in residence at the University of Virginia, Spender visited the Tates in Minnesota. Natasha did not accompany him, as she had returned to England to go with Penelope Betjeman to a horse fair where she was to obtain the horse that Wystan Auden had promised to buy for Lizzie. Auden had always been fond of Lizzie. On one occasion, when he was staying with the Spenders and Lizzie was very young, Natasha took him a morning cup of coffee and was surprised when he said, "I want you to take this money to the store and to buy a pound of rice and to bring me the proper change." It was with some relief that she realized Auden had not been speaking to her but to Lizzie, who was sitting under the desk learning about money and change.[109]

Spender's continuing American lecture tour took him to Northwestern University in Evanston, the University of Minnesota, and various other Midwestern institutions. In May he did some sight-seeing he had always wanted to do in Rome—probably with Reynolds Price, and by the middle of the month he was in London for Stravinsky's eightieth birthday celebration at Chez Laurent with Robert Craft, Simone Signoret, Yves Montand, and other luminaries.[110] There was also a dinner with the Russian poet Yevtushenko in London and a depressing farewell with Price, who was returning to America, leaving Spender and him both "distraught" and "oppressed."[111]

Spender's pursuit of famous friends now became almost relentless. People whom he visited during the summer included Elizabeth Bowen, the Isaiah Berlins, Francis Bacon, Dom Moraes, Oskar Kokoschka, Edith Sitwell, Cyril Connolly, Henry Moore, Margot Fonteyn, and Rudolf Nureyev, who "appeared a gaunt, haggard beatnik with untidy hair and considerable charm."[112] With his good friend Stuart Hampshire he went to a William Coldstream exhibition and was "transfixed" by Coldstream's portrait of his first wife, Inez, done in the thirties. After a Francis Bacon show at the Tate Gallery, however, he decided that "most other contemporary painting seems decoration, doodling, aestheticism or stupidity."[113]

Michael Astor had kindly provided the Spenders with a summer cottage at Bruern in Oxfordshire, which they used for several summers beginning in 1956. There in 1962 they entertained painter Larry Rivers, Lord Kinross, James and Tania Stern, Angus Wilson, and many other friends.

Spender was able to write some poetry at Bruern, but social activities and *Encounter* editing took most of his time. One day Matthew said, "Dad, if I get a scholarship to Oxford will you promise to leave *Encounter*, and do nothing but write poetry?"[114]

June was an especially busy month for Spender. The queen named him a CBE, leading some people to assume he might be in line to be named poet laureate. He delivered a series of lectures at Gresham College, lunched with Philippe and Pauline Rothschild, whom he knew through Hansi Lambert, and had another feud—this one relatively minor—with John Lehmann over the fact that Lehmann had sold the copy of *Trial of a Judge* that Spender had inscribed to him after their *Horizon–New Writing* feud.[115] The Spenders also attended another Stravinsky birthday celebration—this one in Hamburg, where Spender took a walk along the Alster remembering his first trip to Hamburg when he was twenty and now feeling "old."[116] An excursion to Berlin and Munich seemed to stir him to write poetry—more than he had written in some time.

Wystan Auden paid his annual visit in July after having scolded Spender for a review he did not like. "You're a naughty girl," he wrote.[117] This tone was in keeping with Auden's often being called "Mother Auden" by his friends. Enjoying this role, Auden loved reciting Spender's most famous line of poetry, changing the words to "Your mother thinks continually of those who are truly great."[118] The Auden visit coincided with the death of William Faulkner. The two men listened to a recording of *Das Rheingold* and discussed form in poetry. Auden announced that poetry meant "having something truthful to say" and "exploring the possibilities of the English language." What he hated about being a writer was "the whole business of the literary life," which, in effect, had been for some time his friend's life. A few days later Spender woke up thinking, "Getting and spending we lay waste our powers."[119] He was somewhat amused when one morning Auden asked him about "biographical facts for my obituary," which he was writing in advance for the *Times*.[120] He was also writing one for Eliot's future demise.

After Auden's departure, the Spender family took a holiday in Ireland before Stephen travelled to Edinburgh for an inconclusive conference on the novel attended by Mary McCarthy, Lawrence Durrell, Muriel Spark, Angus Wilson, Rebecca West, Henry Miller, and others. Henry Miller finally got up and suggested that the group discuss "something interesting, like painting."[121]

Spender travelled to South America again in the fall for a PEN conference. There, in Brazil, Argentina, and Uruguay, he read *David Copperfield* and Nabokov's *Pale Fire* to pass the free time. The ending of the Dickens novel bored him; *Pale Fire* was "intricate and marvellous."[122]

At Christmastime in Bruern Spender brooded about Christianity. A few months earlier, he had thought about how "Christian writers" like Eliot and Tate were "ironic in their poetry" and how they deemed irony a "necessary 'modern' virtue."[123] Now, working on a long "poem about pronouns," he concluded that "Christianity is about the fact that every individual is to himself or herself 'I.' The figure of Christ crucified is that of the 'I' of each individual. . . . Marxism is the religion of 'he'. . . the objective result of his conditioning by the social class to which he belongs." The real revolutionaries are "we" who work for the ideals of "us." "They" are those who "embody power."[124] Spender seemed determined to find a way of assimilating the Christianity of his friends Tate and Eliot into his own individual and agnostic vision.

Northwestern University in Evanston, near Chicago, became Spender's American base of operations for several years beginning in January 1963. A colleague on the faculty was Richard Ellmann, who would eventually transfer to New College, Oxford, and who remained a much valued friend.

At Northwestern Spender completed work on *The Struggle of the Modern*, a discussion of the modernist movement that had been the basis of the Library of Congress lectures the year before and the Berkeley lectures of 1959. For Spender, the great modernists—Joyce, Eliot, Lawrence, Pound, Woolf, Yeats—and those who have followed them are unified by a sense of difference, a sense that they live in a new age influenced by science. What the modernist artist does is not to attempt to change the world politically or ideologically but to record the newness and to celebrate the individual consciousness through an originality of "arrangements of words or marks on canvas which make a poem or novel, or a painting."[125] The modernist creative act is, in a sense, the subject of modernist works or its central symbol, and it has at its core an almost spiritual belief in the sacredness of civilization and of the individual human experience. Unfortunately, says Spender, the movement is probably dead: "In literature, at any rate, [it] looks today like past history," killed by the hungry beast that is collective, popular culture.[126]

During the late spring, the Spenders returned to southern France and then to Greece, where they took a cruise on a yacht from Athens. In the summer they saw the Lowells in Paris. That fall Spender was deeply saddened by the first death of one of the "Auden group," that of Louis Mac-Neice. And in October it was decided that Matthew would go to New College at Oxford.[127] Spender was pleased at this in spite of what he had said in *World Within World* and elsewhere about his own experience at Oxford.

Early in the next year Spender was in the States again, lecturing in various places and serving on the faculty at Northwestern. He lectured on Woolf, Joyce, Lowell, and Beckett and told William Plomer that he had discovered a congenial gay group there.[128] In April he spent a weekend with the Lowells in New York and complained of boredom and the lack of a social life in Chicago.[129] Lowell had become one of his favourite contemporary poets. He admired Lowell's ability to assimilate experiences and references, to create poetry out of even the most bizarre reality. And he recognized the personal toll this must take.[130]

By 1964 Spender had become very much a part of the American scene, being asked for comments on matters such as the civil rights movement, the Beatles, and Lyndon Johnson. At an afternoon press conference in Washington on February 24, he said he found "our Prime Minister [Douglas-Home] and your president rather embarrassing." Douglas-Home smiled all the time and Johnson was "like something kind of husky that I don't care to eat," and "I much prefer the Beatles to the Prime Minister. I admire their frankness and candor and they are very witty." The poets he liked were "the abstract poets of today who tend to be rather obscene, but they manage to be quite serious by being outrageous."[131] Spender had in mind Allen Ginsberg and the Beat poets, several of whom he had met and liked. He thought of them as, in his sense of the word, real modernists. Perhaps reflecting the irony Eliot and Tate claimed was necessary to the modernist, he suggested in his press conference that to be "serious" one must be "funny" and that Arthur Miller's *After the Fall*, for instance, was finally not serious because it was not funny. Spender was, of course, himself being funny and allowing his audience to decide whether he was being serious: "The best way for a poet to make a living," he announced, "is by giving lectures on how difficult it is for a poet to make a living."[132] Spender was very serious when in September he heeded a plea from the Student Nonviolent Coordination Committee (SNCC) to cancel an engagement to speak at the segregated Mississippi University for Women. "If I had gone, I would have supported something I don't believe in," Spender told the press.[133]

That summer the Spenders bought an old farm in Maussane in the Alpilles region of southern France they had visited a few years earlier. During the next two years, they restored it, Natasha creating a magnificent garden and supervising work in the olive grove. The Mas St. Jerome became a vacation home beginning in 1966.

In August Spender, with the help of Herbert Read, entertained Marianne Moore in London. Later he would write Moore a letter in which he spoke of his admiration for her work,[134] and on October 20 she answered, praising Spender for his work with *Encounter* and for his "discerning the core of a writer's intentions."

Spender was devastated by the news of T. S. Eliot's death on January 4. He had lost his literary father and was now very much the elder statesman himself. The *New Yorker* magazine had recently published one of Spender's most important poems, "One More Botched Beginning," a poem that remembers those who have died, especially those of his university years—Louis MacNeice, for example, and Bernard Spencer. In a sense the poem also remembers Woolf, Eliot, Ottoline Morrell, and all of the other great figures who had meant so much to his life. The last stanza reads:

Their lives are now those poems that were
Pointers to the poems they made their lives.
We read there in the college quad. Each poem
Is still a new beginning. If
They had been finished though they would have died
Before they died. Being alive,
Is when each moment's a new start, with past
And future shuffled between fingers
For a new game . . .
               I'm dealing out
My hand to them, one more botched beginning
There, where we still stand talking in the quad.

Natasha had fallen ill during the autumn, and two operations had been required. After a brief recuperative holiday for her in Marrakesh in January, Spender returned to the United States and Northwestern University, and after a summer in France and England, the Spenders moved to Washington, D.C., in September. There he took up the post of poetry consultant at the Library of Congress, the first foreigner to be named what was, in effect, and is now called the American "poet laureate."

10

THE GENEROUS DAYS

In spite of his Library of Congress appointment, several important American and English university positions, the excitement generated by student revolutions, the development of several new and satisfying friendships, and the publication of several books, the late sixties and seventies were years coloured for Spender by a sense of nostalgia, reminiscence, and sometimes sadness. The deaths of close friends came with increased frequency, and Spender sometimes experienced a sense of decline, both in the context of his abilities as a writer and in what he saw as the gradual demise of the modernist movement he associated with friends such as Yeats, Eliot, Stravinsky, and Auden.

Spender had been chosen in April 1965 by the Library of Congress to be its consultant in poetry, beginning in September. His predecessor was Reed Whittemore, and earlier holders of the post included Allen Tate, Conrad Aiken, Elizabeth Bishop, Louis Untermeyer, Richard Eberhart, Howard Nemerov, Randall Jarrell, Robert Penn Warren, Karl Shapiro, Robert Frost, and Spender's close friend Robert Lowell. The job of the consultant in poetry is to advise the library on its literary collections, to assist in collecting manuscripts, to meet with other poets and scholars, to write a critical essay for the library's *Quarterly Journal*, to present at least one public programme at the library, and to lecture at schools and universities. The stipend for Spender's year in office was $15,000.

There was some criticism of the library for appointing an Englishman to the consultantship, but Spender pleased most people by making a point of accepting as many invitations to speak as possible. There were, of course, the dinners with members of the Washington and New York social and political establishment—Sir Patrick and Lady Dean at the British Embassy, historian Arthur Schlesinger, Katharine Graham of the *Washington Post*, James Reston of the *New York Times*, the Joseph Alsops, the Walter Lippmanns, the Nicholas Nabokovs, the Edmund Randolph Biddles, Alice Roosevelt Longworth, and various congress-men and senators. In late September, for example, the Spenders dined in New York with the Stravinskys and with the Berlins and the Lowells and in November with Truman Capote. And soon after the arrival in Washington Spender attended President Johnson's signing of an arts and humanities bill at the White House. He noted that shaking the presi-dent's hand was like shaking the "hoof of an elephant."[1]

But Spender also entered fully into the less glamorous activities such as high school graduation speeches, college and university lectures, and comments on works sent to him by young poets. These comments revealed both a sense of humour and a certain impatience. He urged one would-be poet to pay attention to details and to look for "something new" to say about them. A poet who was "bad at rhyme" was advised to read Frost, Auden, and Graves. To another, who said she had written over five hundred poems, Spender suggested that while her works were "interesting," they were "frightfully wordy." Perhaps she had written too many poems, he said, with "too many words to each poem." Still another poet was told that his poems were "promising" but that they did not "quite displace or replace Eliot."

Spender made himself particularly available for interviews, a method of communication that always unsettled him. His interviews, like most, were impromptu and full of unstudied remarks that are sometimes revealing. Allen Ginsberg, for whom he had "a qualified admiration," was a "gifted poet . . . given to outpourings." Spender's poems were "not outpourings" but products of much thought and many revisions. The American poets he most admired were Robert Lowell, John Berryman, and Randall Jarrell. There was no "recipe" for writing poetry—"It's like making Irish bread. . . . One just makes it." Novels tended to be "like half-baked autobiography."[2] A poet "cannot write about everything . . . only of those things that move him deeply." It was unfair that in America particularly poets were expected to represent "an idea or a movement."[3] His favourite English poets of earlier times were Shakespeare, Shelley, Browning, and Hardy. Some American poets he admired were Roethke, Crane, Ransom, Frost, Stevens, Marianne Moore, and Tate. He told one interviewer that his favourite of all poems was Thomas Wyatt's "They flee from me that sometime did me seek."[4]

The first official act of the new poetry consultant was to deliver a lecture entitled "Chaos and Control in Poetry." Spender used this occasion to articulate his position in relation to the two literary movements that had been most important to his development as a poet. On one hand was the romanticism, particularly as expressed by Wordsworth and Shelley, that had been so much a part of his early development. Romanticism coincided with Spender's love of nature and his attraction to the confessional mode. "The Romantics," he said, "went to the root of nature, or humanity, and perhaps also to their exacerbated personal emotions." On the other hand were the great modernists—the late Yeats, Eliot, Pound, and Auden—whom Spender admired but who in their understandable eagerness to avoid vagueness and to achieve concreteness had caused modern poetry to become too formal and rule-bound and had thus undermined poetic imagination and originality.

In this speech Spender planted himself firmly on the side of those who felt that in American poetry, for example, there had been too much of the influence of Eliot. In spite of his admiration for Allen Tate, he found himself drawn more to the Walt Whitman, William Carlos Williams, Allen Ginsberg antiformalist radical wing of the American tradition. Of the mainline American moderns, it was Robert Lowell who most appealed to him. For Spender, Lowell represented a satisfying balance between formal restraint and romantic confessionalism, a certain "formulated chaos" that was essential to great poetry, that was the essence of the best works of Yeats, Pound, Eliot, and Auden, in spite of the antiromanticism of their criticism. Theodore Roethke and John Berryman, too, achieved this natural balance between the formal and the more imaginative and original aspects of art and life.

It was necessary to resurrect romantic imagination and originality in contemporary poetry, said the new American poet laureate. It was for this reason that in this and several other speeches during his tenure as poetry consultant Spender did not mock what many saw as the excesses of Allen Ginsberg and the Beat poets. These poets, at least, were not ignoring the "chaos and disorder of modern life" and were freeing themselves from the restrictions of the formal literary conventions that marked many of the followers of the classical modernists. The "Beat" rebellion had much in common with that of the romantics against the rules of eighteenth-century classicism. Like those other "radicals" D. H. Lawrence and Henry Miller, they were attempting to "fit the language of modern society to its fundamental problems."[5] Spender ended his inaugural speech with a quote from Coleridge. Poets "are the bridlers of delight, the purifiers; they that combine all these with reason and order—the true protoplasts—Gods of love who tame the chaos."

Spender was interested in the fact that American poets seemed to pay such a high price for their role as tamers of chaos. He discussed this question frequently with his friend Robert Lowell. In the end the chaos seemed to overwhelm so many of the American poets. Randall Jarrell threw himself in front of a car (this was later denied by Mrs. Jarrell) soon after Spender began his tenure in Washington; Theodore Roethke had committed suicide not long before. Lowell and Berryman were plagued by breakdowns.[6]

Pursuing this line of thought, Spender delivered a series of lectures at Cambridge University during a February leave of absence from the Library of Congress. The lectures would eventually be revised and published as *Love-Hate Relations: English and American Sensibilities*. In these lectures and the book based on them, Spender commented on the fluctuating relationship between American and English culture, beginning with Henry James's leaving the cultural poverty of America to discover a world of manners in Europe, and continuing with what he saw as the Americanization of England and Europe in the postwar period. Spender's own position was that of the Englishman who feels more comfortable in his homeland but who envies American dynamism in spite of its tendency to destroy culture.

The presence of Robert and Elizabeth Lowell in New York and the Berlins and Buttingers in Princeton added a great deal to the year in Washington. Spender made frequent visits to both places. To Lowell he wrote that seeing him often made being in the United States a blessing.[7] When in December Lowell had one of his breakdowns, Spender wrote to him praising him for his willingness to challenge his inner chaos in order to create great poetry.[8]

Spender was frustrated by having little time to work on his own poetry. During the year as consultant, he was frequently called upon to read from his work, and was struck by the predominance of the thirties poems among his choices of what to read. He was far enough away in years from these poems to look at them, even as he read and discussed them, with a certain distance and humour. As he was reading one evening in Chicago, he was struck by a line from "The Express": "But gliding like a queen she leaves the station." The line particularly amused him:

This line always embarrasses me a bit, and I begin visualizing not the express at all but an Oxford queen called M—— gliding down the High when I was still an undergraduate. I was rather willowy myself. . . . I wonder whether anyone has the acuteness to think it absurd—a six-foot-three poet with a limey accent and sibilant voice saying, "gliding like a queen she leaves the station."[9]

The Spenders returned home for the Christmas holidays and New Year celebrations. Nineteen sixty-six was the year of Matthew's twenty-first birthday and the Spenders' silver wedding anniversary. In January Frank Kermode succeeded Spender as editor of *Encounter*, although Spender would stay on as a contributing editor.

Back in Washington after the Cambridge lectures, he lectured on Britten's opera *The Rape of Lucretia*, and on the topic "Modern Poetry,

English and American Traditions." He suggested that the Britten opera, based on a pagan story, was nevertheless a drama of "Christian morality" that reflected T. S. Eliot's idea that an enactment of a morally significant theme "becomes a part of a consciousness outside the time of the events themselves, modifies that later consciousness and can be modified by it." He did a formal reading at the Library of Congress and was elected an honorary member of the American Academy of Arts. In March he was much amused by remarks made by James Dickey, his announced successor at the library. To Howard Nemerov he reported that Dickey had said to him that he was not going to "sit arahnd on mah ass like yew."[10]

In the spring of 1966 Spender taught at George Washington University, and in May he lectured on Wallace Stevens, William Carlos Williams, and Auden at Northwestern. He enjoyed his year in Washington. In his annual report in June 1966 he noted that, having felt that the consultant should think of himself as the " 'gift' of Congress," he had accepted all invitations to speak at schools and to see people who wished to "consult" him. He particularly enjoyed judging the contest in poetry for the secondary schools of the District of Columbia. If he had a disappointment, it was his failure to arouse interest in a conference on translating poetry from behind the Iron Curtain.

By early July the Spenders were in London and soon after that in France, where Spender spent time rereading Joyce. He wrote to the Lowells that he thought Joyce was a writer who really wished he was Mozart but who became Wagner. And by October the usual social round in London had begun again. On October 26, for example, the Spenders entertained William Plomer, Christopher Isherwood, and Francis Bacon at dinner.

In 1967 Matthew married Maro Gorky, the daughter of the painter Arshile Gorky and Magouche Phillips. The couple lived in Italy. Matthew took up a career of painting, sculpting, and writing.

In January Spender was once again in America, this time as a visiting fellow at the Centre of Advanced Studies at Wesleyan University. In the middle of his tenure there – in April – he was contacted by *Ramparts* magazine to say that they had proof that the Congress for Cultural Freedom, the sponsor of *Encounter*, was funded by the CIA through various foundations. Similar charges had been made before, but Spender had been assured by the CCF that they were not true. Now, after the *Ramparts* revelation, they admitted that the charges were based on fact. At about the same time, the details of the case were revealed to members of the CCF board in Paris, a meeting attended by representatives of *Encounter*. What followed was a series of disagreements in London between Frank Kermode and Spender on one side and *Encounter* on the other as to how the latter should meet the charges that implied CIA influence. According to Spender, it became evident that individuals at *Encounter* had known since 1963 about the CIA connection. Also according to Spender, certain Americans at *Encounter* had frequently denied rumours of a CIA connection relayed to Spender and Kermode by Mary McCarthy and Jason Epstein. In any case, with all confidence between the English and American editors ended, Spender and Kermode, both of whom disclaimed previous knowledge of the CIA connection, resigned. Spender was deeply embarrassed and depressed by the whole situation, since he had given many years to *Encounter*, helping to make it one of the most respected literary-political journals in the Western world.[11]

Spender and Kermode received strong support and consolation from Auden, Isaiah Berlin, Stuart Hampshire, and many American friends, and they set about—unsuccessfully, as it turned out—to start a new magazine with Berlin and Hampshire.

In July Auden arrived for his annual visit with the Spenders. This time and for several years that followed, he came to attend the Poetry International Festival in London. Other old Spender friends attending the 1967 event included William Empson, Pablo Neruda, and John Berryman. Spender used the event to drum up support for Russian dissidents on trial in Moscow.

In March 1968 Spender was in Washington to deliver the Seventeenth Annual A. W. Mellon Lectures at the National Gallery of Art. The announced subject of the six lectures was "Imaginative Literature and Painting." This title provided the poet with an opportunity to pursue a favourite topic—the analogy between the much-revised painting and the much-revised poem, and specifically the idea that both are records of the process of creation itself as well as finished products.

Nineteen sixty-eight was tarnished by the death of old friend Herbert Read as 1967 had been by the death of Joe Ackerley. Also in 1968 there was a reeruption of the longtime feud between Spender and John Lehmann. For several years there had been irritation on both sides over the Burgess affair and other quite petty matters. Most recently, Spender had complained to Lehmann about his selling of intimate correspondence to private collectors. Spender's concern over the letters had to do with his fear that intimate details of his life might be revealed. This was odd in a man who seemed so willing to reveal them himself, sometimes quite publicly. Furthermore, he was willing enough to have letters sold to university libraries. Over the years, he sold large amounts of personal correspondence from Eliot, Woolf, Auden, Isherwood, and many others—including Lehmann—to the New York Public Library, Northwestern University, Princeton University, the University of Texas at Austin, the University of California at Berkeley, and many other institutions in the United States.[12] As usual, Lehmann and Spender emerged from a somewhat testy exchange of letters with their very nervous friendship still formally alive.

Among the more important events for Spender in the late sixties and early seventies were those associated with the student revolutions in Prague, New York, California, Berlin, and Paris, and at Kent State and other centres. As had always been the case in his life, Spender seemed to be always at the right place at the right time.[13] In April he climbed through a window at Columbia University to discuss the revolution with students who had taken over buildings there. He followed closely the events surrounding black activist students at Columbia and elsewhere— particularly in the South. Theirs, he felt, was a "serious" purpose beyond revolution for its own sake. He spent the month of May in Paris witnessing the struggle in the streets there. When he was able to leave Paris, he went to Berlin and then to Prague, where he sympathized with the students at Karl University, who were fighting for academic freedom. He admired these students more than those of the middle classes in the "free world" whose "war" he considered sometimes frivolous. Still, the rebellion in all of its manifestations reminded him of the sexual and political "revolution" of his own teens and twenties. That summer in the south of

France he listened in horror to the news of the Russian invasion of Prague and remembered his feelings when Spain had fallen.

Spender recorded his impressions of the student revolution in a book called *The Year of the Young Rebels*. The clear message of *The Year of the Young Rebels* was a call to support the rebellion insofar as it stood for the preservation of basic freedoms and was a clear struggle against the deterioration of humanist values and "the destruction of nature and animal life."[14] The American rebels, whom Spender perhaps knew best through his many teaching positions in the States, were, he suggested, natural descendants of the beatniks, who asserted the importance of their inner selves—their souls—as opposed to the emptiness of the American technological culture. The celebration of the soul by the Beats, hippies, and flower children logically became politicized in the context of soul-starved establishment politics and the Vietnam War.

Spender's support of the students was obvious during his 1969–70 tenure at the University of Connecticut in Storrs. He joined faculty and students in an antimilitarist march on the ROTC building, and his home in Storrs became an evening centre for discussion among students and faculty both from Storrs and Trinity College, Hartford, where he also taught. And Spender participated with Storrs colleagues and old Oxford friend Rex Warner in a semester-long programme called "Semester of the Thirties," which emphasized student radicalism in the thirties and the events surrounding the Spanish Civil War. With Spender's help the university was able to attract several major names as conference participants. These included John Lehmann, Wystan Auden, Paul Goodman, Malcolm Cowley, Carey McWilliams, Granville Hicks, Jack Conroy, Arna Bontemps, Erskine Caldwell, and Sybil Moholy-Nagy.

Natasha Spender joined her husband in Storrs for his sixtieth birthday in February 1969, and there were visits to and from the Isaiah Berlins and the Stuart Hampshires, who were still in America. Spender also paid many calls on Auden, the Lowells, the Buttingers, and Hannah Arendt in New York and Princeton. He felt somewhat isolated in Storrs, although he enjoyed many members of the faculty there, and was glad to be back in Maussane and then London in the summer.

Auden arrived for the Poetry International Festival and everyone remarked on how "difficult" he had become. He made constant patronizing fun of Spender, treating him much as he had treated him in the early Oxford days. Spender had to argue with him at some length before he would agree to visit their friend C. Day-Lewis, who was not well. He called Christopher Isherwood's Vedantism "mumbo jumbo"[15] and told Lizzie Spender to give up her interest in the Zodiac. He was demanding about drink times, mealtimes, bedtimes, and arbitrary about religion and sex.[16] Later in the year Auden came to London for a poetry reading, and afterward Tom Driberg took Auden, the Spenders—including Lizzie—Marianne Faithfull, and Mick Jagger's brother Chris to dinner at the Gay Hussar. The talk was risqué in the extreme. Auden forbade Lizzie to read his poem "The Platonic Blowjob." At one point he asked Marianne Faithfull whether when she smuggled drugs she "packed them up your ass," and he so dominated the conversation that Spender, suddenly irritated, pointed out to him that he spoke of "nothing but yourself." Auden's answer was "What else should I talk about then? What else do I know about?" This exchange and several others are contained in one of a series of "Diary Poems" that Spender wrote in the sixties and included in his published journals.[17]

One evening in 1971 Auden and Spender had a public discussion at the ICA (Institute of Contemporary Arts) in London. The two poets disagreed on whether poets can affect the world. Spender said yes, Auden no. On the dot of 9:30—his bedtime—Auden stomped off the stage, leaving an embarrassed and sheepish Spender to follow him. Spender's passivity in the face of Auden's behaviour sometimes masked a certain anger. In 1971 Spender was asked by Jason Epstein to contribute a poem to a Festschrift for Auden's sixty-fifth birthday. When it became evident that Auden himself knew of the Festschrift and expected a poem, he resisted, resenting having been called upon to act like an attendant at court.[18]

In a light tone Spender suggested to the Lowells that he thought he could begin getting ready for his last years by rudely saying whatever he felt like saying, thus practising the style that Auden had made his own for so long.[19] He did not give in to the temptation often, except perhaps in the very witty letters he wrote his friends and in a certain snideness that prevails in his journals when he discusses the remarks of American students. He reports with glee that one such student raised her hand and asked concerning Eliot's "Prufrock" lines about "ragged claws" and "silent seas," "Don't they mean that he'd like-ter-have-been a lobster and just grab her?"[20]

Spender's great achievement of the late sixties—a celebration, in a sense, of his sixtieth birthday—was the collection of poems entitled *The Generous Days*, first published in a limited edition by David Godine (1969) and then by Faber and Faber and Random House (1971). The theme of this collection is memory—the memory of old and in many cases dead friends. Spender himself noted the "mood of elegiac reminiscence" in the poems.[21] To support the theme, he included the earlier "One More New Botched Beginning," a poem that looks back to late friends Maurice Merleau-Ponty, Louis MacNeice, and Bernard Spencer. There are twenty-one new poems in *Generous Days*. Sanford Sternlicht suggests that the first one, "If It Were Not," "depicts a brooding attitude toward the passing of time" and is "a sharp and poignant reminder of mortality."[22] "V.W. (1941)" is a eulogy for Virginia Woolf. Other poems remember late friends Peter Watson and Herbert Read. Old living friends honoured include Henry Moore, John Lehmann, and especially W. H. Auden in "To W. H. Auden on His Sixtieth Birthday." Auden in the early days had "lobbed squids/Into my solemn dream," that is, had undermined Spender's essential romanticism, but had provided valuable lessons in concreteness.

The new poems, perhaps especially the title poem, reveal a poet much surer of his craft than the poet of earlier collections, one who has accepted and made his own the marriage of the romanticism that comes naturally to him and the almost stark proselike manner that he owes to his modernist mentors—particularly Eliot and Auden. In his poetry Spender had long sought to close the gaps between the public and the private, between poetry and life, between the body and the spirit. In *The Generous Days* he does so with a new efficiency. Doris Eder notices a "new leanness . . . compressing more meaning into smaller compass."[23] The title poem begins:

His are the generous days that balance
Soul and body. Should he hear the trumpet
Shout justice from a sky of ice
—Lightning through the marrow—
At once one with that cause, he'd throw
Himself across some far, sad parapet—
Soul fly up from body's sacrifice,
Immolated in the summons.

Several of the poems in *The Generous Days* reflect on family life. The most famous of these, "Boy, Cat, Canary," is a memory of a day during his son Matthew's childhood:

Our whistling son called his canary Hector.
"Why?" I asked. "Because I had always about me
More of Hector with his glittering helmet than
Achilles with his triple-thewed shield." He let Hector
Out of his cage, fly up to the ceiling, perch on his chair, hop
Onto his table where the sword lay bright among books
While he sat in his yellow jersey, doing his homework.
Once, hearing a shout, I entered his room, saw what carnage:
The Siamese cat had worked his tigerish scene.
Hector lay on the floor of his door-open cage
Wings still fluttering, flattened against the sand.
Parallel, horizontal on the rug, the boy lay
Mouth biting against it, fists hammering boards.
"Tomorrow, let him forget," I prayed. "Let him not see
What I see in this room of miniature Iliad—
The golden whistling howled down by the dark."

Spender felt that *The Generous Days* was one of his best efforts and was hurt by the lack of critical recognition for it. The lack was in part redeemed in 1971 by the award of the Queen's Gold Medal for Poetry.

In the fall of 1970, with the help of Frank Kermode, Spender was given a professorship at University College, London, a position he held until 1975. He found a full-time teaching job, as opposed to the visiting professorships to which he was accustomed, difficult and frequently tedious. But the job in London meant he would not need to travel as frequently to America.

The early seventies brought the annual Auden visits in the summer, other visits from American friends such as the Lowells and the Jason Epsteins, the trips to Maussane and to Italy to stay with Matthew's family—the Spenders had been there for granddaughter Saskia's birth in January 1970—a new interest, the journal *Index on Censorship*, an annual New Year's visit to the Rothschilds in Mouton, and the death of Ezra Pound.

In April of 1972 Spender attended a conference on B. F. Skinner at Yale. He referred to Skinner as a "ridiculous behaviourist," resented what he saw as a waste of time at the conference, and returned to be faced with the death of one of his oldest friends and colleagues, the poet laureate, Cecil Day-Lewis. In spite of his grief, Spender immediately began lobbying to have Auden made laureate.[24] And once again, as in 1968 when Day-Lewis had been appointed to the position, there were rumours that Spender would himself be named. Instead, the queen named Sir John Betjeman.

The summer of 1972 brought a new friendship. The Russian poet Joseph Brodsky arrived in London for the Poetry International Festival on his way to the United States. He arrived from Vienna with Wystan Auden and, like Auden, he stayed with the Spenders. Spender had watched Brodsky's situation, which had included imprisonment, and had worked through PEN to improve it. He had once sent him various gifts through a mutual friend, Anna Akhmatova, when she had been in England to receive an Oxford honorary degree in 1965. In spite of the language barrier, Brodsky and Spender got along well. Brodsky liked Spender's "gentle tentativeness," his "awareness," which Brodsky had, too, "of the provisional, faintly absurd nature of any reality at hand." Auden and the Spenders "mothered" Brodsky during his first days in England. Auden, impatiently, tried to teach him the public phone system; Spender, much more patiently but no more successfully, attempted to explain the underground. In the end, Natasha drove him wherever he needed to go. The Spenders took him to lunch at the Garrick Club with Angus Wilson and Cyril Connolly and to a session of the House of Commons. These days were the beginning of a twenty-three-year friendship.[25]

Nineteen seventy-three was a year of great loss. Old friend Elizabeth Bowen died and so did Spender's longtime confidant William Plomer. Plomer's absence, especially, left a tremendous gap in Spender's life. But a still more difficult gap was that left by the death of W. H. Auden. In October of 1972 Auden had returned to England and made arrangements for what was to be a permanent residency at Christ Church, Oxford. By February of 1973 he had settled there, and Spender had looked forward to spending much more time with him. The relationship with Auden had always been coloured by the combination of Auden's arbitrariness and Spender's passivity in his presence, but the two men had preserved a genuine love for each other that had survived minor wounds and disagreements. Joseph Brodsky later recalled a photograph taken at a party. Spender had said something to Auden that made him laugh. On Spender's face is a "detectable tenderness" and Auden,

> hands in his pockets, is immensely cheered. Their eyes meet; at this juncture, they have known each other for more than forty years, and they are happy in each other's company.[26]

On September 28 the Spenders had been driving to London from Maussane, stopping in Normandy to buy food for a dinner party. They had arrived in London to the news of Auden's death. The dinner party was cancelled and in a few days Spender was at Auden's grave in Kirchstetten, Austria. He would capture that moment later in the sonnet that begins the longer poem entitled "Auden's Funeral," one that echoes Auden's elegy for Yeats.

> *One among friends who stood above your grave*
> *I cast a clod of earth from those heaped there*
> *Down on the great brass-handled coffin lid.*

> *It rattled on the oak like a door knocker*
> *And at that sound I saw your face beneath*
> *Wedged in an oblong shadow under ground*
> *Flesh creased, eyes shut, jaw jutting*
> *And on the mouth a grin: triumph of one*
> *Who has escaped from life-long colleagues roaring*
> *For him to join their throng. He's still half with us*
> *Conniving slyly, yet he knows he's gone*
> *Into that cellar where they'll never find him,*
> *Happy to be alone, his last work done,*
> *Word freed from world, into a different wood.*

On October 27 Spender delivered a memorial address on his oldest friend at Christ Church, Oxford. In a note to E. R. Dodds on November 15 he suggested that Auden's wish that his correspondence be destroyed should be ignored in the interest of literary history. In death as in life, Auden was not above some silliness. On December 7 he delivered memorial remarks at the American Academy. From Loudoun Road in January, again echoing Auden's elegy for Yeats, he wrote to Auden's close friend Hannah Arendt that Auden's death had left a wintry England.[27]

Still, Spender was only sixty-four and life held many promises. *Love-Hate Relations,* dedicated to Isherwood and Don Bacardy, appeared in 1974, and Spender was hard at work on a book for Frank Kermode's Modern Masters Series and Viking on T. S. Eliot, a book that would be published in 1975 and would provide a concise and perceptive overview of his mentor's work. There was the seventieth birthday dinner given by Spender friends Christopher and Elizabeth Glenconner for Cyril Connolly at the Savoy, and a reading with Robert Lowell, Roy Fuller, and I. A. Richards for Allen Tate's seventy-fifth birthday at the Mermaid Theatre.

But death continued to dominate life. On November 29 Cyril Connolly died. There was a funeral on December 2, and at a service on the twentieth Spender took on the now familiar role of delivering the memorial address. For Spender the death of Connolly marked the end of what he thought of as the "*Horizon* era."

For the Christmas holidays the Spenders joined Lord and Lady Noel Annan, Stuart Hampshire, and the Berlins for a trip to Israel. The group travelled in and around Jerusalem, seeing Nazareth, the Yad va-Shem Memorial, Sodom, the Herodium, the Islamic (Mayer) Museum, Rebekah's well, and other sites. They visited Mayor Teddy Kollek, the Armenian archbishop, President Katzir, and the poet Abbay Körner. Spender's position was always pro-Israel, but he felt that perhaps there was "too much of the Wailing Wall about Israel . . . the Holocaust is the negative pole of the positive which is Israel."[28] One of the highlights of the trip was Christmas midnight mass at the Church of the Nativity. Always wary of religion, Spender attended perhaps partly with Auden in mind. He noticed several American hippies, and when he saw them staring at the stations of the cross "with a look of 'Wow!'" he was amused by the thought that they were "contemplating perhaps their own crucifixion as a fabulous last exit."[29]

Auden's longtime companion, Chester Kallman, died in January. Spender was angered by the fact that because Chester had died intestate, Auden's papers would go to his family rather than to Auden's.

On a day in February, during a luncheon party Anne Fleming gave for politicians Roy Jenkins and Paul Channon, the conversation turned to still another death, that of old Oxford friend Dick Crossman, and Spender's mind drifted to the house party years before during which he and Crossman had had a minor "affair." He had been considering the publication of his own journals, and he wondered later whether the suicide of Crossman's only son had resulted in any way from the publication of the Crossman journals.[30]

Early in March the Spenders lunched with Mary McCarthy at the Ritz. After lunch Spender read the Paul Theroux review in the *New Statesman and Nation* of McCarthy's reports on Vietnam and was disturbed to discover that Theroux thought it was "creepy" of Spender to worry about the fare to Hanoi after promising McCarthy to join a group of celebrities who were travelling there to protest Nixon's bombing policy. The fact is, he wrote in his journals, he did not have the necessary money.[31] Negative statements in the press were always extremely bothersome to Spender. One day while shaving he had a thought of which he was "ashamed" but which was, nevertheless, revealing. He realized that he found "confirmation of my 'identity' by reading my name in the news-papers." He envied people who considered publicity "vulgar and obscene."[32]

By mid-March Spender was travelling again. He went to Paris to attend meetings on what many saw as UNESCO's unfair treatment of Israel. While in Paris he also visited David Hockney's studio. He liked Hockney but thought his criticism of the moderns was somehow unre-lated to the essence of the painter's own art.

The end of March and early April found Spender doing a university lecture tour and a book tour for *Love-Hate Relations*—in Newfoundland, New Hampshire, Little Rock, Memphis, and New Orleans, and at Har-vard and Yale. Such trips had become difficult for him, but this time he fell in love with the originality and sensuality of New Orleans. The American trip was described in journals, which Spender published as part of a "Notebook" series in Alan Ross's (formerly John Lehmann's) *London Magazine*.[33]

During stops in New York, Spender met with friends, saw the Francis Bacon show at the Metropolitan Museum, and was saddened by an inadvertent meeting with Robert Lowell on the street. Lowell had recently had one of his breakdowns and was accompanied by nurses. Spender asked him whether it was true that he had taken an overdose of pills. Lowell said it was true but that he would soon be better.[34] Spender was not sure Lowell had recognized him.

While in New York he decided to resign from his position at Univer-sity College, London, and it was with a feeling of relief that he travelled with Matthew to Venice in June and July. The trip is described in an issue of *London Magazine*, on the cover of which there is a photograph of Tom Driberg, Cyril Connolly, and Spender.[35]

The Venice trip was a chance, as Spender wrote in his journals, to recapture "past time" with Matthew. For many years he had been pre-occupied with his writing, his editing, and his teaching jobs, and Matthew had been primarily concerned with his own young family and with his work. The Venice trip was the first time in some years that the father and son had had extended time alone together. In his journal

Spender describes a time of "joyous affection"—Matthew pushing his father up the steeper bridges, their being taken to a palazzo late one evening by a couple whose intentions were dubious and laughing as they escaped, their conversations about the art in various churches and museums. What Spender liked most about this and later trips with Matthew was the reversal of earlier roles. Matthew was now taking care of him.

Spender also enjoyed discussing cubism and surrealism with Peggy Guggenheim at her palazzo, and he was amused to meet one of his American students in Harry's Bar. The student had once told Spender that his dream in life was to be supported by a rich man. Now he could announce that his dream had come true.

In Maussane that summer the Spenders were joined, as they often were, by their friends the Bayleys—John Bayley and author Iris Murdoch. The two couples visited art historian and former Communist Douglas Cooper for lunch in his castle one day and were joined by Renée Laporte, who had written a book about being seduced by Picasso when she was seventeen.[36] Other visitors at St. Jerôme were Philippe de Rothschild and Lord and Lady Annan, and Lizzie came for part of the summer. Spender's reading project that summer was Proust.

In the fall there was another American lecture tour and a semester at the University of Connecticut. In New York Spender met up with Matthew and Maro and played with his baby granddaughter Cosima, "the most smiling contented little starlet."[37] He consulted by phone in late November with Christopher Isherwood about the National Portrait Gallery's plans to hold an exhibition on writers of the thirties, featuring Auden, MacNeice, Isherwood, Day-Lewis, and Spender. Both men felt that the list should be expanded to include others. During his tour, Spender read Montgomery Hyde's biography of Oscar Wilde and was particularly interested in Hyde's picture of Wilde as a fighter for "the cause of a persecuted minority." Like Spender in his youth, Wilde stressed the contrast between the forbidden homosexual world and the "boredom" of the "respectable" world.[38]

At the end of December the Spenders went to Spain for a two-week holiday. While there, Spender wrote a note about marriage in his journal. Marriage was "an agreement—or conspiracy—between two people to treat each other as having the right to be loved absolutely." If that understanding exists, he suggested, aspects of the relationship such as sex and children become "secondary." Thus, it is quite possible for same-sex marriages or marriages without children or even sex to be "immensely binding."[39]

Soon after arriving home, Spender visited Robert Lowell, who was now living in London and was ill with flu. Lowell seemed somewhat unbalanced and told his visitor he was rewriting "I Think Continually" for him. He was changing the first line to "I *would* think continually of those who are truly great" because it was impossible to think of the great continually "though one might wish to do so."[40]

In America in March for a term at the University of Connecticut and a series of lectures elsewhere, Spender learned that Pauline Rothschild had recently died. He did his best to console Philippe, who was also in America. The deaths of close friends were becoming almost common-place. He discussed aging with the painter Robert Motherwell. Both men regretted the deterioration of their bodies. Spender felt that he could have had much more fun with a young body in the 1970s than he had had with his in the 1930s.[41]

Someone told Spender a story about how Auden had once arrived at a faculty party given in his honour, surveyed the situation, and said, "Oh— Well, I have to go to bed. Goodnight."[42] Spender and Edward Mendelson had planned to do a biography of Auden but had decided in the spring of 1976 to drop the idea. There was a reluctance on the part of both men to delve into Auden's personal life, and, as Spender wrote to their potential publisher, Jason Epstein at Random House, he felt that absorbing him-self in Auden would hinder his own creative work.[43] In 1975 a collection of tributes, *W. H. Auden: A Tribute,* had been edited by Spender and pub-lished by Weidenfeld and Nicolson. It was a book that owed its existence to Spender's energetic pursuit of essays by John Betjeman, William Cold-stream, Cyril Connolly, Stuart Hampshire, Hannah Arendt, Lincoln Kirstein, Nicholas Nabokov, Chester Kallman, Joseph Brodsky, Charles Rosen, Christopher Isherwood, Ursula Niebuhr, and many others. It included an introduction by Spender, as well as a diary poem, "Auden in Milwaukee."

In place of the Auden biography, Spender gave Random House his collection of journals and commentaries called *The Thirties and After*. This work, which would be published in 1978, included journals, previously published essays on Yeats, Wyndham Lewis, Louis Aragon, Auden, and Isherwood, and reminiscences about Eliot, Connolly, and others. There were a few memory poems—on MacNeice, on Connolly, and on Stravinsky, for example. In "Late Stravinsky Listening to Late Beethoven," Spender remembers Stravinsky, who had died in 1971, and by picturing him listening to Beethoven, brings together his own divergent poetic inspirations, modernism and romanticism.

> *I see you on your bed under the ceiling*
> *Weightless as a feather, happiness*
> *Glistening through pain. You have become*
> *Purged of every self but your transparent*
> *Intelligence, through which the music turns*
> *In furious wheels. With delectation*
> *You watch Beethoven rage, hammer,*
> *Crash plucked strings, escape*
> *On wings configuring horizons: mock at*
> *The discords of his head that were*
> *The shouting bars of deafness.*

The Thirties and After ends with Spender's moving 1973 Christ Church memorial address on Auden—a "poet of an unanticipated kind—a different race from ourselves—and also a diagnostician of literary, social and individual psychosomatic situations . . . a clinical-minded oracle . . . His only performance was himself."[44]

In May Spender took up residency for several weeks at the University of Florida in Gainesville, and there he met and fell in love with a twenty-year-old ornithology student referred to in his journals simply as "B." "B" was intelligent, affectionate, and reasonable about the limited possibilities of a relationship with a man approaching his late sixties who was committed to his marriage. Much later, in the context of an interview on the subject of Henry James's *The Pupil*—a story about a complex relationship between a tutor and his much younger student—Spender said that at first he had seen "B" as someone who sought a father or a mother in a lover and who was unsettled about his homosexuality. When "B" said on one occasion, "I love you more than you love me," Spender was both surprised and touched. At one point much later, Spender spoke of the friendship with "B" as "the most extraordinary relationship of my life," by which he clearly meant his homosexual life.[45] It was extraordinary because of the age difference, because it was only mildly physical, and because each expected so little from the other during the months and sometimes years of necessary separation. Spender had no intention of ending his marriage for "B," and "B" eventually had other lovers, but the two men remained extremely close, communicated regularly, and saw each other whenever possible until "B"'s early death in 1991. Spender was happier at Gainesville than at most of his other American posts, partly, it is true, because of the intellectual companionship of Richard Eberhart and Robert Dana, who also taught there, but mostly because of "B."

For some time Spender had been attempting to rework his verse drama *Trial of a Judge*, and during the summer of 1976 at Maussane, this was his primary project. In connection with the project he gave a great deal of thought to other modern writers of poetic drama, particularly Eliot, Samuel Beckett, and Harold Pinter. Eliot's "achievement in 'putting poetry on the stage' is remarkable," Spender felt, but flawed by his attempt to make his plays palatable to West End audiences. Beckett's use of "prose rhythms" based on characters who "speak rhythmically" is more successful in the sense that his "poetry comes out of the truth of his characters in their situations." The same could be said of Pinter.[46] But for Spender as a dramatist, the power and concreteness of these great playwrights seemed frustratingly elusive.

Once again in the fall, Spender's writing was interrupted by American university positions. He spent time at Cornell College and Grinnell College, both in Iowa, and then did a Southern tour, which included a happy visit with "B" in Florida.

Nineteen seventy-seven and 1978 saw Spender in Maussane a great deal working on his play, now called *The Corporal*, a memory play of sorts, since the new main character was based on Georg, a boy lover of the Weimar days. David Hockney visited during the summer and so did the Bayleys. In September of 1977 he and Natasha travelled as the guests of PEN (Spender had served a term as president of the English branch of PEN) to Seoul, South Korea, and then went on to Japan, where they visited the Zen temples of Kyoto. On the way home they stopped in Tehran, and toured Isfahan and Persepolis with their friend Cyrus Ghani.

The highlights of 1978 were the publication of *The Thirties and After* and a small book entitled *Recent Poems*. *Recent Poems* contains four works, all of which are reminiscences. The most important of the poems is "Late Stravinsky Listening to Late Beethoven," dedicated to Sacheverell Sitwell, who had died recently and who in the poem is implicitly identified with the dying Stravinsky. Old friends Edith and Osbert Sitwell had died in 1964 and 1969, respectively.

Spender's seventieth year, 1979, was particularly busy. It was a year during which, even as he travelled to and from various American universities, he was preoccupied with the process of aging. He visited Allen Tate in the hospital only days before Tate's death. They talked about poetry and about Natasha. Feeling uneasy and worrying about tiring his friend, Spender left after fifteen minutes. Then he began to think about what his own death would mean to his friends. He thought of how important it would be to have friends present at the end, even if their presence were tiring or even if they were to say nothing. He thought of how "precious it is to see a loved face, let one's eyes travel over it, to read the things the voice has left unsaid."[47]

On the lighter side of the thoughts about aging was the memory of an incident that had occurred in London a few days before he had left in January for an appointment at Vanderbilt University. Walking home from the opera late at night, thinking no one was nearby, he had farted loudly and was amused to hear a group of young people cheering. As it was dark, he was not particularly embarrassed but wondered if he would have been embarrassed had the young people realized who he was.[48]

In his journals Spender wrote about himself and his contemporaries as a "crew of voyagers" who were one by one falling "abruptly off precipices" in the high territories of life. Those who continued to live still attended parties and did their work ignoring the obvious physical changes, the "most obvious" of which was the "loss of memory."[49] People at Vanderbilt and at Houston, where he gave an address, noticed Spender's increased tendency to appear preoccupied and forgetful.[50] This was in part because he was lonely, with no social life, and uncomfortably housed in a Holiday Inn during his first days in Nashville. But Spender himself noticed a difference in his thought processes. He found, for instance, that he could write a draft of something, forget he had written it, write a new draft on the same subject, and only later realize that he had already written it.[51]

Yet when he was with "B," for example, he was happy and alert. In February he was able to get away to Gainesville and to stay with "B" in his trailer. The two friends—one in his twenties, one now nearly seventy—together after a long separation "in meeting again . . . harvested every moment of affection we had ever had together."[52]

On February 28 Spender's seventieth birthday was celebrated with a party at the Royal College of Art in London. Philippe de Rothschild provided the wine, there was a trumpet fanfare, and there were many congratulations from a guest list of over one hundred friends and relatives that included, among many others, the Spender family, Angus Wilson and his friend Tony Bower, the Glenconners, the earl and countess of Snowdon, Anne Fleming and Pat Trevor-Roper, Lucian Freud, the John Pipers, Isaiah Berlin, and William Coldstream.[53]

Spender returned to America in March. He was interviewed on the *Dick Cavett Show*, in preparation for which he gave some thought to his religious views, having been told he would be questioned about them. He decided that he had no religious views, that he certainly could not subscribe to any official or even private religion. He could simply say that Christianity was a "poetic myth . . . which expresses very important truths about life," the primary one being that "humanity can be served by love."[54] With his friend the poet Bill Mazzocco, he discussed what they saw as the foolishness of Auden's belief that homosexuality was a sin.[55]

On his way back to Nashville Spender visited his friend Reynolds Price, now in a proper house with a burglar alarm. He remembered that many years before he had spent a month with Price in a trailer out in a field.[56] He felt a continuing affection for Price and was happy staying with him.[57]

Another stop was New Orleans, where, joined by "B," he met up with Allen Ginsberg and Peter Orlovsky. Ginsberg told Spender that one evening when he had tried to sing for Auden, Auden had begged him to stop. He then took out his keyboard harmonium and sang "Little Lamb Who Made Thee" to a tune he had made up. Spender was both more amused and more tolerant than Auden. He genuinely enjoyed Ginsberg's company and a rather wild day during which Ginsberg and Orlovsky introduced him and "B" to several of their eccentric New Orleans friends.

At Vanderbilt in late March there was a literary conference of poets and scholars, featuring Spender, Helen Vendler, Robert Pinsky, Donald Davie, and Wallace Stegner. Spender was impressed by Vendler who looked like a "governess in a Russian play." He immediately longed "to appear the good boy to her" and "to confess all my sins."[58]

Natasha arrived on April 1 for a month's visit, and Spender was relieved to see her, having felt, until she improved the apartment, "ill-housed and neglected" in Nashville. But he spoiled the visit somewhat by making obvious his feelings for "B."[59] He felt great guilt about this, but in May, after Natasha's departure, he spent another weekend with "B" in Gainesville, days that were "without a shadow in them."[60] In the sections of the journals left out of the published works but given later to "B," and then deposited in the Bancroft Library, Spender talks freely of the depth of this "compulsive relationship" and how the fact that he and "B" had such short times together made the time they did have "miraculous," reflecting, in a sense, the miracle of love between a seventy-year-old and a twenty-two-year-old.

In a lecture at the Sorbonne in late May Spender came to the conclusion that true "modernism and everything one means by symbolism" had ended in the thirties.[61] Soon after that lecture the Spenders visited Henry Moore and his Russian wife, Irina. Spender had come to know Moore in

Hampstead in the early thirties, often in the company of Herbert Read, Edwin Muir, Ben Nicolson, Barbara Hepworth, and Geoffrey Grigson. Moore was now eighty and with his seemingly boundless energy was an inspiration for the seventy-year-old Spender. He also shared Spender's views on modernism and romanticism. In a memorial address for Moore he would give in 1986 at Westminster Abbey, Spender would discuss the sculptor's need, even as he attempted to create an abstract form, to maintain a reference to something "beyond itself." His work, as Moore himself said, "always ended up looking like something." Moore felt, wrote Spender, that "purist movements" always resulted in unnecessary fragmentation, that "all good art contains both classical and romantic elements, order and surprise, intellect and imagination, conscious and unconscious."[62]

After the Moore visit, the Spenders attended the Aldeburgh Festival in honour of Benjamin Britten, one of the many dead modernist "crew of voyagers." At a party given by Lord and Lady Gladwyn, Spender found himself next to Diana Cooper, who bemoaned the fact that she was aging, but who, like Spender, loved to gossip about scandal and sex. She told an amusing story about how, at a recent party in celebration of philanthropist Sir Robert Mayer's one hundredth birthday, she had been approached by a woman who began talking with her. Not being able to see well, she had not at first recognized the woman as the queen and had apologized by saying, "I'm so sorry I didn't recognize you, ma'am. But you see I don't recognize you when you're not wearing your crown." The queen rose to the joke. "I thought it was Sir Robert Mayer's evening," she said, "so I didn't put it on."[63]

During the late summer in Maussane, Spender worked on *The Corporal*. Peggy Ashcroft and others read it and liked it, but there seemed to be little enthusiasm either for publication or production, and, characteristically, Spender began to doubt his own ability.[64] Besides, the heat in Maussane was unbearable, so, after the annual Bayley visit, the Spenders left for various mountain villages and Mouton and eventually travelled to Corfu to visit the Glenconners. Spender was pleased when Harold Pinter and Antonia Fraser came to lunch there one day. He was able to discuss his play with Pinter, whom he admired and liked, and who made various suggestions about making "language the function of (1) situation, (2) character, (3) ideas."[65]

The final outing of the summer was to the Lake District, including a memory-filled pilgrimage to Skelgill Farm, where Spender had first been awakened to the power of Wordsworth. On returning home Spender realized that excessive travel had "disoriented" him.[66] Yet in September he met Matthew in Venice, where the theme of their tour was to be places important to Byron and Shelley. As always, Spender enjoyed being with his son, who looked remarkably like a younger version of himself. The two shared an interest in art particularly. There were also, as always, the opportunities to meet interesting people— Charlotte Bonham Carter, Sir Ashley Clarke, Pound's mistress, Olga Rudge, and Freya Stark at a restaurant in Asolo on the way back to Matthew's home in Avane near Siena. And in Avane there were Matthew's wife, Maro, and the much-loved Saskia and Cosima, who rushed out at the sound of the car to greet their father and grandfather.

The seemingly endless round of American teaching and lecture engagements continued in the fall. Hollins College, Bates College, the University of Maine, and Boston College were among the 1979 stops. More than on any other American trip, Spender was plagued on this one by depression and loneliness. He was not feeling well and had a series of medical tests to look forward to on his return to London. He felt that the three years of work on *The Corporal* might have been a waste of time, like all of the time over the years he had spent on literary criticism and journalism. A young interviewer at Hollins told him her friends all said that poetry, in any case, was "passé," and Spender sometimes felt that he agreed. Yet, when he read William Carlos Williams, for instance, as he did on this trip, he wondered why anyone read anything other than poetry, and he felt panic at the thought that he had so little time left to write poems of his own. He wondered why he found it so difficult to write poetry, and decided it was in part at least because of a lack of recognition on the part of critics. He could not "convince myself that my poetry gives pleasure to anyone." Furthermore, it was difficult being what he thought of as a "minor poet." In the classroom he began to feel that students were "against me." Perhaps he was really more like his father than he had always thought—a man characterized by "incomplete activities enclosed by optimistic rhetoric," a journalist who had not studied his subjects thoroughly enough. In fact, perhaps he was a lesser man than his father; "what makes me different from him is my self-distrust." Spender was reading Virginia Woolf's letters at the time of these ramblings. In a prayer of sorts, he called on her to "help me in my old age not to be a bore. . . . I'm struggling at the end to get out of the valley of hectoring youth, journalistic middle age, imposture, money making, public relations, bad writing, mental confusion."[67]

It was a relief to be home in November. One of the first events of the season was a lunch at the Albany given by Philippe de Rothschild for the queen mother. Other guests were Christopher Fry and Cecil Beaton. With Beaton Spender reminisced about a beautiful gardener at the Rothschilds' in Mouton. With the queen mother he discussed their memories of concerts at the National Gallery during the blitz.[68] He found her interesting because of the combination of her essential dignity and her love of history and beautiful objects.[69] At another party he would discuss the bisexuality of Harold Nicolson and Vita Sackville-West with the archbishop of Canterbury.[70] In a sense, England was more amusing than anywhere else.

In early December Spender underwent some minor radiation therapy at Royal Free Hospital and several days of tests at King Edward VII's Hospital. Although he would recover, the bout with a potentially serious illness led him back to thoughts of the past and of what he felt was a dwindling future.

Christmas in Italy with Matthew, Maro, and the grandchildren was "beautiful, touching"; and the annual New Year's visit to Mouton was restorative. But the lost voyagers were always somehow present. One night Spender dreamed about a reproachful dead friend. He awoke "with that strange feeling that the dead want one to think about them."[71] The one thing that seemed to hold out some hope for the future was the possibility of writing—even if only about the dead. While working on his elegy for Auden in October, Spender had even written in his journal, "I am going to have a final phase."[72]

11

THE FINAL PHASE

During the last fifteen years of his life, Spender was anything but inactive. He continued to travel extensively as a tourist and as a teacher. He published his collected poems and his journals, reworked an early novel, translated Greek tragedies for production, published a final book of new poems, worked for PEN and *Index on Censorship*, fought political oppression, struggled against a biographer, took legal action against a novelist he judged to be a plagiarist, and witnessed the deaths of many more of his fellow "voyagers."

The final phase began with a blow. On a rainy evening in January 1980, Spender was "running" to buy some food for a guest who had unexpectedly arrived at Loudoun Road. He slipped and fell, tearing the ligaments in both knees. Once again in the Royal Free Hospital, he became depressed. Sometimes he found himself crying. Contemplating old age and decline, he had a vision of his life's experience as a "succession of botched beginnings" and "few real achievements." Once again he felt that he had wasted his talents by writing reviews and articles rather than poetry, by constantly seeking pleasure, by passively accepting the opinions of others without real regard for their merit in the context of his

own aesthetic, political, and personal values. He thought of Auden suggesting that a sign from somewhere was often necessary to spur one on to
follow one's true path. He hoped the fall might, at best, be such a sign
and that it was not too late to find the path.[1]

Although the hospital stay was a time for negative thoughts, made
worse by the deaths while he was still there of Renée Hampshire and
Michael Astor, it was also a time to appreciate the loyalty of living
friends. The flow of hospital visitors was constant: Francis Bacon, Stuart
Hampshire, Isaiah Berlin, Peggy Ashcroft, Clifford Curzon, Rosamond
Lehmann Philipps, Juliette Huxley, and many others came frequently.
Most of all, Spender appreciated the presence of his family. Natasha was,
as always, a strong and encouraging source of love and support, Lizzie
brought things she had cooked, brother Humphrey brought his concern,
and Matthew came from Italy for a week and stayed for hours with his
father each day. Matthew's loyalty "nearly broke [his] heart." When
Spender asked his son if there were not other people he might like to see
in London, Matthew said, "No, I just want to be with you."[2]

If the accident was a sign that he should devote the few years left
to poetry, it did not prevent Spender from leaving the hospital in a
wheelchair in mid-April to keep a teaching engagement in Louisville,
Kentucky. As 1980 in America had been proclaimed "Year of the Dis-
abled," the wheelchair seemed appropriate. People noticed, however,
that the injury had aged him and that he seemed more disoriented than
ever. At a conference in Nashville he thought he was in Houston,[3] and
he constantly misplaced important papers and confused dates.

Christopher Isherwood and Don Bacardy came for dinner at
Loudoun Road in late June. Spender was "touched" by the apparent
depth of their relationship. When Isherwood talked, "Don's eyes are
never off him."[4] The Isherwood-Spender relationship had without
much difficulty survived basic differences about religion and other
matters. Spender essentially agreed with Auden's private remark that
Isherwood's Eastern mysticism was "mumbo jumbo," and several somewhat defensive and apologetic reviews he wrote of his friend's work
were irritating to both Isherwood and Bacardy. The most recent was

"My Guru and His Disciple," which would appear in the *New York Review of Books*. Isherwood had a principle that one should only review the work of a friend if one liked it almost unconditionally. Spender had never accepted this principle and had often angered or hurt friends with his reviews of their works. Whatever their differences, however, there was genuine deep affection between Isherwood and Spender that had its roots in Spender's undergraduate days, and most recently both had co-operated in the publication of *Letters to Christopher: Stephen Spender's Letters to Christopher Isherwood, 1929–1939*, edited by Lee Bartlett (1980).

After three weeks in Maussane, Spender was filmed for an introduction to *The Winter's Tale* in Salisbury, and then he and Natasha left again for America, along with Margaret Drabble—this time for a nostalgic return to Santa Fe and the Lawrence shrine and ranch at San Cristóbal, near Taos, for a Lawrence festival. The ranch, which had given Spender so much pleasure some thirty-two years before, had changed so that it was "scarcely recognizable," and the dancing of "white-attired sylphs" before the shrine and the reciting of Lawrence's poems as the rain poured down created an absurd atmosphere that Spender thought would have amused Frieda and given Brett "malicious pleasure."[5]

A brief lecture trip to Maine was followed by a visit with Muriel and Joe Buttinger in Pennington.[6] This was an important time, as Muriel wanted to have a significant conversation with Spender. Understanding this, Margaret and Natasha took Joe, who was suffering from Alzheimer's, for a drive while Muriel and Stephen talked. The conversation was centred on Muriel's questions about Stephen's life and work. Was he satisfied and happy? The questions, coming from one of Spender's closest friends, a woman he had loved and had once hoped to marry, called for something like the conclusion of an autobiography. Spender said that he thought there were two kinds of people among his friends—those who courted fame, love, and money and those who simply enjoyed what life had to offer. Both of these types were certainly present in Spender. He said to Muriel that he knew he had failed in many ways, but that he was luckier than most people, that he "loved life and could say [he] was happy."[7]

In Brussels later in the summer, the Spenders visited the Musée des Beaux-Arts. Spender went immediately to look at Brueghel's *Landscape with the Fall of Icarus*, the source for Auden's poem "Musée des Beaux Arts." He concluded that as "wonderful" as the poem was, it "misinterprets" the painting, in which Icarus is "only an accent. . . . Wystan created a new work of art from his immediate impression of another work of art."[8]

Auden, in fact, continued to be an important figure in Spender's final phase. The poem "Auden's Funeral" (see chapter 10) might well be the major work of that phase. By the summer of 1980 Spender had been working on the poem for some seven years. And he was trying his best to finish an essay on Auden for the use of Edward Mendelson. In a journal entry on September 10, he noted the difficulty he was experiencing in capturing the meaning to him of Auden's absence. He remembered Chester Kallman's putting Wagner's "Funeral March for Siegfried" on the record player after the burial and feeling that through the music Auden's spirit was somehow "carried out." He thought of "the loss of one to us who made his life an instrument for expressing experiences in language, where each of us loses his loneliness, and becomes part of a spiritual community."[9]

That summer Spender read a great deal. In fact, in the late years he found he had more time for reading for pleasure than he had had earlier. This pleased him a great deal and fell into his nostalgic mood. Reading, he felt, was the "passive, receptive side of civilization without which the active and creative would be meaningless." It was the "immortal spirit of the dead realized within the bodies of the living." Reading, like writing, painting, and composing, was "sacramental."[10]

In his reactions to books, however, he often sounded more Auden-esque than sacramental. Iris Murdoch's *Nuns and Soldiers*, which had been inspired by visits to Maussane and was dedicated to the Spenders, was enjoyable but marred by a tendency to exaggerate and to treat characters "as pieces in a game, invented by herself." Edmund Wilson's *Thirties Journals* were "informative, intelligent," but "external . . . like an account of life in a factory." He liked reading Thornton Wilder's *The*

Ides of March because he was interested in things Roman, but after a while he became bored by Wilder, "who is a soft old tabby cat. . . ." But at least Wilder served as a catalyst to make him reread all of Catullus, a "whizz-kid of poetry."[11]

In the fall Spender returned still again to the lecture-reading circuit. There was a reading with Laurie Lee and Patrick Kavanagh in London, and a university lecture tour that took him to Toronto, upstate New York, and Tulsa, Oklahoma, where he stayed with David Plante and met Germaine Greer, "an overgrown schoolgirl."[12] In New York he dined with Stuart Hampshire, attended a concert of the late Beethoven sonatas played "with ice-cold precision" by Charles Rosen, and paid a call on Vera Stravinsky, whose obvious ill health and senility literally made him cry. It was another ending. He thought of Stravinsky with Vera at his side "wheeled off to join the other festive princes of the art of music—Liszt, Wagner, Mozart."[13]

In his journals he describes a nightmarish day during which the flight he was scheduled to take to New York City from Oneonta, New York, was cancelled because of bad weather.[14] As his appointments in the city included the opening of an exhibition, a Rosamund Russell lecture at the Met, and especially a dinner party arranged by his old friend John Russell with Jacqueline Kennedy Onassis and her daughter, Caroline, he was anxious to get there. After two outrageously expensive taxi rides of several hundred miles, including a one-hundred-mile detour to retrieve his wallet, which he had left in a diner, Spender arrived in New York in time for the lecture and the dinner. Jackie Onassis, whom he had met in 1959, was "beautiful like some piece of sculpture," and she "seemed to want to talk seriously."[15]

Spender's final stop on the American tour was Los Angeles, where Christopher Isherwood and Don Bacardy gave him a dinner. Other guests were David Hockney, Gore Vidal, Edward Albee, friend "B," and daughter, Lizzie. Spender was delighted to find Lizzie happy. In his journals he had written of his worries about her, noting that one's child's unhappiness was more than one could bear.[16]

Nineteen eighty came to an end with dinner parties for Alan Pryce-Jones, Rosamond Lehmann, Claire Tomalin, and V. S. Pritchett, a visit to Cambridge to deliver some Auden-Spender papers to Lytton Strachey's friend Dadie Rylands and to dine with the Kermodes and Helen Vendler, and a banquet at New College, Oxford, as the guest of biographer Richard Ellmann and philosopher Freddie Ayer. There was also the funeral of Sonia Orwell. And one evening in December, during a visit from Matthew, the Spenders were at a restaurant where Seamus Heaney, Ted Hughes, and several other poets were eating as well. The poets sent a bottle of champagne to the Spender table, which Spender took as a particular "gesture from fellow poets." It made him anxious to write something "worthy of the attention of colleagues."[17]

But financial needs drove Spender to accept a teaching position for January through May of 1981 at the University of South Carolina at Columbia. The time there was pleasant enough but marked by a series of dreams about dead friends. After South Carolina he went with David Hockney and Hockney's assistant, Gregory Evans, to China for a little less than two months. Beginning in Hong Kong, their trip, which is recorded by Hockney's paintings and photographs and Spender's words in *China Diary*, took them to Beijing, Xian, Nanjing, Hangzhou, Waxi, Shanghai, Guilin, and Guangzhou. They visited all of the major sites and interviewed poets, students, and workers under the watchful eyes and via the translations of their government guides, Miss Li and Mr. Lin. When Spender told Paul Theroux that China was like a school, Theroux suggested that it was more "like the Boy Scouts, and Mao was the Chief Scout."[18] For Spender, going to China was strangely reminiscent of the trip Isherwood and Auden had taken there in 1938. But travelling now was difficult for him physically, and he found the rigidity of the politics and the social structure oppressive. Furthermore, being with Hockney was not always easy. The painter had "a curious indifference to any point of view other than his own,"[19] and Hockney's lifestyle was very different from Spender's. After several hectic days in Los Angeles as the guest of Hockney in April 1982, for instance, he left feeling depressed because of the seemingly constant round of people in the Hockney household. "B" suggested that for Hockney the meaningless and often unnoticed flow of people was analogous to his own parents' keeping the television on all day without necessarily watching or listening to it.

In the spring of 1982, after a visit with Matthew's family in Venice, Spender was once again in America teaching and lecturing—primarily at William and Mary. There he had the first of several painful attacks of kidney stones. The first occurred soon after he had read the negative remarks about himself in the newly published fourth volume of Virginia Woolf's *Diary*, in which he is described as a "rattle-headed . . . young man who thinks himself the greatest poet of all time." On the whole, Spender agreed now with Woolf's early assessment of him. He had been "too much of a journalist, too impressed by the broad generalizations of public reasons and considerations for things, not having at the centre a core of unassailable private values, wanting to justify myself before a court of public evaluation and success."[20] And he was still wrestling with these shortcomings. He felt that Bloomsbury—especially Virginia Woolf—was snobbish, however, in the sense that it could not, finally, tolerate people who were not Bloomsbury, whether that meant working-class outsiders or radicals such as Spender himself in the 1930s. As to Woolf's snobbishness about her own gentility, Spender could understand that, believing himself that one could justifiably appreciate fine old families just as one could enjoy old and elegant things in general.[21]

In connection with the remarks on Woolf's *Diary*, Spender, in the unpublished version of his journals, somewhat justifies them by suggesting that he was and still is in some ways too much like John Lehmann, whom he dislikes. Like Lehmann, he is too concerned with public opinion, though he is not as "cold and calculating" as Lehmann. The people he truly admires are Auden, Stravinsky, Eliot, Isherwood, Woolf, and Lawrence, who seemed to care nothing about public opinion.[22] Not long after making the journal entry, he would have lunch with Lehmann in London and make another entry.[23] Now they were two old men uncomfortable with each other. He remembered having first met Lehmann at Rosamond and Wogan Philipps's home during his Oxford years, how he had rejected Lehmann's sexual advances, and how they had, nevertheless, planned to open a publishing firm together. All of their quarrels seemed to stem from the fact that they were in some basic way "out of sympathy" with each other.

The April visit to Los Angeles and David Hockney, although "disturbing," gave Spender a chance to visit with Christopher Isherwood and Don Bacardy and with "B," who was teaching at UCLA and who now had a partner.

In London in May and June, Spender was upset by the Falklands invasion and wrote a public statement denouncing it. He visited old friends in Oxford, enjoyed watching Lizzie doing a small part in a play, participated in a conference on van Gogh and D. H. Lawrence in Rotterdam, and attended the funeral of his uncle George Schuster, who had written his autobiography at the age of ninety-nine. At a party on the tenth of June a woman asked Spender what his name was. When he told her, the woman said she had only known of one Spender, Stephen Spender, and that "he's dead, I believe."[24]

At King Edward VII's Hospital at the end of June to have his kidney stones removed, Spender remembered that both of his parents had died during operations. And even as these thoughts passed through his mind, he turned on the television to be confronted by the news of Nicholas Nabokov's death during a minor operation. He thought gratefully of the "undeserved" good care Natasha always gave him. During a flulike illness that followed the operation, he once again had despairing thoughts about having failed as a poet and as a husband.[25]

For Spender, 1983 was a year dominated by his work for *Index on Censorship*. To raise money for *Index*, of which he had been a founder, he travelled to America and gave readings in Atlanta with Joseph Brodsky and in New York with Brodsky, Derek Walcott, and John Ashbery. He also raised money at a party in Washington given by the *Atlantic Monthly* owner, Mort Zuckerman, lectured at the Library of Congress, and met with Susan Sontag, David Rieff, Richard Sennett, Elizabeth Hardwick, Barbara Epstein, and others in New York, where he stayed, as he often did, with his friends John and Jill Fairchild.

On May 10 Spender received a letter from Margaret Thatcher's office to say he was being recommended to the queen for a knighthood.[26] He was torn between a long-proclaimed principle that he would not accept a knighthood and the always-present desire for recognition. He realized almost immediately that he would accept the honour "both for myself and for Natasha." And, in fact, in 1983 he became Sir Stephen Spender.

Spender was not, as some had again expected, named poet laureate in 1984 when the post became vacant. Instead, his good friend Ted Hughes was honoured. The Spenders had spent weekends with the Hugheses, and Spender and Hughes had exchanged friendly letters since the 1970s. His friendship with Hughes continued to develop. Spender would be especially supportive of his friend on the subject of the press's negative treatment of him in connection with the marriage to Sylvia Plath and her suicide.[27]

On May 18 there was another in the long series of memorial services—this one for a great Spender friend, the pianist Clifford Curzon, who had died the year before. Spender found that he thought more and more about death and about his wish to write his "immortal work." And, in fact, he was trying hard to write new poetry.

During a trip to Venice he read about his love affair with Muriel Gardiner (Buttinger) in her book *Code Name Mary*. It was strange to have the past revealed from the perspective of a woman who had long ago been a lover and was now a close friend approaching the end of her life. Spender was also interested in the description of Muriel's activities as a Socialist working against the Fascists in Vienna when he had first known her, before the war, and he suspected that she was right in guessing that Lillian Hellman had based her character of Julia in *Pentimento* on her. He would dedicate his *Journals, 1939–1983*, which would be published in 1985, the year of her death, "to Muriel Gardiner."

Nineteen eighty-four found Spender back in California, in Los Angeles, where he saw David Hockney, Christopher Isherwood, Don Bacardy, and, as always, "B." He also delivered an address on culture and politics to the annual meeting of the Bancroft Library at the University of California in Berkeley, and the Bancroft published a limited edition of part of *The Year of the Young Rebels* in honour of Spender for the Friends of the Bancroft Library. Spender returned to California in 1985 to visit Isherwood, who was extremely ill, and while there he attended a birthday party for "B." He also visited the dying Muriel Gardiner that year.

On a more positive note, Fabers published Spender's translation of the *Oedipus* plays in 1985. The plays were produced in Oxford and then in India. And, most important, Faber and Faber brought out the *Journals, 1939–1983* and his *Collected Poems, 1928–1985*. In a sense, the *Journals* are a continuation of the autobiography *World Within World*, and provide us, along with the original version in the Bancroft Library, with a primary source of information on a major part of Spender's life. As for the *Collected Poems*, though some readers have felt that Spender's sometimes considerable revisions undermine the integrity of the poetry in this volume,[28] there are several new poems that by themselves make the book a significant one. The most important of these is the elegy to Auden, "Auden's Funeral," a poetic overview of Spender's memories of his friend. There are also memory poems of MacNeice and Connolly and segments from the *Oedipus* translations, including these ominous words from *Oedipus at Colonus*, the play that covers the aged king's last days:

> *Whoever craves a longer life than his allotted span*
> *That man*
> *I count a fool.*[29]

The *Collected Poems* and the *Journals* spurred a lively correspondence between the two old semiantagonistic colleagues Spender and John Lehmann, both struggling to hold off the end as long as possible and both concerned about their places in literary history. Realizing that Lehmann might be upset by a few negative remarks about him in the *Journals*, Spender sent him all three of his newly published volumes with a note suggesting that the remarks not be taken to heart and noting that in the *Collected Poems* three poems were dedicated to him.[30] Lehmann answered that he appreciated the dedication, was wary of the negative remarks, but wondered why Spender had "censored" the thirties poems, implying that the poet had decided to de-emphasize the homosexuality in his work.[31] Spender replied by assuring Lehmann that the revisions did not represent censorship but were determined by aesthetic concerns. He wished to avoid "gushing" and things "poetically bad." Several of the poems were about love and could be taken to be love between men or between men and women. His job as a poet was not to write specifically heterosexual or homosexual poems.[32]

In November Spender was honoured at a publication party given by Faber and Faber. But all was not well. Ian Hamilton in the *Times Literary Supplement*[33] had offended him by suggesting that he got nothing in return for his friendship with a usually autocratic and demanding Auden. Spender himself had offended his friend Philip O'Connor through negative remarks in the *Journals*.[34] Spender answered O'Connor's complaint by pointing out that he, himself, was "still smarting" over things E. M. Forster had said about him in his *Commonplace Book* and that O'Connor should not take the remarks to heart, especially as he had not been mentioned by name. Spender had been named and was extremely hurt by Forster's comment that he "loses honour constantly through an interminable diarrhoea composed not entirely of words." About Natasha Spender, Forster had said that before her generosity in connection with Tony Hyndman he had "seen [in her] only the climber. . . ."[35]

Christopher Isherwood and Henry Moore died in 1986 and John Lehmann in 1987. Spender delivered a memorial address for Moore at Westminster Abbey. It was published by Fabers. He was one of the very few left from his generation. Of his close friends, only Stuart Hampshire and Isaiah Berlin continued the trek. He became anxious to devote the rest of his life to his own work, hoping to write a novel about his relationship with his sister's governess, Caroline, to complete the reworking of his early novel *The Temple*, and to compile a collection of final poems.

Spender never did finish the governess novel, but he did complete *The Temple* while he taught for a semester at the University of Connecticut in Storrs in 1987. In London during the next year he gave the manuscript to Ted Hughes to read. Hughes felt it was more a series of poems than a novel, and Spender, characteristically, agreed. But the work, in part an expression of nostalgia for the days of sexual awakening in Germany between the wars and in part a record of the rise of Fascism, was published by Faber and Faber in 1988.[36] Some readers interpreted the publication of this novel as a "coming out" for Spender. His friend "B" told him he had become a "hero of the gay rights movement" by publishing it, and Spender was "pleased" by that, as he was "very loyal to homosexuals."[37] Almost simultaneously with *The Temple*, another bit of Spender nostalgia was published as an introduction to *Junge Männer*, a book of photographs by the late Herbert List, Spender's German friend of 1929 and the early 1930s. Spender had got back in touch with List in the 1950s. The photographs juxtapose Greek statues of youths with the boys with whom Spender, Auden, and Isherwood spent time during their early German sojourns. The Spender text is reminiscent of those days and is a highly positive assessment of List's art.

On February 28, 1989, the Spender family and Faber and Faber hosted a party for Stephen Spender's eightieth birthday. He was now the undisputed elder statesman of English letters. His position was such that the *London Review of Books* asked him to write an article entitled "What I Believe," which he did for the October 26 issue.[38] For him, God was the "idea of the absolute 'Thou' who recognizes the 'I' in each of us." The writer of "The Truly Great" realized that his particular faith might be dismissed by many as "elitist" or as "hero worship," because it "makes a hero of the practitioner of sublime art." He believed, he said, "in intellect in the sense in which Proust uses the word" when he speaks of the source of great art.

In 1990 Spender would ask Ted Hughes and others to contribute a short piece to the "ABC" book illustrated by David Hockney, the proceeds from which would go to the AIDS Crisis Trust. The reality of AIDS had been brought home to Spender by the illness of his friend "B." By 1990 the disease and AIDS relief had become a Spender cause. He wrote, somewhat sardonically, to Alan Ross that the French edition of *The Temple* was selling well because of the scantily clad boy on the cover: "Le plaisir sans risqué de CEDA [AIDS]."[39]

A happy event in 1990 was the marriage of Lizzie to Australian comedian Barry Humphries, best known for his television female-impersonator role as the outrageous and bawdy "Dame Edna." Spender liked Humphries a great deal, even allowing him, as a son-in-law, to improve the notoriously shabby Spender wardrobe with some stylish new suits. Most of all, he felt immense relief that Lizzie's life seemed more settled.

In spite of the usual flow of visitors and the trips to Maussane, Spender, who no longer travelled to America to teach, spent a good deal of time in the nineties on his poetry. He knew his time was short. He wrote to Ted Hughes that he was trapped in lifeless poetry because of the deaths of so many friends.[40] He told Alan Ross that he was writing poetry every day. The problem was completion. He decided that he was both a thinking prose writer and a feeling poet. It was difficult to concentrate for long periods of time, and he missed the excitement of his earlier life. He joked with Ross about a character called Spender on the BBC, a detective who observed young drug addicts doing "illicit business" in men's rooms.[41]

The last five years of Spender's life were scarred by the death of "B" in 1991 of AIDS and by two unfortunate disputes over issues that might perhaps better have been ignored. On July 4, 1991, Spender wrote to Michael Hamburger that American poets suffered from "paranoid megalomania" in regard to their position in American life, while English poets were happy enough to isolate themselves in a "little mutually back-biting club." If so, in his reaction to the Hugh David biography *Stephen Spender: A Portrait with Background* (Heinemann, 1992) and to American David Leavitt's fictionalizing of his *World Within World* in *While England Sleeps* (Viking, 1993), Spender behaved more like an American than an English poet.

Spender reacted to what he saw as misinterpretations, false assumptions, and inaccuracies in the biography by making a careful list of them and depositing it in various English and American libraries, notably the Bodleian and the Bancroft. Most reviewers found the book unsatisfactory and said so in no uncertain terms.[42] But rather than allow the reviewers to put the book to rest, the Spenders reacted with outrage. Spender wrote to the poet laureate that he found himself in a Ted Hughes–style fury over what he saw as David's attempt to create dissension between him and old friends like Auden and Isherwood.[43] In an article in the *Times Literary Supplement*, Natasha Spender complained about biographers who pry and mislead and misuse material.[44] Encouraged by Spender, the Society of Authors became involved.[45] The society's chairman, Anthony Sampson, wrote a protest letter to the publisher, Richard Charkin,[46] who politely explained that, although he regretted any inaccuracies, he felt that, in spite of pressure from the "great and the good," there was no good reason not to publish unauthorized biographies.[47] Unfortunately, the whole row gives credence to Spender's often-expressed self-criticism that he was overly concerned with the opinions of others about his life and work. As the writer of the *New Yorker*'s "Talk of the Town" suggested, most reviewers had already judged the book to be "shoddy," and most people had at first felt "considerable sympathy for the Spenders," but that the tone of Lady Spender's article, with its "absurd suggestion that the subject always knows better than the biographer, is so self-righteous that opinion is now drifting the other way."[48]

The commotion over the Leavitt book was larger and more serious and, finally, also more unfortunate. Bernard Knox in the *Washington Post Book World* suggested that Leavitt, a young avowedly homosexual novelist, had made use of material involving Spender and Jimmy Younger (Tony Hyndman) in *World Within World* for his novel.[49] Spender was informed of Leavitt's book and reacted with fury that a fellow writer should make use of his autobiography for a work of fiction in which he and a close friend are depicted in an explicitly sexual context.[50] What followed was what Spender saw as a series of conflicting statements on the part of Leavitt and his representatives, and eventually, supported by the British Society of Authors, he decided to sue, arguing that he had the "moral right" to control the presentation of his own life. He also claimed the legal right given by a 1988 law forbidding the "derogatory treatment" of a writer's work. Faced with the suit, Viking-Penguin decided to withdraw the novel, which was already on bookstore shelves in America, and to pay Spender's court costs. After the settlement Spender said he bore Leavitt "no ill will" and refused to pursue his claim for damages. Inevitably there were those who sympathized with a thirty-two-year-old author in a struggle with the legal and literary establishment in England and America. Unfortunately, the publicity generated by the lawsuit has made the first edition of *While England Sleeps* a valuable collector's item. At the very least, the two literary squabbles cut significantly into Spender's last years, undermining his attempt to devote the end of his life to his poetry.

Ian Hamilton, researching his eighty-fifth birthday profile of Spender for the *New Yorker*, entitled "Spender's Lives,"[51] wondered why Spender had made "such a fuss" about the Leavitt book and the David biography. Frank Kermode and Isaiah Berlin essentially blamed Natasha Spender. Kermode is reported to have said, "When things go wrong, she does the worrying, and Stephen goes on his usual passive way." David Plante, on the other hand, told Hamilton that he thought Spender simply used Natasha as a shield for his own real anger. "Oh, Natasha's very upset," Spender would say, but really, claimed Plante, "he's the one who's making her upset."[52] Speaking for herself, Natasha told Hamilton that it was important to set the record straight. Yet she complained of the high cost in her husband's "declining years" of the kind of stress brought about by the Leavitt and David books[53]—stress greatly compounded, surely, by the vigorous war against them.

In spite of the turmoil, however, Spender did manage to complete a final book. In 1994 *Dolphins* was published by Faber and Faber, who also hosted an eighty-fifth birthday party, which Spender rightly thought of as a drawing of the curtain,[54] and St. Martin's reissued *World Within World*. In October Spender made his last trip to America. He read at the 92nd Street Y and at Brandeis, and delivered a speech on art and literature at a dinner in his honour at the New York Public Library. In November he fell as he was leaving a New York City restaurant and broke his hip. Treatment included the implant of a pacemaker; for some time Spender had suffered from congestive heart failure. It was not until the end of the year that he was able to return home, but he did manage to regain his ability to walk. Back at Loudoun Road, he lived a quieter version of his old life. A hospital stay became necessary during the summer of 1995 and he became frailer, but he continued to write the occasional review and to enjoy lunches at his clubs or at home. As a writer, he knew he had done what he could do.

Dolphins was dedicated to Auden, Day-Lewis, MacNeice, and Isherwood, Spender's closest and oldest literary friends. It is a small book, containing nineteen poems, a few reworked from earlier versions. To some extent, *Dolphins* continues what had become for Spender a process of recollection. Three of the new poems—"Letter from an Ornithologist in Antarctica," "Farewell to My Student," and "Laughter"—are, in effect, elegies to "B," whom he identified by name and described as "one of the best people I have ever met" in an interview with Ian Hamilton for the *New Yorker* profile.[55]

The "Farewell" poem is almost conversational in tone but contains the by now familiar Spender penchant for delicate, almost romantic, nature imagery. It begins:

> *For our farewell, we went down to the footpath*
> *Circling the lake.*
> *   You stood there, looking up at*
> *Egrets nesting in high branches*
>
> *—White ghosts in a green tapestry.*
> *   And I stood silent, thinking of*
> *Images to recall this moment.*

"Air raid" is a World War II memory. "A First War Childhood" looks back to 1916. "Room" describes a space "electric with . . . memories."

"Worldsworth," a favourite *Dolphins* poem of Spender's, is one inspired by the memory of the poet's discovery of Wordsworth in the Lake District as a child. The inspiration came during the 1979 visit to Skelgill Farm with Natasha. He remembered his father reading Wordsworth to his mother, with his play on words that brings together Spender's earliest and primary poetic inspiration and his lifelong commitment to the establishment of a better world.

> *'Worldsworth,' I thought, this peace*
> *of voices intermingling—*
> *'Worldsworth,' to me, a vow.*

In *Dolphins* one feels that the poet has found his own voice, that he is no longer concerned, for instance, with modernism or his part in it.

Dolphins is a relatively conscious farewell from a man who has little time to live and who quietly expresses feelings that are inevitably coloured by the approaching end. The last poem in the volume, a poem called "The Alphabet Tree," dedicated to Valerie Eliot, the wife of his own literary "father," foreshadows the end of the voyager's quest. In the poem a voice urges on the poet:

> *"Today you must climb*
> *Up the rungs of this ladder . . ."*

So the poet climbs and strikes the letter *Z* and reads a poem in his head. But the voice, true to Spender's own tendency to deprecate himself, sees only "a flower/Whose petals will scatter/On the breeze in an hour."

The last stanza is Spender's final celebration of greatness. The voice cries out,

> *"But behold where on high*
> *The entire ink-black sky*
> *Is diamonded*
> *With stars of great poets*
> *Whose language unfetters*
> *Every Alphabet's letters . . ."*

One afternoon in July 1995, the Spenders had lunch, as they had so often before, with a group of accomplished friends. Spender was quiet during the lunch but obviously happy to be where he was, in his natural element. From time to time he said something amusing. The next morning, July 16, when Natasha called him to a meal, there was no answer, and she found her husband dead on the bedroom floor.[56]

On the twenty-first, there was a funeral at St. Mary's, a beautiful Georgian church on Paddington Green. The west window revealed a churchyard bathed in sunlight. There were hymns chosen by Spender—"He who would valiant be," "Let all the world in every corner sing." He had also chosen the Haydn and Schubert played by a string quartet. Harold Pinter and others read some of the poet's work, and Matthew, who, as everyone remarked, looked exactly like his father, spoke. And there was a moving tribute by Stuart Hampshire, which ended with a Spender translation of Hölderlin ("Hölderlin's Old Age"): "In my mad age, I rejoice and my spirit sings/Burning intensely in the centre of a cold sky."

After the service Natasha invited some friends back to the garden at Loudoun Road. As Joseph Brodsky was leaving, a man said to him, "The end of an era." Brodsky managed a "broad, cheerful, Stephen-like grin," and replied, "I don't think so."[57]

The obituaries were predictably laudatory. Nigel Nicolson wrote that "no distinguished man whom I have ever known took more trouble with the undistinguished, particularly the young."[58] For Frank Kermode, Sir Stephen was "absolutely distinctive ... distracted yet accurate, funny yet serious ... the unofficial ambassador of English letters."[59] Reynolds Price called his old friend a "sleeplessly good and watchful man, an entirely original and fearless poet, a grave-eyed watcher of a world far wider than most artists see, a brilliantly generous connoisseur of beauty and loyalty, compassion, and laughter."[60]

A "Service of Thanksgiving to Celebrate the Life and Work of Stephen Spender" was held on March 20, 1996, at St. Martin-in-the-Fields. A Bach chorale was followed by Spender poems read by Harold Pinter, James Fenton, Jill Balcon, and Barry Humphries. There were Haydn and Beethoven quartets, a lesson read by Matthew, and a eulogy by Spender's friend Richard Wollheim. Just before the final music—a Mozart aria sung by Emma Kirkby—and the blessing, the poet laureate read "The Truly Great." The people at the service—representing a wide spectrum of ages and social classes—came to pay homage to a consummate man of letters and a witness to his age, a man who was sometimes so quiet and gentle as to go almost unnoticed but who, like Virginia Woolf's Orlando, was always there. As Spender was so much a representative of the turbulent age of modernism, they came to pay homage not only to him but to that age and to all of its "greats," those voyagers who as painters, as poets, as progressive social and literary thinkers, had broken through the barriers of mediocrity and narrow-mindedness and "wore at their hearts the fire's centre."

NOTES

Throughout the notes, in reference to correspondence, Stephen Spender's name is abbreviated as SS. W. H. Auden is denoted as WHA, Christopher Isherwood as CI, William Plomer as WP, Virginia Woolf as VW, and T. S. Eliot as TSE. Unless otherwise indicated, poems are from the *Collected Poems, 1928–1985.*

Preface

1. Stephen Spender, *Journals, 1939–1983* (London: Faber and Faber, 1985), 259.
2. *Journals*, 52.

Introduction

1. Stephen Spender, comment in *Fact* 4 (July 1937): 18.
2. Stephen Spender, *World Within World* (New York: Harcourt, Brace and Company, 1951), 126, 133.
3. Samuel Hynes, *The Auden Generation* (London: Faber and Faber, 1976), 105.

1. Childhood and Heritage

1. Stephen Spender, *World Within World* (New York: Harcourt, Brace and Company, 1951), 12.
2. Stephen Spender, conversation with the author.
3. *World*, 5.

4. *World*, 294.
5. *World*, 3.
6. *World*, 18.
7. *World*, 292.
8. *World*, 293.
9. *World*, 295.
10. *World*, 79.
11. Stephen Spender, *Dolphins* (New York: St. Martin's Press, 1994), 40–41.
12. *World*, 294.
13. *World*, 295.
14. *World*, 303.
15. *World*, 302.
16. *World*, 5.
17. Stephen Spender, unpublished journal, 1925.
18. *World*, 8.
19. *World*, 6.
20. Stephen Spender, *The Thirties and After* (New York: Random House, 1978), 4.
21. *World*, 24.
22. *World*, 14.
23. *World*, 27–28.

2. Oxford

1. Louis MacNeice, *The Strings Are False: An Unfinished Autobiography* (London: Faber and Faber, 1965), 113.
2. Stephen Spender, *World Within World* (New York: Harcourt, Brace and Company, 1951), 30.
3. *World*, 30.
4. *World*, 31.
5. *World*, 33, 31.
6. *World*, 86–88.
7. *World*, 30.
8. *World*, 58–62.
9. *World*, 61.
10. *World*, 60.
11. SS to CI, fall 1930.
12. SS to WP, July 25, 1930.
13. *World*, 58, 61.
14. *World*, 60.
15. Stephen Spender, *The Temple* (London: Faber and Faber, 1988), 8.
16. Stephen Spender, *Poems* (New York: Random House, 1935), 13.
17. *World*, 92.
18. Humphrey Carpenter, *W. H. Auden: A Biography* (Boston: Houghton Mifflin Company, 1981), 78.
19. *World*, 45–46.
20. *World*, 46.

21. *World,* 46.

22. *World,* 48.

23. *World,* 55.

24. *World,* 53.

25. Stephen Spender, *The Thirties and After* (New York: Random House, 1978), 10.

26. *World,* 52.

27. WHA to SS, summer 1928.

28. Ronald Carter, ed., *Thirties Poets: "The Auden Group"* (London: Macmillan, 1984), 66.

29. SS to Louis Untermeyer, April 1928.

30. Louis Untermeyer, ed., *Modern British Poetry: A Critical Anthology,* 3d ed. (New York: Harcourt, Brace and Company, 1931), 767.

31. *Saturday Review* 11 (November 10, 1934): 274.

32. *World,* 94.

33. Christopher Isherwood, *Lions and Shadows: An Education in the Twenties* (London: Hogarth Press, 1938), 172–173.

34. William Plomer, *The Autobiography of William Plomer* (London: Jonathan Cape, 1975), 261.

35. *Spectator,* August 3, 1929, 152–153.

36. SS to Edward Garnett, August 10, 1930.

37. *World,* 95.

38. *Spectator,* December 1, 1933, 812.

39. *Spectator,* October 19, 1934, 574.

40. *Spectator,* November 2, 1934, 675.

41. Spender, *Thirties,* 155.

42. SS to Wyndham Lewis, August 14, 1929.

43. SS to WP, May 4, 1930.

44. Isaiah Berlin, in *Index on Censorship* 5 (1995): 11.

3. Germany

1. Stephen Spender, *World Within World* (New York: Harcourt, Brace and Company, 1951), 100.

2. *World,* 98–99.

3. *World,* 97–98.

4. *World,* 103.

5. Stephen Spender, from "Hamburg, 1929."

6. *World,* 99–101.

7. WHA to SS, August 29, 1929.

8. *World,* 105.

9. Stephen Spender, *Journals, 1939–1983* (London: Faber and Faber, 1985), 29, 25.

10. SS to WP, November 28, 1929.

11. SS to WP, February 24, 1930.

12. SS to WP, February 24, 1930, and July 25, 1930.

13. SS to WP, March 7, 1930.

14. SS to WP, July 25, 1930.

15. SS to WP, March 7, 1930, and SS to CI, spring 1930.
16. Christopher Isherwood, *Christopher and His Kind* (New York: Farrar, Straus and Giroux, 1976), 46–47.
17. SS to WP, July 25, 1930.
18. *World,* 107.
19. *World,* 112.
20. SS to WP, October 27, 1930.
21. Stephen Spender, from "My parents quarrel . . ."
22. SS to WP, July 25, 1930.
23. SS to WP, October 27, 1930.
24. SS to WP, March 9, 1931.
25. *World,* 110.
26. *World,* 116–117.
27. *World,* 119.
28. *Journals,* 28.
29. *Christopher,* 82.
30. SS to WP, November 12, 1931.
31. SS to WP, January 30, 1932.
32. *World,* 119.
33. Sergei Eisenstein, *Film Essays* (New York: Praeger, 1970), 33.
34. SS to WP, June 15, 1932.
35. *World,* 121.
36. SS to WP, January 30, 1932.
37. *Christopher,* 93.
38. SS to WP, May 6, 1932.
39. SS to WP, July 16, 1932.
40. SS to WP, September 15, 1932.

4. The Man of Letters

1. Virginia Woolf, *The Diary of Virginia Woolf,* ed. Quentin Bell and Anne Olivier (London: Hogarth Press, 1977), September 8, 1930.
2. Harold Nicolson, *Diaries and Letters,* ed. Nigel Nicolson (New York: Atheneum, 1966–1968), June 22, 1930.
3. Stephen Spender, *World Within World* (New York: Harcourt, Brace and Company, 1951), 132.
4. TSE to SS, May 30, 1931.
5. *World,* 132–133.
6. SS to WP, October 27, 1930.
7. WHA to SS, January 14, 1932.
8. *World,* 137.
9. Woolf, *Diary,* November 2, 1932.
10. Woolf, *Diary,* December 21, 1933.
11. Woolf, *Diary,* December 21, 1933.
12. See chapter 2.
13. *World,* 140.

14. *World,* 148–150.
15. *World,* 146.
16. *World,* 151–152.
17. *World,* 90.
18. *World,* 86–88.
19. *World,* 87–88.
20. Stephen Spender, *The Thirties and After* (New York: Random House, 1978), 7.
21. *World,* 132.
22. Harold Nicolson to SS, March 6, 1932.
23. TSE to SS, March 16, 1932.
24. TSE to SS, January 6, 1932.
25. *World,* 158.
26. Christopher Isherwood, *Christopher and His Kind* (New York: Farrar, Straus and Giroux, 1976), 107; and *World,* 158.
27. SS to CI, November 12, 1932, and CI to SS, November 14, 1932.
28. *World,* 125–126.

5. Love and Ideology

1. Stephen Spender, *World Within World* (New York: Harcourt, Brace and Company, 1951), 159.
2. Christopher Isherwood, *Christopher and His Kind* (New York: Farrar, Straus and Giroux, 1976), 222.
3. *Christopher,* 223.
4. SS to WP, June 23, 1933.
5. TSE to SS, November 17, 1933.
6. WHA to SS, June 1933.
7. *World,* 159ff.
8. *World,* 159–161.
9. E. M. Forster to SS, August 25, 1933.
10. VW to Ottoline Morrell, December 31, 1933.
11. Virginia Woolf, *The Diary of Virginia Woolf,* ed. Quentin Bell and Anne Olivier (London: Hogarth Press, 1977), July 24, 1934.
12. VW to Quentin Bell, December 31, 1933.
13. TSE to SS, January 30, 1934.
14. *Hound and Horn,* vol. 7 (April–June 1934).
15. TSE to SS, April 17, 1934.
16. *World,* 175–182.
17. Muriel Gardiner, *Code Name Mary* (New Haven: Yale University Press, 1983), 47.
18. *World,* 177.
19. Gardiner, 54.
20. *World,* 179.
21. *World,* 179.
22. SS to WP, June 19, 1934.
23. *World,* 177.
24. SS to VW, July 4, 1934.

25. VW to SS, n.d., 1934.
26. SS to WP, July 31, 1934.
27. SS to WP, August 1, 1934.
28. SS to Geoffrey Grigson, July 6, 1934.
29. *World*, 174.
30. Gardiner, 54.
31. Sanford Sternlicht, *Stephen Spender* (New York: Twayne Publishers, 1992), 35.
32. *World*, 176.
33. TSE to SS, September 7, 1934.
34. E. M. Forster to SS, September 30, 1934.
35. *New Criterion* 14 (October 1934): 17–24.
36. Stephen Spender, *The Destructive Element* (London: Jonathan Cape, 1935), 121, 131.
37. TSE to SS, October 17, 1934.
38. *Times Literary Supplement,* December 13, 1934.
39. TSE to SS, December 10, 1934.
40. TSE to SS, January 16, 1935.
41. Gardiner, 66.
42. SS to WP, January 11, 1935.
43. SS to WP, July 31, 1935.
44. TSE to SS, March 21, 1935.
45. *Destructive,* 14.
46. *Destructive,* 12.
47. *Destructive,* 98.
48. *Destructive,* 19.
49. Woolf, *Diary,* April 20, 1935.
50. VW to SS, June 25, 1935.
51. Ottoline Morrell to SS, June 6, 1935.
52. TSE to SS, April 25, 1935, and May 9, 1935.
53. WHA to SS, June 30, 1935, and n.d., c. June 1935.
54. SS to John Lehmann, September 21, 1931.
55. SS to John Lehmann, September 25, 1931.
56. SS to WP, January 16, 1932.
57. *Christopher,* 97.
58. SS to R. A. Scott-James at the *London Mercury*, July 1935.
59. SS to John Lehmann, July 15, 1935, and John Lehmann to SS, July 18, 1935.
60. See the Leavitt case, chapter 11.
61. SS to Rayner Heppenstall, December 18, 1935.
62. SS to WP, January 9, 1936.
63. VW to SS, January 15, 1936.
64. SS to WP, January 9, 1936.
65. TSE to SS, February 21, 1936.
66. *World,* 167.
67. Stephen Spender, *Journals, 1939–1983* (London: Faber and Faber, 1985), 326.
68. Stephen Spender, "Errors of Fact and Misreadings of Text in *Stephen Spender: A Portrait with Background* by Hugh David," 24.
69. *World,* 186.

70. *World*, 187.
71. Stephen Spender, *Letters to Christopher*, ed. Lee Bartlett (Santa Barbara: Black Sparrow Press, 1980), 175.
72. *World*, 188.
73. *Christopher*, 259–260.

6. The Crusader

1. Stephen Spender, *The Thirties and After* (New York: Random House, 1978), 44.
2. Stephen Spender, *World Within World* (New York: Harcourt, Brace and Company, 1951), 197.
3. Christopher Isherwood, *Christopher and His Kind* (New York: Farrar, Straus and Giroux, 1976), 322.
4. SS to WP, February 6, 1937.
5. Stephen Spender, "Errors of Fact and Misreadings of Text in *Stephen Spender: A Portrait with Background* by Hugh David," 25.
6. Tony Hyndman notes quoted in *World*, 194.
7. SS to VW, February 15, 1937.
8. Virginia Woolf, *The Diary of Virginia Woolf*, ed. Quentin Bell and Anne Olivier (London: Hogarth Press, 1977), February 18, 1937.
9. *World*, 200.
10. *World*, 211.
11. *World*, 202–203.
12. *World*, 207.
13. *World*, 209–210.
14. *World*, 215.
15. SS to WP, April 12, 1937.
16. SS to WP, April 2, 1937.
17. Woolf, *Diary*, April 15, 1937.
18. Woolf, *Diary*, June 1, 1937.
19. *Herald Tribune*, May 14, 1937.
20. Stephen Spender, *Journals, 1939–1983* (London: Faber and Faber, 1985), 426–427; and *Paris Review* no. 79 (spring 1981): 304.
21. *World*, 217–220.
22. *World*, 219.
23. *World*, 221.
24. *World*, 223.
25. *World*, 205.
26. *World*, 218.
27. *World*, 224–225.
28. Harold Nicolson, *Diaries and Letters*, ed. Nigel Nicolson (New York: Atheneum, 1966–1968), August 9, 1937.
29. SS to Sylvia Beach, September 12, 1937.
30. *World*, 226.
31. *New Republic* 92 (October 13, 1937): 268–270.
32. Woolf, *Diary*, October 19, 1937.

33. *World,* 231.
34. *World,* 234–235.
35. Nicolson, *Diaries,* January 26, 1938.
36. (Dolphin, 1939).
37. SS–Ottoline Morrell correspondence, 1935.
38. SS to Eric Alport, February 25, 1938.
39. *New Statesman and Nation,* March 12, 1938, 408.
40. CI to SS, n.d., 1938.
41. WHA to SS, n.d., 1938.
42. Woolf, *Diary,* March 22, 1938.
43. TSE to SS, March 22, 1938.
44. E. M. Forster to SS, July 23, 1938.
45. John Lehmann to SS, October 15, 1938.
46. SS to John Lehmann, October 17, 1938.
47. Stephen Spender, *The New Realism* (London: Hogarth Press, 1939), 5, 19.
48. Coldstream diary, January 17, 1939. Quoted in Hugh David, *Stephen Spender: A Portrait with Background* (London: Heinemann, 1992), 215–216.
49. SS to Julian Symons, February 3, 1939.
50. Woolf, *Diary,* March 19, 1939.
51. *London Mercury* 39 (April 1939): 613–618.
52. Stephen Spender, *The Still Centre* (London: Faber and Faber, 1939), 10.
53. A. Kingsley Weatherhead, *Stephen Spender and the Thirties* (Lewisburg, Pa: Bucknell University Press, 1975), 177.
54. *Still Centre,* 14.
55. *Still Centre,* 11.
56. Woolf, *Diary,* September 11, 1939.
57. *World,* 237.
58. Woolf, *Diary,* September 24, 1939.
59. *Journals,* 49–50.
60. *Journals,* 44ff.
61. *Journals,* 48.
62. *Journals,* 51–52.
63. *Journals,* 41.

7. War

1. Stephen Spender, *The Thirties and After* (New York: Random House, 1978), 63–64.
2. SS to John Lehmann, October 13, 1939.
3. *Atlantic Monthly* 230, no. 5 (November 1972): 84.
4. TSE to SS, November 3, 1939.
5. TSE to SS, November 21, 1939.
6. "Comment," *Horizon,* vol. 1, no. 1 (January 1940).
7. *Thirties,* 68.
8. Christopher Isherwood, *Christopher and His Kind* (New York: Farrar, Straus and Giroux, 1976), 271.
9. *Thirties,* 66–67.

10. Quoted in Clive Fisher, *Cyril Connolly* (New York: St. Martin's Press, 1995), 186.

11. VW to SS, December 16, 1939.

12. E. M. Forster to SS, October 14, 1939.

13. Virginia Woolf, *The Diary of Virginia Woolf,* ed. Quentin Bell and Anne Olivier (London: Hogarth Press, 1977), January 19, 1940.

14. "Comment," *Horizon,* vol. 1, no. 2 (February 1940).

15. TSE to SS, January 26, 1940; and Woolf, *Diary,* February 15, 1940.

16. Woolf, *Diary,* February 7, 1940.

17. VW to SS, March 7, 1940.

18. "Comment," *Horizon,* vol. 1, no. 2 (February 1940).

19. TSE to SS, April 19, 1940.

20. E. M. Forster to SS, April 18, 1940.

21. John Lehmann, *I Am My Brother* (London: Longmans, 1960), 44.

22. *Horizon* 1, no. 1 (January 1940): 51.

23. *Horizon* 1, no. 1 (January 1940): 55–56.

24. *Horizon* 1, no. 3 (March 1940): 222–223.

25. *Horizon* 1, no. 2 (February 1940): 68.

26. *Spectator,* April 19, 1940, 555.

27. "Absent Intellectuals," *Spectator,* April 26, 1940, 596.

28. *Spectator,* July 5, 1940, 12.

29. Humphrey Carpenter, *W. H. Auden: A Biography* (Boston: Houghton Mifflin, 1981), 288–289.

30. WHA to SS, March 31, 1941.

31. "Letter to a Colleague in America," *New Statesman and Nation* (November 16, 1940): 490.

32. WHA to SS, March 13, 1941.

33. *Horizon* 1, no. 4 (April 1940): 231.

34. *Horizon* 1, no. 5 (May 1940): 360.

35. Woolf, *Diary,* May 6, 1940.

36. Stephen Spender, *The Backward Son* (London: Hogarth Press, 1940), 121.

37. Sanford Sternlicht, *Stephen Spender* (New York: Twayne Publishers, 1992), 90.

38. *Horizon,* vol. 2, no. 9 (September 1940).

39. Stephen Spender, *Journals, 1939–1983* (London: Faber and Faber, 1985), 57.

40. *Thirties,* 68.

41. Stephen Spender, *World Within World* (New York: Harcourt, Brace and Company, 1951), 260.

42. SS to John Lehmann, October 10 and October 18, 1940.

43. Ian Hamilton, "Profiles: Spender's Lives," *New Yorker* (February 28, 1994): 79.

44. SS to Cyril Connolly, January 27, 1941.

45. Hamilton, 79.

46. *Listener,* January 23, 1941, 124.

47. *Horizon* 2, no. 2 (February 1941): 139.

48. *World,* 258–260.

49. SS to Julian Huxley, April 2, 1941.

50. *Horizon* 2, no. 5 (May 1941): 316.

51. *Journals,* 57; and Lehmann, *Brother,* 105–106.

52. SS to John Lehmann, September 1941.

53. *World,* 253–254.

54. *World,* 253.

55. SS to WP, October 29, 1941.

56. WHA to SS, January 16, 1942.

57. *Partisan Review* 9 (January 1942): 63–66.

58. *World,* 251–253.

59. *Journals,* 58.

60. Hamilton, 79.

61. SS to Robert Graves, January 26, 1943.

62. TSE to SS, September 21, 1942.

63. E. M. Forster to SS, August 3, 1942.

64. *Horizon* 3, no. 2 (February 1942): 96–111.

65. *World,* 161.

66. SS to Alex Comfort, August 1942.

67. *World,* 261–262.

68. Stephen Spender, *Life and the Poet* (London: Secker and Warburg, 1942), 127.

69. New Hogarth Library, vol. 2, 1943.

70. Stephen Spender, *Poetry Since 1939* (London: Longmans, 1946), 34.

71. February 28, 1944.

72. *World,* 292.

73. *Thirties,* 73–74.

74. SS to John Lehmann, August 1944.

75. SS to Julian Huxley, July 18, 1944.

76. *Journals,* 58.

77. SS to Edith Sitwell, May 18, 1945.

78. *Journals,* 58.

8. New Worlds

1. John Lehmann, ed. *Penguin New Writing* (London: Hogarth Press, 1940–1950), Series no. 23, 1945, 112–126, and no. 25, 1945, 111–128.

2. *New Writing,* no. 23, 1945, 117.

3. *New Writing* no. 23, 1945, 118.

4. *New Writing,* no. 25, 1945, 128.

5. *Poetry,* November 1945, 88–95.

6. *Poetry,* November 1945, 89.

7. *Poetry,* November 1945, 95.

8. *Poetry,* November 1945, 95.

9. *Partisan Review* 12 (summer 1945): 352–360.

10. *Partisan Review* 12 (summer 1945): 360.

11. Stephen Spender, *European Witness* (New York: Reynal and Hitchcock, 1946), 95.

12. *European Witness,* 130–132.

13. *European Witness,* 134.

14. *European Witness,* 135.

15. Stephen Spender, *The Thirties and After* (New York: Random House, 1978), 76.

16. Stephen Spender, *Journals, 1939–1983* (London: Faber and Faber, 1985), 61–91.

17. *Journals,* 59–60.

18. TSE to SS, February 12, 1946.

19. *Journals,* 162–164.

20. *European Witness,* 45.

21. *European Witness,* 55.

22. *Journals,* 60.

23. SS to Cyril Connolly, December 27, 1945.

24. From Part V.

25. Part IV, 1, 2.

26. From Part VI.

27. Stephen Spender, *Poetry Since 1939* (London: Longmans, 1936), 34.

28. *Poetry Since 1939,* 10–11, 13–14, 17.

29. SS to Hermann Broch, February 14, 1946.

30. *Commentary* 3 (January 1947): 7–12; and *Life* 21 (October 14, 1946): 46.

31. SS to Edith Sitwell, March 13, 1946.

32. SS to Julian Huxley, February 28 and March 12, 1946.

33. *Journals,* 93–94.

34. TSE to SS, February 15, 1947.

35. Bill Read to SS, January 14, 1963, and SS to Bill Read, January 24, 1963.

36. Stephen Spender, *A Choice of English Romantic Poetry* (New York: Dial Press, 1947), 7, 8, 13.

37. SS to William Jay Smith, September 22, 1947.

38. Charles Osborne, *W. H. Auden: The Life of a Poet* (New York: Harcourt Brace Jovanovich, 1979), 223.

39. Stephen Spender, *World Within World* (New York: Harcourt, Brace and Company, 1951), 271.

40. *World,* 274.

41. Stephen Spender, "Errors of Fact and Misreadings of Text in *Stephen Spender: A Portrait with Background* by Hugh David," 30; *Journals,* 94; and Stephen Spender, "On the Road with Lenny," *Times Saturday Review,* November 3, 1990.

42. SS to William Jay Smith, September 3, 1948.

43. *Partisan Review* 15 (November–December 1948): 1194–1211, 1311–1331, and 16 (January–February 1949): 55–56, 188–192.

44. Stephen Spender, "Afterword," in William Goyen, *Selected Letters from a Writer's Life* (Austin: University of Texas Press, 1995), 410–412.

45. Christopher Isherwood, *Diaries: Volume I: 1939–1960* (New York: HarperCollins, 1997), 392.

46. SS to Dorothy Brett, October 31, 1948.

47. SS to Dorothy Brett, December 8, 1948.

48. SS to Dorothy Brett, January 1, 1949.

49. SS to Margaret Marshall, January 9, 1949.

50. SS to Geoffrey Faber and TSE, n.d., University of Texas, Austin, papers.

51. SS to John Hayward, March 15, 1949.

52. Mary Lago and P. N. Furbank, eds., *Selected Letters of E. M. Forster,* vol. 2 (London: Collins, 1985), September 18, 1953.

53. Stephen Spender, unpublished journals, 1949.

54. *Journals,* 99–103.

55. Spender, unpublished journals, 1949.

56. Theodore Roethke to SS, October 13, 1957.

57. SS to Margaret Marshall, April 1949. In the *Journals,* Spender assigns his tour to 1948. In fact, it took place in 1949; his chronology in hindsight was often inaccurate.

58. *Journals,* 103.

59. SS to Dorothy Brett, May 31, 1949; and Isherwood, *Diaries,* 394.

60. SS to Dorothy Brett, April 28, 1950.

61. Isherwood, *Diaries,* 676.

62. "To Think of Peace as Well as War," *New York Times,* August 12, 1951, 12.

63. *Thirties,* 132.

64. Stephen Spender, "Notebook X," *London Magazine* (June–July 1976): 8–24.

65. SS to William Smith, November 6, 1949, and SS to Dorothy Brett, April 28, 1950.

66. *Journals,* 103–104.

67. SS to Dorothy Brett, June 27, 1950.

68. Richard Crossman, ed., *The God That Failed* (New York: Harper and Brothers, 1949), 269–272.

69. *Thirties,* 136.

70. Sanford Sternlicht, *Stephen Spender* (New York: Twayne Publishers, 1992), 69.

71. Sternlicht, 70.

72. *World,* vi.

73. SS to Saxe Commins, September 18, 1948.

74. *Twentieth Century* 149 (May 1951): 405–411.

75. CI to SS, September 13, 1950.

76. *Nation* 5 (April 21, 1951): 376–377.

77. *New Statesman and Nation* (April 14, 1951): 426–427.

78. *Listener* (December 1952): 670.

79. *Observer,* April 8, 1951, 7.

80. *Sunday Times,* April 8, 1951.

81. *New York Times Book Review,* April 8, 1951, 1.

82. Frieda Lawrence to SS, September 5, 1951.

83. For example, Harold Clurman, *New Republic* 125 (July 2, 1951): 19.

84. WHA to SS, June 20, 1951.

9. Spender I and Spender II

1. *Sunday Times,* April 8, 1951, 3.

2. *Partisan Review* 29 (summer 1962): 350–365.

3. Library of Congress, 1962.

4. SS to Julian Huxley, June 12, 1951.

5. Humphrey Carpenter, *W. H. Auden: A Biography* (Boston: Houghton Mifflin, 1981), 370.

6. WHA to SS, June 14, 1951.

7. Carpenter, 369.

8. Charles Osborne, *W. H. Auden: The Life of a Poet* (New York: Harcourt Brace Jovanovich, 1979), 236.

9. Stephen Spender, *Journals, 1939–1983* (London: Faber and Faber, 1985), 95–96.

10. *Journals,* 95–96.

11. John Lehmann to SS, June 1951, and various other letters, including a June 26 letter from Lehmann's solicitor.

12. *Journals,* 95–96.

13. SS–John Lehmann correspondence, November 1965.

14. John Lehmann, *The Ample Proposition* (London: Eyre and Spottiswoode, 1966), 127–132.

15. SS to Julian Huxley, June 12, 1951.

16. SS to Lynette Roberts, August 23, 1951.

17. *Journals,* 106.

18. E. M. Forster to SS, December 9, 1951.

19. *Journals,* 107.

20. *Journals,* 109.

21. *Journals,* 109.

22. *Journals,* 105.

23. SS to WP, September 20, 1952.

24. SS to WP, October 11, 1960.

25. SS to Dorothy Brett, June 26, 1952.

26. Allen Tate to Katherine Anne Porter, June 13, 1952, in Ann Waldron, *Close Connections: Caroline Gordon and the Southern Renaissance* (New York: G. P. Putnam's Sons, 1987), 291.

27. Waldron, 291–304, 316–317, 331; and Nancylee Novell Jonza, *The Underground Stream: The Life and Art of Caroline Gordon* (Athens, Ga., and London: University of Georgia Press, 1995), 310, 321.

28. SS to Allen Tate, July 30, 1952.

29. SS to Allen Tate, July 30, 1952.

30. Jonza, 321; and Waldron, 316.

31. *Index on Censorship* 5 (1995): 16.

32. SS to Allen Tate, October 9, 1952.

33. SS to Allen Tate, December 21, 1952.

34. SS to Allen Tate, January 16, 1953.

35. Stephen Spender, *The Thirties and After* (New York: Random House, 1978), 137–138.

36. Elliston brochure for lecture series.

37. Stephen Spender, *The Creative Element* (London: Hamish Hamilton, 1953), 11.

38. *Journals,* 118–119.

39. SS to Allen Tate, February 22, 1953.

40. *Journals,* 97.

41. SS to Tate, February 22, 1953, and n.d c. March 1953.

42. *Journals,* 125–126.

43. Mary Lago and P. N. Furbank, eds., *Selected Letters of E. M. Forster,* vol. 2 (London: Collins, 1985), May 1, 1953.

44. SS to John Lehmann, May 18, 1953.

45. SS to John Lehmann, June 4, 1953.
46. E. M. Forster, *Commonplace Book* [1975], ed. Philip Garner (London: Scolar Press, 1985), 192.
47. SS to John Crowe Ransom, June 11, 1953.
48. Waldron, 304.
49. Jonza, 321.
50. Waldron, 351.
51. SS to Allen Tate, March 1, 1954.
52. *Encounter,* vol. 5, no. 3 (September 1955).
53. SS to Allen Tate, April 3, 1953.
54. *Journals,* 137–139.
55. *Journals,* 141.
56. TSE to SS, December 27, 1954.
57. *Journals,* 144–145.
58. *Journals,* 146.
59. *Atlantic Monthly* 230, no. 5 (November 1972): 86–89.
60. WHA to SS, June 15, 1955.
61. WHA to SS, n.d., 1955.
62. Stephen Spender, unpublished journals, 1955; and *Journals,* 161–162.
63. *Journals,* 169.
64. *Journals,* 162ff.
65. SS–Tom Driberg correspondence, November 1955.
66. Stephen Spender, *The Making of a Poem* (London: Hamish Hamilton, 1955), 60.
67. Stephen Spender, *Collected Poems, 1928–1953* (New York: Random House, 1955), 194.
68. Christopher Isherwood, *Diaries: Volume I: 1939–1960* (New York: HarperCollins, 1997), 565–566.
69. Isherwood, *Diaries,* 566.
70. Isherwood, *Diaries,* 583.
71. Isherwood, *Diaries,* 594–595.
72. Isherwood, *Diaries,* 566.
73. Isherwood, *Diaries,* 590.
74. Isherwood, *Diaries,* 584.
75. *Thirties,* 141.
76. Reynolds Price, "Appreciation: The Poetic Ideal," *Washington Post,* July 18, 1995, C1.
77. Joe Ackerkey to SS, November 26, 1958.
78. *Journals,* 151.
79. *Journals,* 159.
80. *Journals,* 158.
81. *Journals,* 156.
82. SS to Gerald Hamilton, July 12, 1956.
83. *Journals,* 179.
84. *Journals,* 183.
85. SS to WP, October 5, 1959.
86. *Journals,* 183–184.

87. Reynolds Price, "Appreciation."

88. SS to Robert Frost, May 1957.

89. TSE to SS, May 24, 1957.

90. Margaret Drabble, *Angus Wilson: A Biography* (New York: St. Martin's Press, 1995), 232–234.

91. Drabble, 235.

92. Drabble, 235.

93. Stephen Spender, *World Within World* (New York: Harcourt, Brace and Company, 1951), 149.

94. Isherwood, *Diaries,* 747.

95. *Journals,* 190.

96. *Journals,* 189–190.

97. SS to WP, June 8, 1958.

98. SS to James Burns Singer, July 9, 1958.

99. Isherwood, *Diaries,* 802–803.

100. Isherwood, *Diaries,* 806.

101. *Journals,* 250.

102. *Yale University News Bulletin,* November 9, 1959.

103. *Journals,* 210ff.

104. *Journals,* 225–226.

105. SS to Sylvia Plath, May 10, 1960.

106. Osborne, 253.

107. SS to Allen Tate, July 21, 1960.

108. Natasha Spender to Allen Tate, October 4, 1961.

109. Carpenter, 385.

110. *Journals,* 227.

111. *Journals,* 228.

112. *Journals,* 237.

113. *Journals,* 229.

114. *Journals,* 227.

115. SS to John Lehmann, June 6, 1962.

116. *Journals,* 237–238.

117. WHA to SS, postcard, n.d., c. June 1962.

118. Carpenter, 411.

119. *Journals,* 243.

120. *Journals,* 244.

121. *Journals,* 252.

122. Spender, unpublished journals, October 14, 1962.

123. *Journals,* 248.

124. *Journals,* 254–255.

125. Stephen Spender, *The Struggle of the Modern* (London: Hamish Hamilton, 1963), 13.

126. *Struggle,* 256.

127. SS to WP, October 11, 1963.

128. SS to WP, May 14, 1964.

129. SS to Robert Lowell, April 21, 1964, and May 15, 1964.

130. SS to Robert Lowell, May 28, 1964.
131. *Evening Star,* February 25, 1964.
132. *Washington Post,* February 25, 1964.
133. *Christian Science Monitor,* September 16, 1964.
134. SS to Marianne Moore, September 2, 1964.

10. The Generous Days

1. Stephen Spender, *The Thirties and After* (New York: Random House, 1978), 177.
2. Various interviews in Library of Congress Archives, January 1966.
3. Interview in *Largesse,* Bishop O'Connell High School, January 1966, 22–23.
4. *Vagabond,* June 1966, 6–7.
5. *Baltimore Sun,* November 18, 1965.
6. *Thirties,* 177.
7. SS to Robert Lowell, November 29, 1965.
8. SS to Robert Lowell, December 13, 1965.
9. *Thirties,* 181.
10. SS to Howard Nemerov, March 19, 1966.
11. SS to Nicholas Nabokov, July 21, 1967; and Stephen Spender, *Journals, 1939–1983* (London: Faber and Faber, 1985), 257.
12. SS to John Lehmann, March 8, 1968, John Lehmann to SS, March 15, 1968, and SS to John Lehmann, August 8, 1968.
13. *Journals,* 257–258.
14. Stephen Spender, *The Year of the Young Rebels* (London: Weidenfeld and Nicolson, 1969), 185.
15. SS to Humphrey Carpenter, June 6, 1990.
16. Humphrey Carpenter, *W. H. Auden: A Biography* (Boston: Houghton Mifflin, 1981), 433; SS to Humphrey Carpenter, June 6, 1990; and *Journals,* 269–274.
17. *Journals,* 269–270.
18. SS to Jason Epstein, December 28, 1971.
19. SS to Robert Lowell, May 1970.
20. *Journals,* 274.
21. Stephen Spender, *The Generous Days* (London: Faber and Faber, 1971), 45.
22. Sanford Sternlicht, *Stephen Spender* (New York: Twayne Publishers, 1992), 80.
23. D. L. Eder, "Stephen Spender," in *The Dictionary of Literary Biography,* vol. 20 (New York: Dutton, 1983), 362.
24. SS to Jason Epstein, June 3, 1972.
25. Joseph Brodsky, "English Lessons from Stephen Spender," *New Yorker* (January 8, 1996): 58ff.
26. Brodsky, 61.
27. SS to Hannah Arendt, January 7, 1974.
28. *Journals,* 286–287.
29. *Journals,* 283–284.
30. *Journals,* 294.
31. *Journals,* 296.
32. *Journals,* 293.

33. Stephen Spender, "Notebook," *London Magazine* 15, no. 3 (August–September 1973): 47–56.
34. *Journals,* 301–302.
35. Stephen Spender, "Notebook VII," *London Magazine* 15, no. 5 (December 1975–January 1976): 12–29.
36. *Journals,* 303.
37. *Journals,* 311.
38. *Journals,* 312.
39. *Journals,* 313.
40. *Journals,* 314.
41. *Journals,* 316.
42. *Journals,* 316.
43. SS to Jason Epstein, July 3, 1976.
44. *Thirties,* 229.
45. SS interview with author, October 1987.
46. *Journals,* 319–320.
47. *Journals,* 340.
48. *Journals,* 336.
49. *Journals,* 323.
50. Conversation with Peter Stitt, February 1998.
51. *Journals,* 358.
52. *Journals,* 340.
53. Margaret Drabble, *Angus Wilson: A Biography* (New York: St. Martin's Press, 1995), 534; and *Journals,* 342.
54. *Journals,* 344–345.
55. *Journals,* 346.
56. *Journals,* 348.
57. Stephen Spender, unpublished journals, 1979.
58. *Journals,* 352.
59. Spender, unpublished journals, April 24, 1979.
60. *Journals,* 358.
61. *Journals,* 359.
62. Stephen Spender, *Henry Moore: A Memorial Address* (London: Faber and Faber, 1987), 2.
63. *Journals,* 361.
64. *Journals,* 363.
65. *Journals,* 369.
66. *Journals,* 371.
67. *Journals,* 375–385.
68. *Journals,* 386.
69. SS to Ted Hughes, October 21, 1990.
70. *Journals,* 389.
71. *Journals,* 392.
72. *Journals,* 378.

11. The Final Phase

1. Stephen Spender, *Journals, 1939–1983* (London: Faber and Faber, 1985), 399–400.
2. *Journals,* 399–401.
3. Conversation with Peter Stitt, February 1998.
4. *Journals,* 402.
5. *Journals,* 403–404.
6. *Journals,* 404.
7. *Journals,* 404.
8. *Journals,* 407.
9. *Journals,* 411.
10. *Journals,* 399.
11. *Journals,* 410–412.
12. *Journals,* 424.
13. *Journals,* 421–422.
14. *Journals,* 422ff.
15. *Journals,* 422–423.
16. Stephen Spender, unpublished journals, September 1980.
17. *Journals,* 437.
18. Stephen Spender and David Hockney, *China Diary* (New York: Henry Abrams, 1982), 198.
19. *Journals,* 447.
20. Virginia Woolf, *The Diary of Virginia Woolf,* ed. Quentin Bell and Anne Olivier vol. 4, 1931–1935, (London: Hogarth Press, 1977) p. 129; and *Journals,* 439.
21. SS interview with author, October 1987.
22. Spender, unpublished journals, March 1982.
23. Spender, unpublished journals, June 1982.
24. *Journals,* 451.
25. *Journals,* 455–457.
26. *Journals,* 481.
27. SS to Ted Hughes, March 14, 1988.
28. See, for example, Sanford Sternlicht, *Stephen Spender* (New York: Twayne Publishers, 1992), 85.
29. Stephen Spender, from *Oedipus at Colonus, Oedipus Trilogy* (London: Faber and Faber, 1985), 196.
30. SS to John Lehmann, October 14, 1985.
31. John Lehmann to SS, October 16, 1985, and November 25, 1985.
32. SS to John Lehmann, November 27, 1985, and December 4, 1985.
33. *Times Literary Supplement,* November 22, 1985, 1307–1308.
34. Philip O'Connor to SS, November 20, 1985.
35. E. M. Forster, *Commonplace Book* [1975], ed. Philip Garner (London: Scolar Press, 1985), 120, 192.
36. SS to Ted Hughes, March 1, 1988.
37. Ian Hamilton, "Profiles: Spender's Lives," *New Yorker* (February 28, 1994): 84.
38. Stephen Spender, "What I Believe," *London Review of Books,* October 26, 1989, 24–25.
39. SS to Alan Ross, November 27–29, 1989.

40. SS to Ted Hughes, October 21, 1990.

41. SS to Alan Ross, November 27, 1990.

42. See, for example, Hilary Spurling in the *Daily Telegraph*, October 18, 1992; Peter Ackroyd in the *Times*, October 18, 1992; Peter Parker in the *Times Literary Supplement*, October 16, 1992; and Julian Symons in the *Sunday Times*, October 11, 1992.

43. SS to Ted Hughes, October 11, 1992.

44. *Times Literary Supplement,* October 9, 1992, 13.

45. SS to Anthony Sampson, November 12, 1992.

46. Anthony Sampson to Richard Charkin, November 27, 1992.

47. Richard Charkin to Anthony Sampson, December 4, 1992.

48. "Talk of the Town," *New Yorker* (October 26, 1992): 35–36.

49. Bernard Knox, *Washington Post Book World,* September 12, 1992.

50. *Washington Post,* February 17, 1994, A39.

51. Hamilton, *New Yorker,* 72–84.

52. Hamilton, *New Yorker,* 83.

53. Hamilton, *New Yorker*, 84.

54. SS to Ted Hughes, February 10, 1994.

55. Hamilton, *New Yorker,* 82.

56. Letter from a Spender friend in England to one in America, August 12, 1995.

57. Joseph Brodsky, "English Lessons from Stephen Spender," *New Yorker* (January 8, 1996): 67.

58. *Spectator,* July 29, 1995, 41.

59. *Guardian,* July 17, 1995.

60. *Independent,* July 23, 1995.

BIBLIOGRAPHY

Works cited and/or of general interest in connection with Stephen Spender.

Works by Stephen Spender—a Chronological List by Genre

Poetry Collections

Nine Experiments. [London: SS home press, 1928]; Cincinnati: University of Cincinnati (facsimile edition), 1964.

Twenty Poems. Oxford: Blackwell, 1930, 1936.

Poems. London: Faber and Faber, 1933; New York: Random House (revised edition), 1934.

Vienna. London: Faber and Faber, 1934; New York: Random House, 1935.

The Still Centre. London: Faber and Faber, 1939.

Selected Poems. London: Faber and Faber, 1940, 1944, 1945, 1947.

Ruins and Visions. London: Faber and Faber; New York: Random House, 1942.

Spiritual Exercises. [To C. Day Lewis]. London: private, 1943.

Poems of Dedication. London: Faber and Faber; New York: Random House, 1947.

Returning to Vienna, 1947: Nine Sketches. New York: Banyan Press, 1947.

The Edge of Being. London: Faber and Faber; New York: Random House, 1949.

Sirmione Peninsula. Illustrated by Lynton Lamb. London: Faber and Faber, 1954.

Collected Poems, 1928–1953. London: Faber and Faber; New York: Random House, 1955.

Inscriptions. London: Poetry Book Society, 1958.

Selected Poems. New York: Random House, 1964.

The Generous Days. New York: Random House; London: Faber and Faber (augmented edition), 1971.
Recent Poems. London: Anvil Press, 1978.
Collected Poems, 1928–1985. London: Faber and Faber; New York: Random House, 1986.
Dolphins. London: Faber and Faber; New York: St. Martin's Press, 1994.

Drama

Trial of a Judge. London: Faber and Faber; New York: Random House, 1938.
Danton's Death. Adaptation from Büchner. London, 1939.
Mary Stuart. Adaptation from Schiller. London, 1959.
Rasputin's End. With Nicholas Nabokov. Milan, 1963.
Oedipus Trilogy. Adaptation from Sophocles. London, 1985.

Fiction

The Burning Cactus. London: Faber and Faber; New York: Random House, 1936.
The Backward Son. London: Hogarth Press, 1940.
Engaged in Writing, and The Fool and the Princess. London: Hamish Hamilton; New York: Farrar, Straus and Cudhay, 1958.
The Temple. London: Faber and Faber; New York: Grove Press, 1988.

Autobiography and Journals

European Witness. London: Hamish Hamilton; New York: Reynal and Hitchcock, 1946.
"Oxford and Germany." *Partisan Review* 16 (September 1949): 924–936.
World Within World. London: Hamish Hamilton; New York: Harcourt, Brace and Company, 1951.
Learning Laughter. London: Weidenfeld and Nicolson; New York: Harcourt, Brace and Company, 1953.
"September Journal" and "Rhineland Journal" in *The Golden Horizon.* New York: University Books, 1955.
"Pages from a Journal." *Sewanee Review* 63 (fall 1955): 614–630.
The Thirties and After. New York: Random House, 1978.
Letters to Christopher: Stephen Spender's Letters to Christopher Isherwood, 1929–1939. Ed. Lee Bartlett. Santa Barbara: Black Sparrow Press, 1980.
China Diary. With David Hockney. New York: Henry Abrams; London: Thames and Hudson, 1982.
Unpublished journals. Berkeley: Bancroft Library.
Journals, 1939–1983. London: Faber and Faber, 1985.
"Errors of Fact and Misreadings of Text in *Stephen Spender: A Portrait with Background* by Hugh David." Berkeley: Bancroft Library.

Criticism and Commentary

The Destructive Element. London: Jonathan Cape, 1935; Boston: Houghton Mifflin, 1936.

Forward from Liberalism. London: Victor Gollancz; Random House, 1937.

The New Realism. London: Hogarth Press, 1939.

Life and the Poet. London: Secker and Warburg, 1942; New York: Haskell House, 1974.

Citizens in War—and After. London: George Harrap, 1945.

Poetry Since 1939. London: Longmans, 1946.

A Choice of English Romantic Poetry. Edited by Spender. New York: Dial Press, 1947.

See Crossman, Richard.

Shelley. London: Longmans, 1952.

The Creative Element. London: Hamish Hamilton, 1953.

The Making of a Poem. London: Hamish Hamilton, 1955.

The Imagination in the Modern World. Washington: Library of Congress, 1962.

The Struggle of the Modern. London: Hamish Hamilton; Berkeley: University of California Press, 1963.

The Year of the Young Rebels. London: Weidenfeld and Nicolson; New York: Vintage, 1969.

Love-Hate Relations. London: Hamish Hamilton; New York: Random House, 1974.

Eliot. London: Fontana; New York: Viking, 1975.

Henry Moore: A Memorial Address. London: Faber and Faber, 1987.

Henry Moore: Sculptures in Landscape. New York: Clarkson N. Potter, 1979.

W. H. Auden: A Tribute. London: Weidenfeld and Nicolson, 1975.

See List, Herbert.

See Upward, Edward.

Works by Others

Ackerley, J. R. See Braybrooke, Neville.

Ackroyd, Peter. *T. S. Eliot.* London: Hamish Hamilton, 1984.

Bell, Quentin. *Virginia Woolf: A Biography.* London: Hogarth Press, 1972, revised edition, 1990.

Braybrooke, Neville, ed. *The Letters of J. R. Ackerley.* London: Duckworth, 1975.

Brodsky, Joseph. "English Lessons from Stephen Spender." *New Yorker* (January 8, 1996): 58ff.

Carpenter, Humphrey. *W. H. Auden: A Biography.* Boston: Houghton Mifflin, 1981.

Carpenter, Humphrey. *The Brideshead Generation.* London: Weidenfeld and Nicolson, 1989.

Carter, Ronald, ed. *Thirties Poets: "The Auden Group."* London: Macmillan, 1984.

Connors, J. J. *Poets and Politics: A Study of the Careers of C. Day-Lewis, Stephen Spender and W. H. Auden in the 1930's.* New Haven: Yale University Press, 1967.

Crossman, Richard, ed. *The God That Failed: A Confession.* By Stephen Spender, Arthur Koestler, et al. New York: Harper and Brothers, 1949.

Cunningham, Valentine. *British Writers of the Thirties.* London: Oxford University Press, 1988.

Davenport-Hines, R. P. T. *Auden.* London: Heinemann. 1995.

David, Hugh. *Stephen Spender: A Portrait with Background.* London: Heinemann, 1992.

Day-Lewis, Cecil. *The Buried Day*. London: Chatto and Windus, 1960.

Drabble, Margaret. *Angus Wilson: A Biography*. New York: St. Martin's Press, 1995.

Driberg, Tom. *Ruling Passions*. London: Jonathan Cape, 1977.

Eder, D. L. "Stephen Spender." *The Dictionary of Literary Biography*. Vol. 20. New York: Dutton, 1983, 351–365.

Eisenstein, Sergei. *Film Essays and a Lecture by Sergei Eisenstein*. New York: Praeger, 1970.

Finney, Brian. *Christopher Isherwood: A Critical Biography*. London: Faber and Faber, 1979.

Fisher, Clive. *Cyril Connolly*. New York: St. Martin's Press, 1995.

Forster, E. M. *Commonplace Book* [1975]. Edited by Philip Garner. London: Scolar Press, 1985.

Forster, E. M. See Lago, Mary.

Gardiner, Muriel. *Code Name Mary*. New Haven: Yale University Press, 1983.

Hamilton, Ian. "Profiles: Spender's Lives." *New Yorker* (February 28, 1994): 72–84.

Hewison, Robert. *Under Siege: Literary Life in London, 1939–45*. London: Weidenfeld and Nicolson, 1977.

Holroyd, Michael. *Lytton Strachey: A Biography*. London: Penguin, 1971.

Hoskins, Katherine. *Today the Struggle: Literature and Politics in England During the Spanish Civil War*. Austin: University of Texas Press, 1979.

Hynes, Samuel. *The Auden Generation*. London: Faber and Faber, 1976.

Isherwood, Christopher. *Christopher and His Kind*. New York: Farrar, Straus and Giroux, 1976.

Isherwood, Christopher. *Diaries: Volume I: 1939–1960*. New York: HarperCollins, 1997.

Isherwood, Christopher. *Lions and Shadows: An Education in the Twenties*. London: Hogarth Press, 1938.

Jonza, Nancylee Novell. *The Underground Stream: The Life and Art of Caroline Gordon*. Athens, Ga., and London: University of Georgia Press, 1995.

King, James. *Virginia Woolf*. London: Hamish Hamilton, 1994.

Lago, Mary, and P. N. Furbank, eds. *Selected Letters of E. M. Forster*. Vol. 2. London: Collins, 1985.

Lago, Mary. *E. M. Forster: A Literary Life*. New York: St. Martin's Press, 1995.

Leavitt, David. *While England Sleeps*. New York: Viking, 1993.

Lee, Hermione. *Virginia Woolf*. New York: Knopf, 1997.

Leeming, David A. "A Conversation with Stephen Spender on Henry James." *Henry James Review* 9, no. 2 (spring 1988): 128–135.

Leeming, David A. "Stephen Spender." *British Writers: Supplement II*. New York: Scribner's, 1992, 481–496.

Lehmann, John, with Roy Fuller, ed. *The Penguin New Writing*. Harmondsworth: Penguin, 1985.

Lehmann, John. *The Ample Proposition*. London: Eyre and Spottiswoode, 1966.

Lehmann, John. *Christopher Isherwood: A Personal Memoir*. New York: Henry Holt, 1987.

Lehmann, John. *Folios of New Writing*. London: Hogarth Press, 1940–1941.

Lehmann, John. See Woolf, Virginia.

Lehmann, John. *I Am My Brother*. London: Longmans, 1960.

Lehmann, John. *The Whispering Gallery*. London: Longmans, 1955.

Lewis, Percy Wyndham. *The Apes of God* [1930]. Baltimore: Penguin, 1965.

List, Herbert. *Junge Manner.* Text by Stephen Spender. Altadena, Ca.: Twin Palms Publishers, 1988.

MacNeice, Louis. *Modern Poetry.* Oxford: Clarendon, 1938.

MacNeice, Louis. *The Strings Are False: An Unfinished Autobiography.* London: Faber and Faber, 1965.

Maxwell, D. E. S. *Poets of the Thirties.* London: Routledge and Kegan Paul, 1969.

Mendelson, Edward. *Early Auden.* New York: Viking, 1981.

Nicolson, Harold. *Diaries and Letters.* Edited by Nigel Nicolson. New York: Atheneum, 1966–1968.

Osborne, Charles. *W. H. Auden: The Life of a Poet.* New York: Harcourt Brace Jovanovich, 1979.

Pandey, Surya Nath. *Stephen Spender: A Study in Poetic Growth.* New Delhi: Arnold Heinemann, 1982.

Plomer, William. *At Home.* London: Jonathan Cape, 1958.

Plomer, William. *The Autobiography of William Plomer.* London: Jonathan Cape, 1975.

Plomer, William. *Double Lives: An Autobiography* [1956]. Freeport, N.Y.: Books for Libraries Press, 1971.

Rosenthal, M. L. *The Modern Poets.* London: Oxford University Press, 1965.

Scarfe, Francis. "Stephen Spender: A Sensitive." *Auden and After: The Liberation of Poetry, 1930–1941.* London: Routledge, 1942.

Schuster, Sir George. *Private Work and Public Causes.* Cowbridge: D. Brown and Sons, 1979.

Shelden, Michael. *Friends of Promise: Cyril Connolly and the World of Horizon.* London: Hamish Hamilton, 1989.

Spender, Harold. *The Fire of Life.* London: Hodder and Stoughton, 1926.

Spender, J. A. *Life, Journalism and Politics.* 2 vols. London: Cassell and Company, 1927.

Stanford, Derek. *Stephen Spender, Louis MacNeice, Cecil Day-Lewis: A Critical Essay.* Grand Rapids: Eerdmans, 1969.

Sternlicht, Sanford. *Stephen Spender.* New York: Twayne Publishers, 1992.

Thurley, Geoffrey. "A Kind of Scapegoat: A Retrospective on Stephen Spender." *The Ironic Harvest: English Poetry in the Twentieth Century.* London: Edward Arnold, 1974, 79–87.

Tolley, A. T. *The Poetry of the Thirties.* London: Victor Gollancz, 1975.

Untermeyer, Louis, ed. *Modern British Poetry: A Critical Anthology.* 3d rev. ed. New York: Harcourt, Brace and Company, 1931.

Upward, Edward. *Journey to the Border.* Introduced by Stephen Spender. London: Enitharmon, 1994.

Waldron, Ann. *Close Connections: Caroline Gordon and the Southern Renaissance.* New York: G. P. Putnam's Sons, 1987.

Weatherhead, A. Kingsley. *Stephen Spender and the Thirties.* Lewisburg, Pa.: Bucknell University Press, 1975.

Wilde, Alan. *Christopher Isherwood.* New York: Twayne Publishers, 1971.

Wilson, Edmund. *The Fifties.* New York: Farrar, Straus and Giroux, 1986.

Woolf, Virginia, John Lehmann, et al. *The Hogarth Letters.* Introduction by Hermione Lee. London: Chatto and Windus, 1985.

Woolf, Virginia. *The Diary of Virginia Woolf.* Edited by Quentin Bell and Anne Olivier. London: Hogarth Press, 1977.

Woolf, Virginia. *Letter to a Young Poet.* London: Hogarth Press, 1932.

Woolf, Virginia. *The Letters of Virginia Woolf.* Edited by Nigel Nicolson. New York: Harcourt Brace Jovanovich, 1977–1982.

Worsley, T. C. *Fellow Travellers: A Memoir of the Thirties.* London: London Magazine Editions, 1971.

ACKNOWLEDGMENTS

I wish to thank Allison Singley, who has been my primary research assistant on this project. I have also had research help from Betty Gubert, Roslyn Foy, and Katie Drowne. Several interviews with Stephen Spender during the late 1980s have provided me with invaluable material, and I am grateful to Spender for his 1994 letter of support with permission to quote from his published works. The primary sources—letters, journals, manuscripts, and other materials—for my work were found in the following centres: the Durham University Library, the Bodleian Library at Oxford University, Christ Church Library at Oxford University, University College Library at Oxford University, King's College Library at Cambridge University, the Royal Society of Literature, the BBC Written Archives Centre, the University of Leeds Library, the British Library, the John Rylands University Library at Manchester, the University of Sussex Library, the University of Reading Library, the University College Library, the National Library of Scotland, the University of Birmingham Library, the Columbia University Library, the Berg Collection at the New York Public Library, the Princeton University Library, the Harry Ransom Humanities Research Center at the University of Texas in Austin, the Houghton Library at Harvard University, the Rosenbach Museum and Library in Philadelphia, the University of Michigan Library, the Getty Research Institute in Los Angeles, the Cornell University Library, the Schlesinger Library at Radcliffe College, the Dartmouth College Library, the Rice University Library, the University of Iowa Library, the State University of New York at Buffalo Library, the Northwestern University Library, the University of Washington Library, the Washington University Library in St. Louis, the Virginia Polytechnic and State University Library in Blacksburg, the University of Virginia Library, the Duke University Library, the Washington and Lee University Library, the University of Pennsylvania Library, the Bancroft Library at the University of California in Berkeley, the Research Library at the University of California in Los Angeles, the Emory University Library, the University of Cincinnati Library, the Wichita State University Library, the Temple University Library, the University of Connecticut Library, the Beinecke Library at Yale University, the Lincoln Center Library for the Performing Arts, and the Library of Congress. The librarians at all of these institutions were most helpful. I wish to thank the University of Connecticut Research Foundation for generous financial support; Jim and Pamela Morton and my wife, Pamela, for moral support; Carlos Freire and Rollie McKenna for photographs; and my agent, Faith Childs, and my editors, Ray Roberts and Jack Macrae, for their suggestions and encouragement.

INDEX